W9-ACX-068

EDWARD PLANTAGENET

(EDWARD I.)

EDWARD I.

(From "Fœdera," Rymer Edition.)

EDWARD PLANTAGENET

(EDWARD I.)

THE ENGLISH JUSTINIAN

OR

THE MAKING OF THE COMMON LAW

BY

EDWARD JENKS

Select Bibliographies Reprint Series

BOOKS FOR LIBRARIES PRESS
FREEPORT, NEW YORK

First Published 1901
Reprinted 1969

STANDARD BOOK NUMBER:
76-95069

LIBRARY OF CONGRESS CATALOG CARD NUMBER:
8369-5070-4

PRINTED IN THE UNITED STATES OF AMERICA

PREFACE

IF ever there was a national hero, it was Edward of England. In his person, his character, his position, and his policy, are summed up the essential elements of that great English nation which came into existence during his lifetime. How far Edward was its creator, how far its creature, is a shrewd question, which each student of history must answer for himself; but I trust that this little book may help him to form a sound conclusion. Whatever be the answer, there can be little doubt, that it would be impossible to find a truer symbol of the English nation, in the days of its glorious youth, than the king whose life is sketched in the following pages.

Perhaps it is necessary that I should offer a word of apology for the intrusion of a mere lawyer upon a scene so dominated by great historians. My explanation is, that I have long been unable to understand, how any one but a lawyer can possibly appreciate the true inwardness of Edward's reign. The Common Law which came into existence during his lifetime was, and is, the very picture of English national life, the concrete form into which the national spirit crystallises with the moving centuries.

Some of Edward's most brilliant achievements in legislation and statecraft are wholly missed by lay historians, simply because these achievements are expressed in highly technical language. If I have essayed the perilous task of striving to make technical matters clear to the general reader, as in Chapters IX. and XIII., I have done so because I have felt, that it was idle to attempt, in any other way, to bring out Edward's real greatness. But, even with this conviction, I should hardly have ventured the task, had I not been encouraged, by those whose opinions are entitled to greater weight than my own, to hope that I might in some degree succeed in persuading my readers, that Law is a dull subject only to those who do not understand it.

Although I have not thought it advisable, in a work intended for the general reader, to cumber my pages with references, I trust that I shall be believed when I assert, that the book is written absolutely from first-hand sources, a few of which will be found enumerated in the List of Authorities. The one exception to this rule has been in the matter of military details, of which I know very little, and in which I have been content to follow the learned authority of Professor Oman, to whose work, *A History of the Art of War*, I am greatly indebted. To my colleague, Professor Goudy, I owe thanks for his kindness in discussing with me the Roman side of our legal history; and to my friend, Mr. R. Lane Poole, for his constant readiness to place at my disposal his stores of medieval learning. Finally, my former colleague, Professor Tout, of the Owens

College, Manchester, has laid me under deep obligation, by bringing his great knowledge of all things connected with Edward I. to bear upon my proof-sheets, to the great advantage of my readers and myself.

E. J.

OXFORD, *August*, 1901.

CONTENTS

CHAPTER III.

CHAPTER IV.

CHAPTER V.

CHAPTER VI.

LIST OF MAPS, PLANS, AND PEDIGREES

MAP.

PLANS.

PEDIGREES.

ILLUSTRATIONS

[1] From "Fœdera," Rymer Edition.
[2] From Dugdale's "Monasticon."
[3] From Viollet le Duc's "Dict. du Mobilier Français."
[4] From Stothard's "Monumental Effigies."
[5] From Hewitt's "Ancient Armour."
[6] From Strutt's "Dress and Habits."
[7] From Viollet le Duc's "Descript. Château de Coucy."
[8] From Fairholt's "Costumes."
[9] From Crull's "Antiquities of St. Peter's."

[1] From Viollet le Duc's "Dict. du Mobilier Français."

[2] From Stothard's "Monumental Effigies."

[3] From Dugdale's "Monasticon."

[4] From Nicholas' "Annals of Wales.

[5] From Hewitt's "Ancient Armour."

CHRONOLOGICAL SUMMARY.

1239 June 17. Edward born.

1240 Death of Llywelyn ab Jorwerth, and Edmund Rich (archbishop).

1241 Successful invasion of Wales by King Henry. Treaty of Rhuddlan. Death of Pope Gregory IX. Great victories of the Tartars in Hungary and Poland.

1242 Outbreak of the French war; Henry defeated at Taillebourg and Saintes.

1243 Election (after interval of two years) of Innocent IV. (Fieschi).

1244 War with Wales and Scotland. Death of Gruffyth ab Llywelyn.

1245 Council of Lyons. Renewal of quarrel between Papacy and Empire.

1246 Death of David ab Llywelyn. The Pope turns a deaf ear to complaints of Papal taxation.

1248 Montfort made viceroy of Gascony.

1249 Death of Alexander II. of Scotland.

1250 Defeat of French Crusaders at Mansourah, and capture of St. Louis. Death of the Emperor Frederick II.

1251 Marriage of Edward's sister, Margaret, with Alexander (III.) of Scotland.

1252 Complaints of Montfort's government in Gascony.

1253 Civil war in Gascony. Disastrous campaign of Henry. Betrothal of Edward to Eleanor of Castile. Death of Bishop Greathead.

1254 Ireland, Wales, Gascony, Channel Islands, Chester, etc., settled on Edward. Henry accepts kingdom of Sicily ("Apulia") for his second son Edmund. Edward's marriage. Death of Innocent IV., succeeded by Alexander IV.

1256 Revival of Welsh war. Richard of Cornwall made King of the Romans.

1258 League of Scotland and Wales against Henry. The Parliament and *Provisions* of Oxford.

1259 Henry renounces his claims to the lost possessions of his father. Quarrel between Montfort and Gloucester.

1260 Birth of Margaret of Scotland (Edward's niece). *Provisions of Westminster.*

1261 Henry obtains Papal absolution from the Provisions of Oxford; Edward refuses. Montfort and Gloucester reconciled. Montfort summons knights of shire to St. Alban's; the King bids them assemble at Windsor.

1262 Death of the Earl of Gloucester.

1263 Disastrous Welsh campaign. Massacre of foreigners and outbreak of the Barons' War. Temporary reconciliation; St. Louis to arbitrate.

1264 Jan. 23. Mise of Amiens. The barons decline to accept it. The Londoners pillage the house of Richard, the King's brother. Renewal of the Barons' War. (May 14.) Battle of *Lewes;* defeat of the King. Montfort governs in King's name.

1265 First Parliament with special members for the boroughs. Quarrel of Montfort and (the younger) Gloucester. Edward makes a party in the west. Campaign on the Severn. Edward captures Kenilworth and wins the battle of *Evesham* (Aug. 4). Montfort and many of the baronial leaders slain.

1266 Grant of the Customs revenue to Edward.

1267 Treaty of Shrewsbury (or Montgomery) with Llywelyn. *Statute of Marlborough* (modified version of the *Provisions of Oxford*).

1270 Edward starts on crusade. Death of St. Louis before Tunis. Edward in Sicily.

1271 Murder of Henry of Cornwall by the Montforts. Edward at Acre.

1272 Death of Richard of Cornwall. Attempt to assassinate Edward. Robert Kilwardby, Provincial of Franciscans, made Primate by Pope. Death of King Henry.

1273 Llywelyn refuses to do homage to Edward's representatives. Edward journeys leisurely home. Renews the charters. Visits Gascony and Paris.

1274 Council of Lyons; nominal reunion of Greek and Latin churches. Peace between England and Flanders. Edward lands in England (23 July). Great enquiry into private franchises.

1275 *Statute of Westminster the First.* Permanent grant of the "ancient" Customs. Llywelyn again refuses to do homage. Eleanor of Montfort (his betrothed) captured off the Welsh coast. The *Hundred Rolls.*

1276 War declared against Llywelyn.

1277 Victorious campaign in Wales. Treaty of Aberconway.

1278 Kilwardby made Cardinal, and Peckham appointed Primate by Pope. Alexander III. of Scotland does homage to Edward. The *Statute of Gloucester.*

1279 The *Quo Warranto* enquiry. Edward acquires Ponthieu by the death of his mother-in-law. Provincial council at Reading. The *Statute of Mortmain.*

1280 Marriage of Margaret of Scotland (Edward's niece) with Eric of Norway. (Michaelmas) Important direction concerning Parliamentary petitions.

1282 Renewal of Welsh rising. The English defeated at Menai Straits (Nov. 6). Victorious at Orewin Bridge (December 11). Llywelyn slain.

1283 Death of Margaret of Scotland (Queen of Norway) leaving an infant daughter (the "Maid of Norway.") *Parliament of Shrewsbury.* David of Wales condemned and executed. *Statute of Merchants* (or *Acton Burnel*).

1284 *Statute of Rhuddlan* (settlement of Wales).

1285 *Statutes of Westminster the Second* and *Winchester.*

1286 Death of Alexander III. of Scotland (March 19). The League of Turnberry.

1287 Conservators of the Peace to enforce the Statute of Winchester.

1288 Edward in Gascony. Narrow escape from death by lightning. Valuation of Pope Nicholas IV.

1289 Treaty of Salisbury (concerning the "Maid of Norway.")

1290 Treaty of Brigham ("Maid of Norway" to marry Edward's son). Great punishment of corrupt officials. Quarrel between Hereford and Gloucester. Expulsion of the Jews from England. Death of the "Maid of Norway" and of Edward's wife, Eleanor of Castile.

1291 Formal submission of the Scottish succession to Edward. The trial begins at Norham. Deaths of Edward's mother, Eleanor of Provence, and of Robert Burnel.

1292 Completion of the Scottish trial. Award in favour of Balliol. The Normans attack Dover, and the Channel fleets drift into war.

1293 Philip of France, having obtained temporary surrender of Aquitaine (Gascony) from Edmund, King's brother, refuses to restore it. War is declared.

1294 Seizure of clerical treasure. The "maletolte" on wool. Great military preparations. Winchelsey made Primate by the Pope.

1295 Election of Boniface VIII. Death of the elder Bruce. Balliol enters into a league with France and Norway against England. ORGANIZATION OF THE COAST GUARD. Meeting of the MODEL PARLIAMENT (Nov. 27).

1296 The Bull *Clericis Laicos*. Balliol renounces fealty. Edward invades Scotland. Battle of DUNBAR. (June.) At Parliament of Bury St. Edmund's, the clergy refuse a grant.

1297 The clergy are outlawed. Quarrel between Edward and the earls. The clergy submit. The earls refuse. Farewell at Westminster. Edward in Flanders. *Confirmation of the Charters.* Reconciliation between Prince Edward and the earls.

1298 Peace between England and France on terms suggested by Pope Boniface. The Scots rise under WILLIAM WALLACE, and harry the north. Totally routed by Edward at FALKIRK. (July 22.)

1299 Edward marries Margaret of France. Pope Boniface claims Scotland as a fief of the Papal See.

1300 Great reformation of the coinage. Commission of Trailbaston. Enquiry as to forest grievances. *Articles upon the Charters.*

1301 Great Parliament at Lincoln. The magnates repudiate the Papal claim on Scotland. Ineffectual campaign in Scotland.

1302 Crushing defeat of the French by the Flemings at COURTRAI.

1303 Segrave and the English defeated at Rosslyn. The Scots capture Stirling. Edward obtains grant of "new" Customs from foreign merchants; the native merchants refuse.

1304 Many of the Scottish nobles submit to Edward. Siege and capture of Stirling castle by the King. Second Commission of Trailbaston.

1305 Important Parliament. Capture and execution of WALLACE. Meeting of English and Scottish representatives in London, and scheme for government of Scotland (Sep. 15). New Pope (Clement V.) releases Edward from his oath to the charters.

1306 Scottish rising under Bruce (grandson of the Competitor). Murder of John Comyn. Prince Edward knighted with great pomp. Great expedition to Scotland. Bruce defeated at Methven (June 25). The Pope makes large grants of ecclesiastical revenues to Edward. Execution of Earl of Athol and two Bruces.

1307 *Parliament of Carlisle.* Statute against Papal taxation. Banishment of Piers Gaveston. Bruce defeats the English at Loudon Hill. Edward starts out to meet him, and dies on the road (July 7). Buried at Westminster (Oct. 18).

RULERS OF CHRISTENDOM

1239-1307

ENGLAND.	Henry III.
1272.	Edward I.
SCOTLAND.	Alexander II.
1249.	Alexander III.
1286.	The Maid.
1290–2.	Interregnum.
1292.	John Balliol.
1296–1306.	Interregnum.
1306.	Robert Bruce.
FRANCE.	St. Louis (IX).
1270.	Philip III.
1285.	Philip IV.
EMPIRE.	Frederick II.
	William of Nassau (1248).
1250.	Richard of Cornwall (opp. by Alfonso of Castile).
1273.	Rudolf of Habsburg.
1292.	Adolf of Nassau.
1298.	Albert of Austria.
CASTILE.	Ferdinand III.
1252.	Alfonso X.
1284.	Sancho IV.
1295.	Ferdinand IV.
ARAGON.	James I.
1276.	Peter III.
1285.	Alfonso III.
1291.	James II.
NAVARRE.	Theobald I.
1253.	Theobald II.
1270.	Henry I.
1274.	Jeanne (m. Philip IV. of France. ob. 1314).
1305.	Louis (X. of France).
HUNGARY.	Bella IV.
1270.	Stephen IV.
1272.	Ladislas IV.
1292.	Andrew III.
1301–5.	Wenceslas.
1305.	Otto I.
BOHEMIA.	Wenceslas I.
1278.	Wenceslas II.
1305.	Wenceslas III.
1306.	Henry of Carinthia m. Anne of Bohemia (opp. by Rudolf of Austria).

NORWAY.	Hakon IV.	1268–71.	Vacancy.
1263.	Magnus VI.	1271.	Gregory X.
1281.	Eric II.	1276.	Innocent V.
1299.	Hakon V.		Adrian V.
	——		John XXI.
SWEDEN.	Eric III.	1277.	Nicholas III. (Orsini.)
1250.	Birger Jarl.	1285.	Honorius IV. (Savelli.)
1266.	Waldemar.	1288.	Nicholas IV.
1279.	Magnus I.	1294.	Celestine V. (Morrone.)
1290.	Birger II.		Boniface VIII. (Gaetani.)
	——	1303.	Benedict XI. (Bocasi.)
DENMARK.	Waldemar II.	1305.	Clement V. (Goth.) At Avignon.
1241.	Eric IV.		——
1250.	Abel.	EASTERN EMPIRE.	
1252.	Christopher.		John III.
1259.	Eric V.	1254.	Theodore II.
1286.	Eric VI.	1258.	John IV.
	——	1261.	Michael VIII.
POPES.	Gregory IX. (Ugolino.)	1282.	Andronicus II.
1243.	Innocent IV. (Fieschi.)		
1254.	Alexander IV.		
1261.	Urban IV. (Pantaleone.)		
1265.	Clement IV. (Foulquois.)		

EDWARD PLANTAGENET

EDWARD PLANTAGENET

CHAPTER I

THE MIDDLE AGES IN EUROPE

THE first lesson to be learnt by the student of the past is, resolutely to close his eyes against the conditions of the present. Just as the wise traveller leaves behind him his home life, adopts, so far as possible, the ways and thoughts of the people amongst whom he sojourns, and becomes, for the time being, a stranger to his own country, so the student of history must strive by all means to reach the point of view of the period which he studies, to become, as far as possible, a man of the age on which his eyes are fixed. The objects of study and travel are very much alike. They aim at widening the view, storing the mind, deepening the experience of life. It is common knowledge, that much of the keenest pleasure of travel comes when the travel is over, and the traveller, safely returned, studies the familiar objects with an eye sharpened by the force of contrast. So with the student of history.

Returned from his visit to the thirteenth century, he will be the better able to understand the twentieth. And the more completely he has forgotten, for a time, the century in which he lives, the more forcibly will it appeal to him on his return. For this is one of the secrets of history, that in studying the past we also unconsciously study the present.

Barbarism of medieval Europe.

And so, in turning our eyes upon Europe in the Middle Ages, we must try to grasp a fact so alien from present ideas that the first effort will probably be in vain. We have for so long looked upon Europe as the centre of civilisation, that we cannot, at first, realise it as the home of barbarism. To us, the East has so long been the prey of the European adventurer, the easy plunder of European courage and brains, that we cannot think of the positions reversed. Although our book of books, the Holy Bible, is admittedly a gift from East to West, yet we look upon our science, our literature, our art, our thought—in a word, our civilisation generally, as immeasurably superior to anything which the East can shew. As for our material resources, we should smile with contempt if any benighted Oriental ventured to dispute our supremacy. And yet, in the ninth century Europe was to Asia, very much what Central and Southern Africa now are to Europe.

The Middle Ages.

Much of this difficulty arises, no doubt, from certain phrases which we absorb unconsciously in the days of which nothing is forgotten. We speak of the 'Middle Ages,' till we convince ourselves that they are a stage in the onward march from the civilisation of Greece and Rome to the civilisation of England and America. The phrase is really an accident of chronology. The Middle Ages began when Constantine moved the seat of his empire from Rome to Constantinople; but that very step transferred the centre of Roman civilisation to the borders of Asia, and left Western Europe helpless before the inroads of the barbarians. Even the Greek civilisation, with all its intellectual and physical beauty, was never a great material civilisation; and no civilisation which is not material can hope to win the masses of men. At any rate, when the Roman Empire fell, the treasures of Greek life and thought became sealed to Europe for many centuries. With the Middle Ages then, we *begin* the history of Western Europe; for history is the record of civilisations, not the mere annals of different lands.

A.D. 330.

The downfall of the Roman Empire left all Europe north of the Alps as truly a prey to adventurers as ever was America in the sixteenth century, Australia in the eighteenth, or Africa in the nineteenth. The thin varnish of material civilisation spread over it by the empire of the Cæsars, only made the prize more tempting. The dying organisation of the Roman government was powerless to withstand the westward march of the barbarians. For the space of five hundred years, from the fifth century to the tenth, the history of Europe is little more than one prolonged scramble for the land; and the only question of serious interest is—who will come out victorious?

The settlement of Europe.

At first there seems to be no clue to the dazzling mass of confusion which seethed in Europe during those years. Kings and chiefs come and go, lands are conquered and exchanged, aimless battles disturb the peace, family quarrels breed long wars which seem to end in nothing. Bands of warriors, led by fierce adventurers, burst through the Alps, swoop down on the remains of Italian industry, eat the land bare, hurry on into Gaul, meet other bands of warriors, plunge into deadly conflict, disappear from sight. A swarm of pirates, coming from the unknown North, sails up the mouth of a great river, harrying, burning, plundering. Allured by the charms of the land, these pirates may send for their wives and children, or intermarry with their wretched victims, and found a permanent State. Or, again, fired by rumours of yet richer booty, they may sail away when the spring comes, and be heard of no more. What is to be the end of it no one can foresee ; only one thing is clear, that neither by land nor by sea is there safety for honest labour. The peasant sows his corn; but the warrior devours his crops. The trader ventures all on his voyage; the ship is captured ere she reaches port.

But, looking steadily at this confusion, we can see at last what is the great question that is settling itself amid so much suffering and wreck. The many rivals for the soil of Europe are seen to fall into two great groups, divided from each other by two great barriers, one of climate, the other of religion. On the one hand are the pale races of the North, not of Europe

The dividing lines.

Climate.

only but of Asia,—Scandinavians, Goths, Lombards, Franks, Saxons, Lithuanians, Poles, Avars, Bulgarians,—representing roughly, the cold or temperate climates of the world. On the other are the dark races of the South, the Arabs, Moors, and Syrians, the fierce and subtle products of the burning deserts of northern Africa and Asia. In a sense, all were uncivilised races; the true civilisations of the world as it then stood, the Egyptian, Hindu, and the distant Chinese, stood aloof from the scramble. But the southern races had acquired from their contact with these a thin covering of arts and sciences, to which the rude tribes of the North could lay no claim.

Religion.

The other barrier which divided these contending groups, was the barrier of religion. The efforts of the Christian missionaries had succeeded, by the end of the ninth century, in converting at least to a nominal acceptance of the Christian faith, the lands of Western and Northern Europe. The limits of Christendom included the countries now known as Italy, France, Western Germany, Denmark, England, and Northern Spain. The conversion of the conquering Franks at the end of the fifth century had set an irresistible impulse at work; and, as the Frankish power grew, it was natural that men should begin to think of an united Christendom under the dual leadership of the Frankish King and of that great ecclesiastic of the West who still dwelt in the city of the Cæsars, the Pope of Rome. The union was for a long time very slight; its members quarrelled and fought among themselves. But as the struggle

Conversion of the Franks.

with the invaders from the South became more and more terrible, men came slowly to realise that this was a fight, not only for lands and homes, but for the faith of Christ against the followers of the Prophet.

For the real danger of the invasion from the South lay in the fact that it at last ceased to be a mere
Mahometanism. rabble of scattered bands, each bent on plunder; it became an organised development of a great religious system. The triumphs of Mahomet had not ended with his death. Within
632. fifty years of that event, the mighty
Caliphate of the Omayyads had been founded at Damascus; and in the eighth century its conquests spread rapidly over Asia Minor, India, Northern Africa, and Spain. It was this last and most daring development which finally roused a militant Christendom; and Charles Martel, Chief of the Franks, fairly earned his title as leader of Christian Europe and champion of the northern races, by
732. defeating the Saracen hosts at Tours, just
a century after the death of the Prophet. Not that we are to suppose any definite recognition of his claims by his northern rivals. The hands of Charles' predecessors had been heavy on their neighbours; and his successors continued the tradition. But, almost unconsciously, the Frankish King drifted into the position of champion of Christianity; and every enlargement of the Frankish borders, against Avars, Bohemians, Saxons, and Lombards, meant an increase of the boundaries of Christendom. At length the great idea, which had

been so long vaguely floating in the minds of men, was seized and made material by a great Pope and a great warrior; and Charles the Great was solemnly crowned in Rome, on Christmas Day, 800, not as German King, but as Emperor and King of the Romans, the destined reviver of the Christian Empire of Rome, under whose sway the world had once enjoyed peace. The Christian Church of the West had broken away from the Eastern Church at Constantinople; the Pope had renounced allegiance to the Eastern Emperor. The desertion of four hundred years was to be avenged. Once more the seat of Empire was to be on the Seven Hills. And if the secular rulers of the Empire were to be found oftener at Aachen, or Trier, or Köln, on the march or in the camp, than in the palaces of the Cæsars, still, in the person of the Pope the spiritual head of the Empire would still watch over the Eternal City, and guard the gates of Christendom. The Sword of the Flesh would be aided by the Sword of the Spirit.*

Leo III.

It was a brilliant idea, perhaps the most brilliant ever conceived by the Western mind; but it was only possible in a world in which fiction was stronger than fact, which lived in the dim tradition of the past, rather than in the steady light of the present. Charles himself had been a man of genius; and the very essence of genius is its rarity. He had carried his victorious arms from the Spanish Mark to the Elbe and the Weser, from

The Empire of Charles.

* For a full account of the life and reign of Charles the Great, the reader is referred to the work by Mr. Carless Davis in this series.

Hungary to the western shores of Gaul. He had even, with more doubtful right, absorbed the Christian kingdom of Lombardy, whose heresy was an eyesore to the neighbouring Popes. And during his lifetime, he somehow held together, by an elaborate revival of the Roman provincial system, the vast territories which owned his sway. But his empire perished, as all revivals must, when the sudden enthusiasm died, which called it into being. In less than a century from the death of Charles, it seemed as though all his work were to do over again. The mighty structure he had reared fell all to pieces. Once more Europe was a mass of petty chiefships and communities, each doing that which was right (or wrong) in its own eyes. Once more was it girt by a ring of threatening heathenism,—northern pirates, eastern Wends, and Magyar horsemen, worst of all, in the south, by the dread Moslems. In the eighth century the Omayyad Caliphate of Damascus had fallen, only to be replaced by the still more splendid Abbaside Caliphate of Bagdad. The great
786-808. Harun al Rashid had sought the friendship of the great Emperor Charles; but would his successors respect the petty princes who divided the empire of Charles amongst them? True, Mahometanism was not so strong as it seemed. The Emir of Cordova refused to acknowledge the Caliph at Bagdad; and the latter, in his anxiety to maintain his dynasty, had taken a step which was at last to prove its ruin, by arming the Turcoman tribes on his border, and enlisting them under the banner of the Prophet. Like the Prætorians of old Rome,

these had turned against their masters. But against the foes of Islam they were a new and awful terror. Not without reason have historians agreed to call the two centuries which followed the death of Charles the Great, emphatically, the Dark Ages. The reign of peace seemed as far off as ever.

Feudalism.

Out of the wreck there arose the two great pillars on which were laid the foundations of modern civilisation,—feudalism and monasticism. The vast empire of Charles the Great could not be governed from a single centre; it needed an elaborate system of local officials, entrusted with great powers. In his scheme of government, Charles had, no doubt, been guided largely by the only model within his reach, that Roman Empire which he believed, at the last, that it was his mission to revive. Whether his eyes were fixed more on the old Western Empire of Marcus Aurelius and Alexander Severus, or on the later Eastern Empire of Theodosius and Justinian, it is difficult, without a minute study of the period, to determine. But it is fairly clear, that the system of Charles contained fatal defects, from which the Roman system, in its better days, had been free. In the first place, the great officials of the Roman provinces had been sent out from the seat of Empire, and kept carefully free from local influences. They were not allowed to marry among their provincial subjects, nor to acquire landed property within the limits of their governments. Charles' officials, on the other hand, were often chosen from among the very chiefs and

Defects of the Carolingian system.

Local influences.

petty rulers whom he had subdued, and who bore against him an undying grudge for their loss of independence. No doubt the plan seemed an easy solution of a difficulty; no doubt a conquered territory accepted the rule of its old chiefs with less bitterness than the government of strange officials. But it was fatal to the central power. For, while the dukes and counts of Charles' Empire were willing enough to overawe their dependents by the use of imperial titles and symbols, they were still more willing to use their old local influence to defy the orders of the Imperial Court, and to scheme for the recovery of their lost independence. Again, such officials as these could not be treated as mere temporary agents, who could be recalled at pleasure and transferred to distant posts. The wise Roman administration never allowed a provincial governor to grow warm in his seat. To the cosmopolitan Roman or Byzantine, all countries were more or less alike, or rather, his preference for this or that sphere of labour was dictated solely by prudence. But the barbarian chief, transported from his native soil and his own folk, would have been a wretched exile among a people whose language he did not understand, and whose country and mode of life were utterly alien from him. And so, almost inevitably, the officials of Charles and his successors became permanent in their offices. Charles himself refused to give them anything more than a life tenure; but his weak successors went further, and admitted the right of a son to succeed to his father's position. The date usually assigned to this

Heritable offices.

vital mistake is the year 877; but it is more than likely that the decree of that year only recognises a practice which appeared so soon as the strong hand of Charles himself was withdrawn by death.

Add to this the fact, that the Frankish system, again unwisely (but perhaps inevitably) departing from the Roman model, provided no sala-
ries for its local officials, but allowed them 814.
to retain a fixed proportion of the revenue arising from their districts—the fines for bloodshed and disturbances, such scanty remains of the Roman system of tribute as were still enforced, and the various other claims of the imperial treasury. This fatal practice was even formally sanctioned by Charles the Great himself, on his conquest
of Lombardy, though with many strict 790.
safeguards. But it soon spread far beyond the limits which he assigned to it; for it descended to the European system as one of the worst legacies of the Middle Ages. Again it seemed so obvious, to encourage the activity of the imperial officer by rewarding him according to the fruit of his labours; but again the practice proved fatal to the central government. The ideas to which it gave rise were fostered too by another practice of the Frankish monarchs, which allowed their officials to farm the royal domains within their districts at profitable rates, in the hope that they would thus be tempted to keep the land in good order. The result was, of course, that the officials, while carefully guarding themselves against any admission of larger profit, strove by every means to increase that part of the

Payment by results.

revenue which fell to their share. And so it was not very wonderful that, in less than a century from the death of Charles, the governors whom he had set up, the dukes, marquises, and counts of the Frankish Empire, had come to look upon themselves, not as officials to carry out the orders of a central government, but as *proprietors*, or, as the ideas of the time had it, *lords*, of fiefs or benefices. These they held at a fixed rent or "render" from their suzerain, to whom they owed nominal allegiance; but in them they acted as independent rulers, and from them they and their heirs could only be displaced on one or two well-defined grounds, and then only if the central government happened to be strong enough to enforce its rights.

Military authority.

The final touch to the position of the feudal noble was given by his military duties. In the Roman system, the civil administrator had nothing, at least in later days, to do with the soldiery. The armies of the later Roman Empire were professional, and were placed under the command of purely military officials, kept carefully apart from the ordinary provincial governors. Dangerous as the principle may have been on general grounds, it at least was a great safeguard against the evils of feudalism, the very essence of which is, that all the powers of government, military and civil, shall be concentrated in the hands of a single ruler, permanently fixed in a certain district. The military policy of the Franks led precisely to this result; for, reverting to the older idea of citizen service, they demanded of all their free subjects unpaid service in the host, and left the enforcement of their demands to those same officials to whom they also entrusted the collection of their revenues, and the maintenance of order. Again, as inevitably happens in primitive systems of government, the number of soldiers to be furnished by each official to the host, soon became fixed by custom; and, so long as he was ready on demand with the prescribed number, no questions were asked about his mode of raising them. Thus the famous distinction between feudal and militia service grew up. The feudal official retained in his pay the regular number of fighting men, either humbler officials who, in their subordinate places, repeated his position, or simple retainers, men-at-arms who lived at his table and fought in his quarrels without asking questions. Only in great crises, and in well-governed countries, was the levy of the peasantry revived. The continual, ordinary, fighting which went on, was done by the professional fighting class, noble, knightly, or merely hireling; the peasant had other work to do in the social scheme.

Thus it is not hard to understand how Europe once more fell to pieces after the deaths of the great Frankish rulers. The Frankish Empire was so brilliant in its day, that the shortness of its life is not always recognised. From the coronation of Pepin the Short, at Soissons, to the death of Lewis the Pious, are less than one hundred years; and these are liberal limits for the Frankish Empire. What wonder that the great Charles himself only succeeded in keeping

The Dark Ages.

752.

840.

his Empire together by the use of vigorous measures, by the steady supervision of his distant domains through his *missi*, or confidential officials, by his insistence on his local deputies making frequent journeys to his court to report upon the state of their districts. Under the feeble rule of his son, the great building rocked to its foundations; at his death it fell
843. to pieces. Even the partition of Verdun failed to check the rush of dissolution. Once more Christendom became a mass of warring chiefdoms, the throne of Charles the Great an empty honor, which carried no real power.

The legacy of the Frankish Empire.

But the brilliant episode of the Frankish Empire was not without results. Not only had it revived a great idea, which for centuries haunted the mind of Europe, and, on the whole, worked for good; it had contributed to the practice of men two definite rules, which did much to help the cause of progress, and to redeem the anarchy of the ninth and tenth centuries from the utter hopelessness of the sixth and seventh.

The homestead.

The first of these was fixity of abode. The homestead, with all the possibilities which it implies, was largely the result of the fostering care of Charles the Great. The wild races who had invaded Europe in the fifth and sixth centuries had really been shepherds, not farmers. Among the dim causes which started the westward march of the northern hordes, certainly was that hunger for broad pastures which, as population increases, is sure to beset a pastoral folk. But as Europe filled up, the same trouble reappeared, and this time the choice lay between the Atlantic and a new scheme of life, which should enable the land to feed the increase of people. In those days the Atlantic was, of course, a barrier which none might pass. Instinctively men felt that there was no turning back. East and north were blocked by fierce races, only too willing to repeat the history of those who had gone before them. Under the eyes of men lay the answer to the problem, in the vineyards and cornfields of the Roman provincials. At first these were, of course, mere plunder, to be harried and consumed in reckless waste. And as each barbaric horde ate a conquered district bare, it rushed off on one of those wild raids which are the most terrible features of the early Middle Ages. But slowly the lesson was learned. In one code of barbarian customs we are shewn a formal, if simple, system by which the barbaric conqueror is quartered on his provincial "host," who renders him a fixed share of the produce in return for his protection against other foes. From regarding agriculture as a mere chance of plunder, the barbarian came to protect it as a source of wealth, or, at least, of existence. The brief Peace of the Frankish Empire was the turning-point in the change. With all his power Charles the Great strove to protect the husbandman, and to revive in his domains those priceless relics of Roman agriculture, which had well-nigh perished in the chaos of the invasions. But a good system of farming means years, perhaps centuries, of patient work at the same land. The rough scratching of the soil by a migrating tribe, which is here one year and gone the next, is worthy only of barbarians. And so, under the fostering care of Charles, the village homestead, with the peaceful life of unvaried toil, became the ideal of life for humble folk. All men who were not warriors or clerks, spent their lives in tilling the soil.

The warrior.

The other result of the Frankish Empire was, as we have said before, the warrior class, formed in the long wars of Charles Martel, of Pepin, and of Charles the Great himself, and organised by the great emperor into a definite scheme for the guard of his borders against the heathen. No doubt the old Frankish idea of the host, the assembly of the freemen, survived as a refuge against overwhelming danger. At the royal ban, every free subject of the Empire was bound to appear before the royal presence. But, as the Empire grew, it came inevitably to rely more and more on the professional soldier, and less and less on the armed peasant. And so the great bargain of the later Middle Ages was struck,—the peasant to till the land and provide food for the warrior, the warrior to protect the peasant against the hostile raid. Each village of farmers had its lord, whose grim castle looked down upon it from a neighbouring height. The king or emperor was far off; the lord was near. Even if he were a harsh lord, he would, for his own sake, see that no one else plundered his villages. If he were a great lord, so much the better; his arm would be stronger for defence, and, being a great lord, he would not look so sharply after his dues of labour and of corn. But if he were a small lord, he might still have over him a great lord, who would protect his vassal's villages.

Thus, when the Empire of Charles fell into fragments, each fragment, each *fief* (as it was called) was, in a sense, a real unit, capable of making some defence, however feeble, against the dangers of life. And so the feudalism of the ninth and tenth centuries, anarchic though it was, was not the hopeless anarchy of the sixth and seventh. Though, to all seeming, a reaction against the brilliant progress of the Frankish Empire, it was yet a real step in advance, all the safer that it did not make too great demands on human nature. It was only the retreating curve of the spiral.

Monasticism.

Of the other great pillar of later medieval civilisation we can speak but briefly. There are by nature, and have always been, men fit neither for the hard life of the peasant, nor for the career of the soldier. For these the one home during the Middle Ages was the monastery. The ordinary parish priest was himself much as the peasantry amongst whom he laboured. He was, in fact, part of the village life. Taking his tithes "as the plough traversed the tenth acre," he worked in the physical, no less than in the spiritual field. Until the reforms of Pope Gregory VII. in the eleventh century, he married, and begat children, who, likely enough, succeeded to his own office. He spoke the tongue of his people, and was a true son of the soil. His clerkship sat lightly upon him; and, if he could read his breviary, he had enough learning to command the respect of his parishioners. The great ecclesiastic, on the other hand, the archbishop or bishop, was of the knightly class, statesman and warrior in one, the companion of kings and

princes, at home in court and camp. He fitted well enough into the framework of feudalism. But for many men the recluse life seemed the only refuge from the anarchy of the world. Coming originally from the East, where the life of the body is easily sustained, and where the long hours of leisure foster a tendency to meditation and retirement, monasticism made its appearance in the West, even before
St. Benedict. the fall of Rome. But it was in the dark
days of the sixth century that Benedict
of Nursia fixed his cell on Monte Cassino, and
528. planted the fruitful seed which was so
soon to grow into a mighty tree. His Rule, or Order of Life, seems to us almost commonplace, so thoroughly does it accord in most respects with modern ideals, if not with modern practice. But, to the men of the sixth century, it must have appeared a scheme of almost impossible holiness. It was the Rule of a community, not of a solitary ascetic. Chastity, obedience, temperance, frugality, religious exercises are enjoined ; but hospitality and a modest enjoyment of the pleasures of the table are permitted, and, above all, the value of honest labour manual and mental, is insisted upon. The words of the Rule are well known, but will bear repetition. "Idleness is the enemy of the soul. And therefore ought the brethren to be employed at fixed hours in labour of their hands ; and again at other hours in the study of things divine." And then the Saint goes on to prescribe regular hours for meals, labour, study, and worship, with a minuteness necessary in days of universal scepticism, when men longed for the

BENEDICTINE MONK.

(*From Dugdale's "Monasticon."*)

simple voice of command to lead them in the right way.

Noble results flowed from the Rule of St. Benedict, which spread over all Europe in the two centuries that followed his death, and which planted in many a fertile valley, as a foil to the frowning castle on the height, a house of labour, sacred and profane. The services of the Benedictines to the cause of learning in those dark times have been told by one well qualified to speak.* In the scriptorium of the abbey, the priceless relics of ancient literature were preserved from fire and water, and multiplied for succeeding ages. In the same place, the chronicle of deeds, good and evil, slowly growing from year to year, has preserved for us our chief literary record of the ages gone by. From the charter room of the abbey came also those priceless examples of early legal documents, to which we are indebted for almost all that we know of the social life of the early Middle Ages. Round the abbey sprang up schools, grammar schools, and, later, schools of philosophy and science, as well as schools of theology. Charles the Great himself, urged on by one of the noblest of England's sons, Alcuin of York, shaped the good custom into a system, and regulated it by ordinance. But the labour of the hands was not forgotten. Priceless as were the services of the monastery to learning, they were no less vital to agriculture. The Roman tradition, where it survived at all, probably survived through the channel of a great religious house. One of St.

* G. H. Putnam. *Books and their Makers in the Middle Ages,* Part I., Cap. I.

Benedict's cherished objects had been, to replace the wandering groups of monks which infested Italy in his day, by communities of ordered and settled men and women, cleric and lay. Of the wandering monks he cannot speak strongly enough, of their idle, aimless life, given up to the pursuit of pleasure and unlawful self-will; and therefore he thinks it better to be silent. His monks are to set an example of settled, organised life, under the permanent rule of abbots, whom they may, indeed, elect for themselves, but whom, having elected, they must implicitly obey. They are to make the wilderness blossom as the rose, and to bring order out of chaos.

And so the monasteries appeared as little centres of peace, discipline, industry, and labour, in a stormy age. But as they prospered and became rich, they shewed the same tendency to break loose from all control as the secular princes who were their rivals. From Gregory the Great, at the Lateran Synod of 601, some had procured freedom from episcopal visitation—a doubtful boon, and afterwards the cause of fierce dispute. From the Frankish kings and emperors they secured immunity from the control of feudal officials. In all this they were thoroughly in accord with the spirit of the times. And so, alongside the great fief with its domains and villages appeared the great abbey with its villages and domains; and the abbot sat in his judgment seat and levied his taxes, and collected his men at the royal ban, and maintained his pomp and luxury, even as the neighbouring baron did. But the domains of the abbot compared well with the land

Decay of monastic influence.

BENEDICTINE NUN.

(From Dugdale's "Monasticon.")

of the baron; and the justice of the abbey was better than the justice of the castle.

It is not a little curious that the fall of the Frankish Empire was followed by a great revival of monasticism. In the peaceful years of the Empire, the Benedictine Order, rich and prosperous, had sunk into sloth. The Rule had been forgotten, or explained away. Rioting and luxury took the place of modest hospitality. Stately buildings, jewelled furniture, costly plate, were in strange contrast with the homely simplicity of the little chapel on Monte Cassino. But, in the evil days that followed the fall of the Frankish Empire, men's minds turned once more to the earlier and purer days of the Order. In the famous abbey of Cluny, founded by William of Aquitaine, Berno, its first abbot, began a mighty reform which, a century later, spread the Cluniac houses through France, Spain, Italy, and England. More than this, there was to be no more isolation. The old Benedictine houses had allowed no interference from without; theirs was the true barbaric ideal of independence. But the Cluniac foundations preserved the spirit of the Frankish Empire, and the priors of the daughter houses owed fealty and obedience to the "Abbot of Abbots" at the mother house of Cluny. The exaggeration of chroniclers fixed the number of priors attending a Cluniac General Chapter at three thousand. Making all allowances, we can realise the force wielded by such a power. A still further reaction against the decay of primitive ideals, brought into existence, in the eleventh century, the ascetic Order of

Revival of monasticism.

910.

the Carthusians, and the still more ascetic Order of the Cistercians. The last is of special interest
1084. to English-speaking folk, for it owes
1098. its foundation to an Englishman, St.
Stephen Harding; though the fame of its founder has been overshadowed by the greater fame of his illustrious disciple, St. Bernard of Clairvaux. Still, it was an Englishman whose dogged perseverence carried the little community, in the swamps near Dijon, through the hard years of its early life, and established the White Monks with their Charter of Charity, which received the Papal sanction in 1127. By the Rule of St. Stephen the growing idea of union is still further expressed. Not only is any simple monk of the Order eligible for the abbacy of any house, but at the annual General Chapter, held at Cîteaux, the assembled abbots control the policy of the whole Order, even, it may be, to the removal of the Father Abbot himself. Thus we have something very near a system of representative government. And thus we are prepared to trace the working of a new spirit in the affairs of western Europe.

CLUNIAC MONK.

(*From Dugdale's "Monasticon."*)

CHAPTER II

THE EMERGENCE OF MODERN EUROPE

850–1250

SLOWLY, very slowly, the outlines of modern Europe began to emerge from the chaos of the earlier Middle Ages. This time, the power making for peace and order had the better chance of success, in that it came from below, not from above. Modern Europe was at last formed, not by the hand of an universal conqueror, but by the slow and halting unions of petty tribes and fiefs against heathen foes. In the north-west, the citizens of Paris, hard pressed by the plundering Northmen, threw off the nominal yoke of the degenerate successor of Charles the Great, and chose their valiant Count Odo (Eudes) as King of Paris. The plan was taken up, with some misgivings, by the feudal chiefs of Western Europe ("the Frank, Burgundian, and Aquitanian princes," as they are called by a chronicler of the times), and, after some little wavering, the descendants of Odo became recognised as lawful kings of the Western Franks. Thus the future kingdom of France, the country west

France.

888.

of the Meuse and north of the Pyrenees, (a Latin-speaking country with a German name,) became an ideal to be striven for by the Kings at Paris. But for long generations it was a mere league of very independent princes, who had chosen
987. Hugh Capet to lead their defence against the "unbelieving nation of the Huns" (*i. e.*, the Northmen), which, "drunk with slaughter, rapine, and all kinds of cruelty, poured itself over the Gauls." How hard his task, may be judged from the fact that the Northmen had already, when Hugh was chosen King, made good their claim to one of the most fertile tracts of Gaul, and form-
912. ally established the almost independent province of Normandy.

East of the Rhine, the no less terrible dread of the Magyars, the founders of modern Hungary,
Germany, soon led to the choice of Conrad the
911-919. Franconian, and, after his death, of Henry the Fowler, by the feudal princes of what we should now call Germany, but which was destined, for nearly a thousand years, to be still a mass of petty princedoms, held together only in vaguest fashion by a nominal allegiance to a titular emperor. Thus we see the foreshadowing of two of the great States of modern Europe. Far
Spain. away, in the south, the heroic Counts of Castile, often hard pressed in those fortresses (*castillos*) from which their land takes its name, were waging a gallant struggle against the Moslem, who held the richest part of what we now call Spain. For long centuries here, also, the balance of power

CARTHUSIAN MONK.

(*From Dugdale's " Monasticon."*)

was destined to vibrate among a crowd of little principalities—Castile, Galicia, Leon, Barcelona, Navarre, Aragon; but here, also, we can see the beginning of the movement which was to result, in the sixteenth century, in the brilliant kingdom of Spain. The long agony of the process of union is revealed by the solemn list of titles appended, even in the thirteenth century, to the official style of the King of Castile, who must be addressed, in all formal documents, as "King of Castile, Toledo, Leon, Galicia, Seville, Cordova, Murcia, Guienne, and Algarve." Far away again, in the north, the three kingdoms of Denmark, Sweden, and Norway slowly emerged, not, it is to be feared, without much hard fighting and bloodshed,* out of the mass of petty chiefships. And, not least, England, after centuries of internal strife, and harryings by northern pirates, was being rapidly welded into a strong and compact State by the genius of her Norman kings. Strangely enough, it was in Italy, the true home of European empire, that the anarchy of the Middle Ages lingered longest. Perhaps the prize was too rich, or the claimants too many. But with wars of Norman and Lombard, rivalries of Pope and Emperor, incursions of Saracens, and dying struggles of the Eastern Empire, Italy was destined long to remain a standing menace to the peace of Europe.

Scandinavia.

England.

Italy.

The movement for union, once started, soon

* One of the by-products of the struggle was the foundation of the little colony of Iceland, by men who loved the old anarchic days, and had no fancy for a strong government.

caught the imaginations of men. While, on its practical side, it was being slowly adopted in the painful consolidation of the States of Europe, on its ideal side it had again a brilliant and adventurous career. The empire of Charles the Great still haunted men's thoughts, and it needed but the electric spark to fire the sleeping mine. The gallant adventures and generous aims of Otto the Great, who succeeded his father as German King in 936, proved to be the magic spark; and, again, as it were out of nothing, sprang the dream of universal empire. Otto was crowned Emperor in Rome, not *an* Emperor, but *the* Emperor, the successor of Charles the Great and the Cæsars. But the dream was far less perfect this time. Though still the Emperor retained, by the glory of his name and office, the precedence and respect due to the first potentate in Europe, though he still, in theory, exercised rights which nothing short of imperial power could sanction, he was, in fact, little more than a German prince with a magnificent title. He was not King, even of Germany; he was but Duke of Saxony and King of the Germans. The Western Franks, the French as we should now call them, regarded themselves as freed for ever from the rule of German Emperors, by the final election of Hugh Capet. "And so" (says the French chronicle) "the kingdom of the Franks was disjoined from the line of Charles the Great, Emperor and King of the Franks." It seems to us a subtle difference; but it pointed to a momentous fact, the definite separation of the

The Holy Roman Empire.

962.

987.

peoples east and west of the Rhine. With France closed to his troops, the Emperor could do nothing with Spain; the most romantic of all the deeds of Charles the Great, the defence of Roncesvalles, passed from German to Spanish history, and the glories of Charles' paladins were eclipsed by the glories of Cid Campeador. In later centuries, a Spanish King (Charles V.) might become Emperor; but Spain remained outside the Empire. From the very first, the Norman Kings of England openly disavowed all allegiance, both to their former overlords at Paris, and to their ancient suzerains at Aachen. They were, as they and their statesmen proudly claimed, "absolute," *i. e.*, independent of any foreign power. Scandinavia never acknowledged the Empire, even though Otto carried his victorious arms into Denmark. So the empire of Otto, the "Holy Roman Empire," was a very different thing from the empire of Charles the Great: Roman only by virtue of its shadowy claims on the Lombard lands, Holy only by virtue of its alliance with the Pope. And when, in the year after Otto's coronation, men saw the strange sight of the Emperor deposing the very Pope (John XII.) who had crowned him, and, in later years, saw Europe convulsed by the quarrels of Gregory VII. and Henry IV., and by the implacable hatreds of Gregory IX. and Frederick II., such odour of sanctity as the Holy Roman Empire once enjoyed vanished from it; and Pope and Emperor became little more than earthly potentates of the

Quarrels of Pope and Emperor, 1076.

1227–1240.

ordinary self-seeking type. Poets like Dante might dream again of a beneficent world-swaying Empire, working in spiritual harmony with the
1265-1321. Papacy. But common men saw only the petty and purely mundane strife of Guelf and Ghibellin.

Far more powerful in advancing the cause of European unity, and the march of European civilis-
The Crusades. ation, was the movement which resulted in the Crusades. The reforming zeal
Hildebrand, 1073-1085. of Gregory VII. (Hildebrand) had not ceased with his victory over the Empire. He had been the first to realise the magnificent possibilities dormant in the institutions of the Church. He saw that by uniting, organising, above all by reforming and purifying the existing materials, he and his successors might raise up a power, beside which any one of the struggling States of Europe would be as dust in the balance, a power which, by playing off one of these States against another, or by combining them all under one direction, might render itself supreme in Europe. Gregory had that rare union of imagination with hard practical sense, which makes the ruler of men. He did not despise the secular arm; he could make use of Norman soldiers if necessary. But he realised the great truth, that the world is ruled by ideas rather than by armies; and he deliberately pitted the frock of the priest against the armour of the knight. The scene in the courtyard of Canossa, where the Emperor meekly awaited the absolution of the Pope, shews the result in a flash. By insisting on

CRUSADING GALLEY.

(*From Viollet le Duc's "Dict. du Mobilier Français."*)

the celibacy of the clergy, Gregory raised up in all the countries of Christendom a host of agents, detached from worldly ties, and looking ever more and more, for direction and reward, to the Chair of St. Peter. By sternly denying, or, at least, limiting the secular rights in the matter of patronage, he not only purged the grosser scandals of simony in the Church, but created a vast source of wealth for the furtherance of his policy. By forcing the too secular bishops to submit to the visits of his legates, sent direct from headquarters, he revived the famous *missi* of Charles the Great, and established a firm hold over his nominal subordinates. The religious Orders were ready to his hand; he himself had been a monk of the famous Abbey of Cluny. By fostering the growth and ordering of a great system of Canon Law, he made the Church a formidable rival to the growing power of the royal administration of justice. In the long run, his policy proved fatal to the unity of that Church which it was his one object to exalt. But, for the time, his twelve brief years of power changed the face of Europe.

Capture of Jerusalem. 1076.

In the midst of Gregory's great career came news which struck Christendom to the heart. The Turks under Malek Shah captured Jerusalem, and, though Malek's rule was great, and professedly founded on justice and mercy, the Christian world believed, rightly or wrongly, that the Christian pilgrims to the Holy Places were treated with brutal cruelty by the Moslem conquerors. Here was Gregory's chance. With a curious blending of materialism and imagination, so typical of the Middle

Ages, the Christian world had become more and more passionately attached to the physical relics of the life of Christ on earth. And a pilgrimage to Jerusalem was becoming almost as much a duty of the Christian as a pilgrimage to Mecca of the good Moslem. Gregory saw, that if he could work up the passionate frenzy of Europe into a practical rescue of Jerusalem, the Papacy would come out of the enterprise unquestioned leader of Christendom in matters temporal and spiritual. The struggle with the Empire disappointed his hopes; but he bequeathed the plan to his successors, and, aided by the fiery zeal of Peter the Hermit, Urban II. succeeded in organising, less than a quarter

1096. of a century from Gregory's death, the armies of the first Crusade.

This is not the place in which to record the strange story of the Crusades. Like all things medieval,

The Crusades. perhaps like all things human, it is a strange mixture of high motives and base, of good and evil. Side by side with the purest devotion, the loftiest self-denial, the most patient endurance, went the most sordid self-seeking, the most open indulgence in sensual pleasures, the utter recklessness of the adventurer, and the bitter jealousy of the disappointed miser. The tale of the Crusades reads like the story of a dream. Old men, women, even children, jostle side by side with armoured knights and brutal men-at-arms. The Christians go to free the pilgrim's way, and they set up feudal principalities in the Holy Land, and perfect the maxims of feudal law under the shadow of the Temple. They go to uphold the banner of Christ against the infidel, and by the way they overthrow the one Christian Power of the East, the Empire of Constantine and Justinian, which still claimed to be *the* Roman Empire. Two great religious Orders are founded to succour Christian pilgrims, the Knights Templars and the Knights Hospitallers of John; and they are found to turn their arms against each other in pitched battle. A third Crusading Order, the Teutonic Knights, is destined to find its lasting work in the wresting of lands from the heathen Prussians, and in the establishing of a Christian State on the shores of the Baltic.

But, in spite of all these dazzling inconsistencies, the Crusades mark, in more ways than one, the beginning of modern Europe. In the first place, they are the turning of the tide which at last, after thousands of years, shifted the centre of human progress from East to West. For the second time in the world's history, the West had turned upon that prolific East, which was ever sending out her countless hordes to ravage and enslave the peoples of Europe. And if the political results of the Crusades in the East were not so striking or apparently so lasting as those of the invasions of Alexander the Great, yet, in fact, they were more profound. Europe had found her courage at last; and it can hardly be doubted, that she learned in the Crusades the real weakness of the East, and so came to challenge, finally to despise and plunder her ancient foe.

Results of Crusades.

Yet here again, it is to be feared, too many of us

miss the real danger which threatened European civilisation at the close of the Middle Ages. We

The Mongol danger.

have heard of the great Saladin *; and we know how our Crusaders were hard put to it to maintain their hold on Jerusalem against him—nay, how they failed at last, and how

1187.

Jerusalem fell again into the hands of the Moslem, after the battle of Tiberias. The pages of Scott have made us familiar from our school-days with the battles of the two great heroes

1191-2.

of Eastern and Western chivalry, Saladin and Richard Cœur de Lion. As we come to read of St. Louis, we shall see how he, in one sense the greatest of all the Crusaders, was foiled by the Mameluke Emir Bibars in Egypt. But, before the defeat at Mansourah, the Eastern danger to Europe had apparently passed from the Saracens to the Mongols; and it was only by a series of almost miraculous events, that Europe was saved from the horrors of a Yellow invasion.

The Mongols occupy a middle rank between the fair northern races and the dark southern races,

Zenghis Khan.

which have threatened Europe from the East. Their original home seems to have been somewhere in what we should now call southern Siberia, or northern China, far away to the extreme East. They seem to have been almost the earliest of the wandering races to start for the plunder of the West; for we hear of them attacking the rich provinces of China about two hundred years

* The story of his life is told in No. XXIV. of this series, by Mr. Stanley Lane-Poole.

A TEMPLAR.

(From Stothard's "Monumental Effigies.")

before the birth of Christ. Driven back by the native rulers, who built the Great Wall to defend themselves against their attacks, they then retired for some centuries to their ancient seats, in the wild mountain country. Sallying out again in the fifth century after Christ, they dashed with resistless force westward across Asia, and, under their great chief, Attila, burst like a whirlwind upon the dying Roman Empire, by whose general they were, however, at
last defeated, at the great battle of Chalons- 451.
sur-Marne. With the death of Attila, they
disappeared almost as suddenly as they had come, leaving, it may be, some traces of their presence in the Avars and Magyars of Hungary, and, it may be, in the Turkoman tribes which afterwards became the great fighting force of the Mahometan Caliphs. Again were they buried in obscurity for nearly seven hundred years, and then once more they emerged into terrible fame under their ruler, Zenghis Khan, who, having inherited the vague leadership of a few scattered tribes, succeeded, in the early years of the thirteenth century, in hammering these into a compact fighting mass. Then he turned fiercely to a career of conquest. The Tartar Mongols, like their forerunners, the Huns, were no builders of States. Theirs was simply a fighting power, which quartered itself on the wealthiest countries within its reach, and lived at free quarters while the plunder lasted. Unlike the followers of Mahomet, they had no faith to preach, save the gospel of slaughter and rapine. In their own land they had been shepherds, worshipping, like true patriarchal folk, the spirits of their ancestors.

Issuing from his native mountains, the Khan swooped first on the tempting prize of China, already trembling before the impending rumours of Tartar invasion. By the year 1215, the Tartar conquest of China was as complete as such conquerors could make it; and China has been the one conquest which the Tartars have permanently retained, imparting to the policy of the Celestial Empire that savage ferocity whose periodical outbursts horrify the world, and which is wholly alien from its native character.

Attacks China.

At this point, the Khan seems to have hesitated between an attack on the South and a march to the West. He even made offers of friendship to the Mahometan rulers of Persia, the Khorasmian dynasty, one of the fragments into which the mighty Mahometan Empire of Haroun al Raschid had dissolved in the twelfth century. Happily for Europe, his advances were met with insult, and the furious Tartar, swayed by the impulse of the moment, plunged into a deadly struggle with the Mahometan power. Nothing could withstand the shock of his invasions; Persia fell before him, and, after a few fierce battles, he took and pillaged the cities of Otrar, Khogend, Tashkend, Bokhara, and Samarcand. Then, turning south, he pursued the last representative of the once mighty kingdom of Alp Arslan, at Merv, into Afghanistan and North-Western India, leaving traces of his presence in Ghazni and the ruined city of Herat, and foreshadowing that terrible invasion of his race which, in

Invades Persia.

1220.

India.

the next century, carried devastation under Tamerlane into the fairest provinces of India, and finally resulted in the establishment of the Moghul Empire of Akbar.

Meanwhile, the Khan's generals had marched westward, and, carrying their arms beyond the Caucasus, had inflicted a terrible defeat **Russia,**
on the Russians near Kazan. Having **1222.**
completed his conquest of China, the great Khan was about to follow up the new track opened out by his generals, when his superstition **1227.**
was alarmed by an unfavorable appearance of the planets, and he turned home to die.

But his successors only awaited his death to carry on the system of conquests which were to make the name of Tartar a sound of **Ogodai.**
terror, from the China Sea to the Danube. Zenghis' son Ogodai was hardly inferior to his father in warlike prowess, and, only waiting to secure his hold on China, he dashed across Turkestan into Asia Minor, capturing Tiflis and Kars, **1237.**
and ravaging Georgia and Armenia. Here he detached his nephew and general, Batu, for the conquest of Europe, and the latter's lieutenant overran Bulgaria, while the main body of the host, under Batu himself, charged into Russia, capturing Riazan, Moscow, Vladimir, Kozelsk, and Kieff, and inflicting unheard-of atrocities on the wretched inhabitants. By this time, Europe was at least partly awake to the awful danger which threatened it; and the Emperor Frederick II. issued a general appeal which, whatever may have been his motives, and

however turgid his style, shews him to have been by far the ablest and most far-seeing statesman of his day. He even maintained an army under his son Conrad to watch the threatened invasion; but, in spite of all his efforts, and the exhortations of the
1241. Popes, the armies of Batu inflicted a crushing defeat on the Hungarians at Mohi, sacking Pesth and Gran; and, in the same year, carried their victorious arms into Poland, defeating Duke Henry of Silesia at Liegnitz, with terrible slaughter.

It now seemed as though nothing could save Europe but a desperate victory, such as that which
Death of Ogodai. had turned back Attila from the plains of Chalons, eight hundred years before. But again the hand of Providence interfered on behalf of Christendom; and the death of Ogodai,
1241. in the very year of Mohi and Liegnitz, drove the Tartar generals hurrying back to the head camp in Asia, to take part in the choice of a successor to the great Khan. A mere conquering horde like that of Zenghis loses its conquests as soon as its leaders disappear; and, in the brief breathing-space
The policy of Europe. afforded by the death of Ogodai, Europe adopted a policy which, in the long run, saved it from Tartar conquest. Instinctively the Moslems felt, that neither they nor the Christians were strong enough to stand alone against the looming storm, and they so far sank their quarrels as to offer alliance against the common foe. But Christendom could not so far forget its traditions as to accept help from the Power which held the Holy

Places. An alliance between the Head of Christendom and the descendant of the Prophet would have been regarded with horror. One of the gravest charges brought against the Emperor Frederick himself was, that he had tampered with the faith of Christendom. Better by far make common cause with the barbaric Mongol, who might be won to the faith of Christ, and who, as a fact, had proved himself a marvel of tolerance, or, at least, indifference, in matters of religion, protecting at his court Buddhist, Christian, and Mahometan teachers, with cynical impartiality. And so mission after mission was despatched to the Khans by Popes and Emperors, and, in the end, however crude their diplomacy may seem to us, they succeeded in their objects. The Tartars did not loose their hold on Russia till the days of Peter the Great, and their conquests in Asia forced the Ottoman Turks into Asia Minor and south-eastern Europe, which lived in terror of their
name till the days of the heroic John 1683.
Sobieski. Thus the Tartars may be said
to have left, as their legacy to Europe, the two great Eastern Questions, the problem of Constantinople and the problem of Pekin. But the weight of their fury was turned against the Mahometan South, and the invasion of Hulagu, the grandson of Zenghis,
resulted in the capture and sack of Bag- 1258.
dad, and the shearing away of the rich
eastern domains of the Caliphs. After this, the centre of Mahometanism was shifted for a while to Africa, where it was far less dangerous to the existence of Europe; and the greedy eyes of the Tartar

chiefs were turned on the riches of India. Thus to the West, at last, came, in some degree, the blessings of peace. There can be no doubt that the instinct of Europe was right. From the rude Mongol the Christian had nothing to fear beyond physical suffering and destruction; and from these a prudent alliance might save him. From a friendship with the subtle Moslem, he had to fear the far more deadly risk of the undermining of his faith, and the degradation of his life. And from these no treaty could save him.

Commerce.

To the Crusades Europe owes also that expansion of trade and commerce, which did so much to break up the crust of feudalism. As the earliest home of civilisation had been the East, so the earliest trade routes had run from east to west. Even before the fall of the Roman Empire, caravans brought the riches of China (Cathay) and India across the deserts to Egypt and Syria, whence they were carried by Phenician sailors to the mouth of the Danube, and the ports of Italy and southern Gaul. But the anarchy which set in with the Middle Ages had delivered over the Mediterranean and the Euxine to pirates; and the selfish policy of the Emperors at Constantinople had made the land route through Asia Minor costly and slow. The Eastern Emperors sat at the gate of Asia, and took heavy toll of the supplies of Europe. Such scanty commerce as Europe enjoyed struggled slowly up the Danube, through the walled cities of Ratisbon, Forchheim, Erfurt, and Magdeburg. But the Crusades opened up new routes. The Venetians, who had already broken in

The new routes.

upon the trading monopoly of the Eastern Empire, dealt a master stroke when, in 1198, they came to the rescue of the Crusaders with an offer of ships to convey the hosts to Palestine. The needy Crusaders were unable to find all the money demanded by the Republic, and the Doge, playing skilfully upon their hopes and fears, involved them in a quarrel with the Eastern Empire. This led to the Latin conquest of Constantinople, and the rise of Venice as a sea power. The invaders even offered the Empire to the aged Dandolo; but he wisely preferred for his city the substantial privileges of the carrying-trade. Venetian factories were established in Asia Minor, and even, following in the wake of the Crusaders, in Mahometan lands. Thousands of ships brought the treasures of the East to Venice, whence they were sent through the Alpine passes into Germany, thus avoiding the long Danube route. Augsburg, Nuremburg, and other cities sprang up as centres of distribution; and the merchants of the Teutonic Hanse built their houses in all the great cities of Northern Europe. When the Eastern Empire was restored in 1261, Michael Palæologus, burning to revenge the injuries inflicted on his line by the Venetians, transferred their trading privileges in his dominions to the Genoese, their great rivals in the Mediterranean. The Venetians retaliated by opening up a new route from India, through Arabia, by the coasts of the Red Sea and the Isthmus of Suez, through Cairo to Alexandria. But Genoa became also a mighty port, and behind her and Marseilles sprang up the trade of Avignon, Nismes, and Lyons, with the fairs of Champagne and Burgundy. Finally, even the Atlantic coasting route, used long ages before by the Phenician merchants who came to Cornwall for tin, was revived; and the wines of Gascony found their way into the cellars of the London vintners. The expansion of commerce was shewn in the rise of the great houses of the Italian cities, half merchants, half bankers,—the Spini, the Friscobaldi, the Medici, and the Aldobrandini of Florence, the Ricardi, the Ballardi, and the Betti of Lucca,—and of the many Jews, to whom the Christian dislike of usury had opened the possibilities of finance. To these, and to the great religious houses, many of the Crusading nobles had pledged their lands, to procure outfit for the journey, and, as often as not, had failed to redeem them. In both cases, the results were fatal to the spirit of feudalism, the essence of which was that each acre of land should represent a definite liability to military service. The monks themselves were, of course, exempt from military duty; and, though they admitted, in theory, a liability to provide as many soldiers as the baron whose lands they held, yet, in practice, by a skilful confusion of lands thus acquired with lands given to them by pious founders "in free alms," they evaded the liability. Hence the bitter policy of "mortmain," by which kings and princes strove to hinder the acquisition of lands by the Church.* The merchant and the Jew

The great commercial houses.

Mortmain.

* The rule against mortmain strictly forbade the alienation of land to any person or body having perpetual succession, *i. e.*, as we should now say, to any "corporation." The word "mortmain" (*mortua manus*) refers to the "dead hand" of the patron saint.

creditor, of course, merely looked upon the pledged land as so much money value. Though the Jew, as an alien, could not himself become tenant of the soil, he could and did succeed in breaking down the laws aimed at restricting the free alienation of land; and thus the great estates were broken up. Unable to enforce their feudal claims, kings and rulers accepted money payments instead, and thus the money rent took the place of personal service. With the money obtained, the kings hired mercenary troops, and the feudal knight, with his tenants marching under his pennon, threatened to become almost as rare as the armed peasant of the old militia. His place was taken by the Italian *condittiere*, the German *lanzknecht*, and the Brabançon pikeman, who would go anywhere, and fight for anyone, if the prospects of pay and plunder were good. Though the great development of industry did not take place till the fourteenth century, the increased supply of Eastern luxuries, — silk, spices, dyes, jewels, ivory, and gold,—created a new and higher class of craftsmen,—silk-weavers, goldsmiths, confectioners, and tailors, — whose productions and whose guilds, or clubs, added another attraction to the growing life of the towns.

Decay of feudalism.

But the effect of the Crusades was not wholly material. Under the enlightened rule of the great Moslem Caliphs and Sultans, the science and the philosophy of the East had flourished; and Arabian learning, in spite of the evil taint of heresy which clung to it, spread widely among the awakened spirits of Europe. The

The new learning.

capture of Constantinople by the Franks had dispersed a host of treasures, the priceless manuscripts containing the literature of the great days of Greece and Rome, which Europe was now just beginning to understand. No doubt, at first, the new learning tended to rivet still tighter the fetters of that scholastic philosophy which then bound the intellect of Europe, and which was destined to flourish for nearly two centuries more. But, alongside the philosophy of the ancients, the first beginnings of experimental science began to make their way in from Arabia; and mathematics, astronomy, botany, chemistry, and medicine, though long disguised by the mists of wonder and superstition which always accompany the birth of new sciences, sowed the seed of that mighty tree of knowledge which is but now putting out its fairest fruit. Before the years of the thirteenth century had run out, Marco Polo had made his wonderful voyages from Venice to the far East, and lifted the veil which had so long hidden from Europe the wonders of the Orient, while Roger Bacon had laid the foundations of modern experimental science.

The Roman Law.

The Crusades too had brought to Europe one work of priceless value, destined, during the next few centuries, to exercise a profound influence over the minds of men. The Law of the Roman Empire, the slow accretion of centuries, which was, in truth, the great bequest of that Empire to modern civilisation, had hitherto been studied only in the garbled versions of the Barbarian Codes. The Roman Law of the Burgun-

ENGLISH SOLDIERS OF THE TWELFTH CENTURY.

(*From Hewitt's "Ancient Armour."*)

dians, of the Visigoths, of the Ostrogoths under Theodoric, had been barbarous travesties of the treatise of Gaius and of the Code of Theodosius, cut and hacked about to suit the needs of barbarian warriors. The full, harmonious splendour of the Roman ideal of citizenship was to be found in the *Corpus Juris* of Justinian, given to the world long ages after the seat of empire had passed from Rome to Constantinople. In it the writings of the golden age of Roman Law, the days of Paulus, Ulpianus, Modestinus, Papinianus, Gaius, Pomponius, had been polished and harmonised by subtle Greek casuistry into the *Digest* or *Pandects*, that storehouse of moot cases in which, as it seemed to the student of the thirteenth century, every conceivable difficulty had been anticipated and explained. Alongside of this priceless effort of practical philosophy came the mighty Code of statutes, in which a long succession of emperors had provided for the daily needs of the world which they governed. It may well be that the vague survival of the Empire in Europe, through the hands of Charles the Great and Otto, conferred upon the Imperial *Code* the quasi-sanctity of historical tradition. But the modern conception of Law, as the command of sovereign authority, to be obeyed as such, regardless of its inherent virtue or vice, was a conception alien from the common ideas of medieval Europe. The Roman Law claimed the devotion and the study of men, just as, but much more than, their own local customs claimed their obedience and respect, because it seemed to them to express the highest possible results of earthly wisdom. It was the Bible of the layman, just as the Sacred Scriptures were the Bible of the cleric,—a thing to be pored over, studied, glossed, expounded, and preached, with all the fervour of missionary zeal. And when the jealousy of the Church strove to ostracise it in favour of her own Canon Law, which, to no small degree, was borrowed from it, the sting of persecution only added zest to the study; and the Church made a grave mistake when she forced into existence, alongside of her own clerks, who had long enjoyed a monopoly of intellectual work, a second and rapidly growing profession of lawyers, none too friendly to the Order from which they had seceded, and destined, in the long run, to oust that Order from its most valued and profitable offices. Of the fate of the Roman Law in Europe we shall have more to say at a later stage; but here it is well to remember, that the enthusiastic reception given to it in the newly founded universities, or homes of higher learning, in Bologna, Siena, Padua, Paris, and Oxford, proves beyond a doubt, if proof were needed, that, with the thirteenth century, the long night of the Dark Ages of Europe had passed into a brilliant dawn, and that the mind of Europe was emerging into the full vigour of manhood.

CHAPTER III

ENGLAND IN THE THIRTEENTH CENTURY

IF we pass now, from the general picture of Europe in the thirteenth century, to that of England, we begin naturally with the condition of the peasant. For, in spite of the stirrings of foreign trade, and the growth of town life which had already begun, England in the thirteenth century was still an almost purely agricultural country. Bread and ale were the great necessaries of life; and these could only be produced by the ploughing of fields and the reaping of corn. Food-supply from abroad was still a thing undreamt of; and such was the isolation of life in the villages, that even a famine in Norfolk hardly brought corn from Kent. Owing, also, to the still primitive farming, the return of the farmer was, to our ideas, very small. Walter of Henley, a famous authority on farming in the thirteenth century, considers threefold to be an average harvest; in poor years, if the farmer gets back his seed corn with as much again, he may count himself lucky. So that, to feed the two millions of people, or there-

Agriculture.

Walter of Henley.

abouts, in the England of the thirteenth century, not much less than five-sixths of the entire population must have been directly at work, for part of the year at least, on the soil. And so, above all things, we must think of the England of the thirteenth century, not as a land of mighty cities and trim villas, but as a land of fields and villages, in which everything centred round the great event of the year, the corn harvest.

The medieval village.

Picking our way slowly along the road which, if it be not one of the great trunk routes maintained for the passage of the royal armies, is probably a mere track in the forest, we arrive at last at the village of which we are in search. The cottages of the peasants are huddled together in the centre; and we notice at once how roughly they are built, and how they all appear of much the same size. Perhaps a larger house, built of brick and timber instead of wattle and clay, and roofed with shingles instead of thatch, marks the dwelling of the bailiff; possibly another substantial house is the rectory, but it is an even chance that there is no resident parson. Mayhap the church, lately rebuilt in that glorious Gothic which is one of the surest marks of the greatness of the time, stands in the centre of the village; but, as likely as not, it cowers under the shadow of the castle or manor-house hard by.

If it be not one of those saints' days * which were,

* Walter of Henley reckons the number of holidays in the year at fifty-six. The enormous stimulus given to money-getting by the Puritan attitude towards saints' days has never been fully appreciated.

as their name implies, the "holidays" of the time, and which, with their frequent recurrence, earned for the country, in pre-Reformation times, the title of "merrie England," we will follow the villagers afield, and watch them at their tasks. The first thing which strikes us is the absence of those lovely hedges, thick with bursting shoots, and studded with wild flowers, which, in the spring and summer, are now the chief glory of the English countryside. In their places we see only great balks, or strips of unploughed turf, dotted with trees, under which sheep are lazily feeding, and with those uncouth windmills which, in the thirteenth century, are just being introduced as an Eastern novelty. But these balks by no means take the place of the modern hedges. They are far fewer in number, and, practically, only divide the ploughed land of the village into three great fields (or, it may be, only two), while these are left entirely open, being merely intersected by wandering footpaths. If it is during the time of haygrowth, from Hokeday * to Lammas, † the meadows may be divided off into sections by a sort of rude fencing, which consists, probably, only of long poles laid across heaps of stones—the ancestors of the modern "post-and-rail." ‡ But after hay harvest even these are removed; and all the winter long the fields of the village are as open as a chessboard.

Open fields.

* The second Tuesday after Easter.

† August 1st.

‡ This temporary fencing may be seen in Sweden at the present day.

Beyond the arable and the meadow, there is fairly sure to be a wide expanse of scrub and woodland, which shuts the village off from the outer world, and which provides rough food for its humbler inmates—the hogs which rout up the acorns, and the geese which pick the coarse grass from the waste.

The waste.

Looking again at the villagers as they work, we shall notice further points of difference from the countryside of to-day. Instead of the light plough, guided by a single ploughman, with, maybe, a lad to lead the pair of horses which draw it easily along the clean land, we see huge wooden frames, drawn by six or even eight oxen, each yoke guided by its master; for the land is heavy, and thick with coarse weeds. Oxen are cheaper to work with than horses; they eat less in the winter, and they do not require shoeing. Each villager of the better sort has his yoke of oxen, which he will bring to the common ploughing in due turn. As to the ploughs, no one exactly knows to whom they belong: there have been ploughs in the village from time immemorial, and, when they need repair, they are mended by the village carpenter or the village smith, who, in turn, receives a certain amount of corn from each of the husbandmen. The seed corn is probably provided by the "lord" of the village, whose land lies intermixed with that of the villagers in the open fields, and whose bailiff watches the daily labour of the villagers, to see that the "demesne" receives its due share of ploughing, weeding, and reaping. The oxen, sheep, and

The village at work.

pigs of the villagers feed together on the common wastes; and are looked after, not by their respective owners, but by officials acting on behalf of the village as a whole, and maintained by the produce of certain strips of land set aside for the purpose from time immemorial. In the rare event of any new departure from the traditional arrangements, the matter is discussed by the villagers gathered around the moot tree. But the real guiding and controlling force, checked only by the impenetrable thicket of custom, is the "lord."

The lord.

For the distinction between capital and labour was just as clear in the English village of the thirteenth century as in the English village of to-day. But it was in an earlier stage of development, which is both interesting and suggestive. It depended, not on contract, but on custom. In some mysterious way, the precise nature of which is still a matter of grand dispute, the forces which went to the making of feudalism had resulted in binding the peasant to the soil, and rendering him the servant, the "serf," of the neighbouring noble or knight. No doubt it was part of the unconscious bargain struck in the evil days of Continental anarchy, when the one hope of safety for the husbandman lay in placing himself under the protection of the strong man armed. In return for this protection, the peasant set aside part of his holding for the support of the lord's household; and this in time became regarded, quite naturally, as the "demesne" or own

The serf.

land of the lord. Or the peasant rendered his protector, at stated intervals, a fixed portion of the produce of his lands, naturally in kind, for in those days money was almost unknown, except in the coffers of kings and great men. Then, as States grew up, and kings made regular demands of tribute from their subjects, the noble made himself answerable to the king for the dues of the peasants near his "manor," or abode; and the King, glad to be saved the labour and inconvenience of collecting miscellaneous produce from thousands of little homesteads, willingly allowed the noble to pay a fixed or fixable sum, as representing the produce of a given district, and to recoup himself as best he might. Thus the familiar features of medieval serfdom gradually revealed themselves. The serf could not be personally ill-used, or arbitrarily removed from his holding; for his ancestors were, in all probability, settled on the land long before the days of feudalism. On the other hand, he could not depart without his lord's license, for who then would render the lord's dues in labour and in kind? He could not change the course of husbandry, for that would be to disconcert a system which depended for its success upon the harmonious co-operation of all its members. He could not send his son to school, nor give his daughter in marriage beyond the village, for that would be to diminish the number of labourers on the lord's domain. But the claims of the lord could not be arbitrarily increased, merely because the capacity of the village land and the profits of farming improved. There was as yet no

" economic theory of rent," which regarded all margin beyond a bare working profit as the natural perquisite of the owner of the soil. It is even doubtful if the question of " ownership " had ever definitely presented itself to people's minds. Still less was the average peasant a mere journeyman, without a hold upon the soil, who could be employed at a daily wage if his labour were required, and turned adrift to starve if it were not needed. Perhaps the Norman Conquest, with its introduction of Continental ideas, which hardly tallied with the facts of English history, had unduly depressed the great mass of the English peasantry in the social scale. But the gulf between the manorial lord and the cottager with his little patch of land, who might not know in the morning what work he would have to do before the evening, was bridged over by the substantial class of " virgaters," who held farms of thirty acres, scattered in strips over the open fields, and who, if they owed week-work and boon-work to their lords, had yet at least half their time to themselves, and by the still higher " freemen " or "socagers," who only worked at harvest time on the lord's domain, and sent occasional presents of eggs and butter to the castle.

Isolation.

The great feature of medieval village life, at any rate in the thirteenth century, was not poverty but isolation, an isolation rendered all the more hopeless by the rigid system of custom by which each village conducted its affairs. It was this which rendered any unforeseen calamity, such as a famine or a fire, so terrible a scourge.

Each village provided only for its own wants; its aim was to be self-supporting. Each autumn saw the total produce of the fields stored in the great common barns, there to be thrashed as wanted during the long winter months. Such of the oxen as were not needed for the plough were killed off and salted down for the winter's food; for there were no roots and very little hay in store. The few sheep furnished a supply of coarse wool, which was woven into the rough garments of the villagers. The small ale, which was almost the universal drink, was brewed by the women from the barley, which alternated with the wheat in the course of husbandry. Salt and iron, brought by pedlars on pack-horses, were almost the only articles imported; and to procure money for these the bailiff would, perhaps, send a small quantity of corn to the nearest market, where it was bought for consumption by the Court, or by the few townsmen who did not grow their own food-supply.

But there were signs, even in the thirteenth century, that this ancient system was breaking down.

Signs of change.

The advent of peace (and this peace, despite the interlude of anarchy under Stephen, came sooner in England than elsewhere), gave the peaceful arts a chance; and, even in the thirteenth century, the spirit of reform was in the air. The three or four agricultural treatises of the period which have survived to us, and which were the classical text-books of the landowner for the next two centuries,—the work of Walter of Henley, previously referred to, the anonymous *Husbandry*

ENGLISH ARTISANS OF THE THIRTEENTH CENTURY.

(*From Strutt's "Dress and Habits."*)

and *Seneschaucie* of about the same date,*—shew that men were beginning to look on agriculture, not merely as a means of subsistence, but as a means of profit. The much-vexed question of the relative advantages of the "three-field" and the "two-field" system of farming was settled in favour of the former, by the triumphant proof that the same area, thus worked, yielded thirty-three per cent. more produce than under the rival system, while it actually involved twelve per cent. less ploughing. Still more important was the change in the condition of labour which was being gradually introduced. The value of labour and kind dues had long been *reckoned* in money; with the increase in the supply of coin brought about by the Crusades, and the keenness to increase the productiveness of the soil shewn by the new lords or mortgagees of estates, it was beginning to be *commuted* for money. And thus a new class of farmers was slowly growing up, a class of men who rendered their dues only in money, and spent their time and cultivated their lands as they pleased. The change at first only touched the higher ranks of the peasantry, and drew a sharp line between the "free" tenant, whose bargain with his lord was fixed and definite, and would be protected, if need be, by the King's courts, and the "villein" or "base" tenant, who still rendered his dues in kind, whose holding was still governed by the custom of the village, and

Money payments.

* These have been published together, in a handy form, under the editorship of Professor Cunningham and the late Miss Lamond. Longmans, 1890.

whose affairs were dealt with only in the manorial court of the lord himself. But it enabled the great proprietors to carry out experiments in farming, which would have been impossible in the days when customary service was universal. Gradually there appeared a class of paid labourers, whom the lord's bailiff employed when he thought fit, and who, when their services were not required on the land, drifted away to the growing towns, and formed the nucleus of the modern proletariat. But all this was only in its infancy in the thirteenth century.

The castle.

At that time, the evil results of the bad days of Stephen were still to be seen, in the strong castles which dotted the land. If the lord of the village were a great lord, it was more than probable that he lived in a fortified place, not in a simple manor-house. For, in spite of all the efforts of Henry of Anjou, who strove with might and main to undo his predecessor's work, the feudal castle was a very genuine thing, even in his days; and it did not tend to disappear under the weak rule of his two sons, or in the feeble minority of Henry III. One of the most serious features of the situation was, that the art of defence was gaining on the art of attack. Not only had the steady development of defensive armour rendered the knight, and even the man-at-arms, almost impervious to ordinary weapons ; but a castle built on thoroughly advanced principles was wellnigh impregnable, except to a surprise. The Crusaders had brought back with them to Europe a knowledge of fortresses which could defy all the clumsy weapons of the

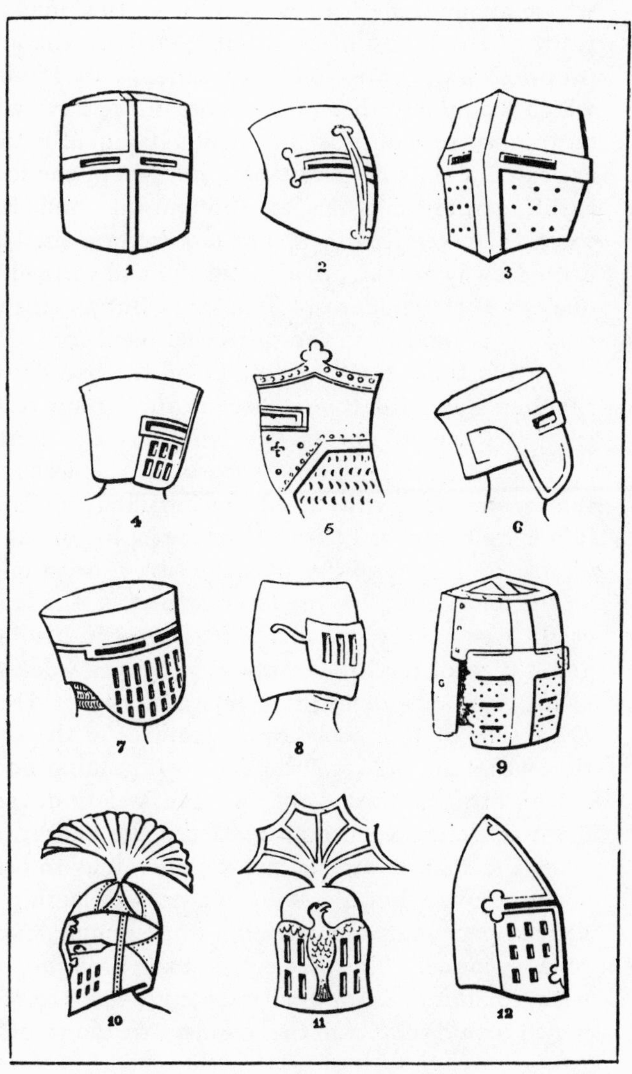

HELMETS OF THE THIRTEENTH CENTURY.

(*From Hewitt's "Ancient Armour."*)

siege train, as it then was known. In its desperate defence against the Saracens, the Eastern Empire had slowly evolved a perfection in the art of defence which was beyond the imagination of the architects of Europe. The main features of this defence were studied by the Crusaders, and reproduced on their own lands, more with a view of rendering themselves independent of royal control, than with any definite prospect of requiring such elaborate protection against a foreign foe. Beyond the old Norman keep, or donjon, protected by a wall of comparatively slight strength, the "curtain," or outer wall now covered an immense area, within which sheep and cattle could be kept and fed, barracks, workshops, and even houses built, and enormous quantities of food and drink stored. This outer wall itself was guarded against attack by strong towers planted at intervals. Later on, a further development brought into existence one more "outer wall," absolutely detached from the inner castle, which, surrounded by a moat, could only be approached by temporary drawbridges which were easily destroyed, or at least rendered useless, by manipulation from within. Thus, if the besieger, after a hard struggle, succeeded in breaking through the outer defences, the garrison withdrew to the inner ward, hoisted the drawbridges, and were still very far from surrender. Here, supplied with all the necessaries of life, physical and spiritual, the defenders might prolong the siege indefinitely, till help came from without, or till the besieger, worn out with impatience, raised the siege. To realise the prospects of a force attacking a well-victualled fortress in the thirteenth century, one has only to think of an attempt to capture Windsor Castle without the aid of gunpowder or any other explosive.

It is not improbable, that this triumph of the art of defence may have had something to do with the

The rise of infantry.

appearance of another great change in military life during the thirteenth century. We have seen, in a previous chapter, that the original Teutonic idea of universal military service had given way before the feudal idea of a warrior class. Only in England and, perhaps, in the Low Countries, where feudalism was always comparatively weak, had the ancient *fyrd* survived as a real fighting force. Henry of Anjou had taken the useful hint afforded by the Battle of the

A.D. 1138.

Standards, where the Yorkshire militia under Archbishop Thurstan had done so much to defeat his mother's ally, the King of Scots; and the Assise of Arms, in which he gave minute directions for the organisation of the militia system,

A.D. 1181.

is important evidence of his policy. But the peasant, armed with feudal weapons, and these naturally inferior in kind, would have had little advantage over the feudal knight, save that, as infantry, he cost less to move about. It is true that, unlike the feudal knight, he had not succeeded in establishing any definite limits to his period of service. But, on the other hand, there was an awkward theory that he could only be called out for the defence of the realm, perhaps only of his own county. What was wanted by the monarchs of the

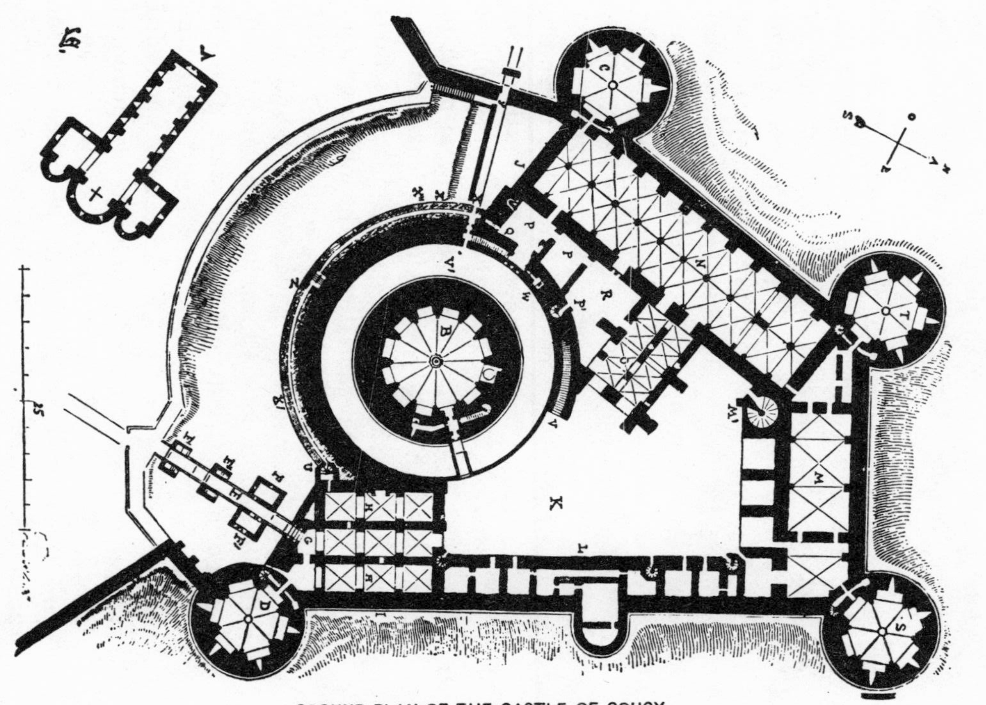

GROUND PLAN OF THE CASTLE OF COUCY.

(*From Viollet le Duc's "Descript. Château de Coucy."*)

thirteenth century was a force which would not throw up a siege or a campaign at the end of forty days, would not object to be sent across the borders of its own county, and would be armed with serviceable weapons.

Such a force was found in the professional archers of the thirteenth and fourteenth centuries. The crossbow had been a common weapon in Europe for ages, although, unlike most inventions, it does not appear to have come from the East. The Genoese crossbowman was as well-known a figure among the mercenary troops which were rapidly becoming familiar to men's eyes, as the Brabançon pikeman. But the long bow seems to have been a discovery of the twelfth century, and to have come from the neighbourhood of South Wales. Henry II. employed it freely, and with success, in his conquest of Ireland; and by the middle of the thirteenth century it had almost become the national weapon. It was exactly suited to the character of the Englishman — simple in construction, requiring great strength in action, but to be used with deliberation. It was the cheapest of weapons, and as handy in sport as in war. Naturally, it could not batter down the walls of castles; but it could pick off any defender who dared to show his head above the parapet, and its hardy wielders would starve into submission the garrison around which they lay in wait.

The long bow.

1169-1175.

In its religious aspect, the English countryside was, perhaps, during the thirteenth century, less satisfactory than in its physical condition.

The policy of Gregory VII. had borne evil fruit. Even before Gregory's accession to the Papal throne, the Norman Conqueror had taken a momentous step in withdrawing ecclesiastical causes from the ordinary local courts. It was the first stage in the process of separation between Church and State. Its immediate effect, combined with the rule of celibacy enforced against the parochial clergy, was to render the priesthood a caste apart from ordinary life, and, as a natural consequence, to disgust the abler among the parochial clergy with the narrow routine of village existence. The ordinary man, neither much better nor much more learned than his neighbours, might have settled down peacefully to family life in a country parsonage. Only a man of exceptional piety, or a man too weak to push his way in the world, would be found to be content with this narrow lot, uncheered by the presence of wife and children. In the thirteenth century we see clearly at work the causes which, in the fourteenth and fifteenth, were to render the Church so unpopular, that the brutal spoliation of Henry VIII. could pass without serious protest. Although the quarrel between Henry of Anjou and Becket, over the jurisdiction of the ecclesiastical courts, had ended, nominally, in a royal victory, the mad folly which murdered the Archbishop, and enshrined him as the great popular saint of the succeeding centuries, had robbed the victory of its fruits. Even for grave crimes, such as murder and theft, the cleric could not be punished like an ordinary criminal.

The clergy.

For venial offences, such as adultery and peculation, he was punishable only by the courts of the Church; and the Church held it to be good policy to avoid scandals. The great religious houses begged the tithes of parish livings from their patrons, and merely sent monks from time to time to perform the offices of the Church. The enormous patronage of the Crown was used to reward political services. In the dire need of money, which their temporal ambition had brought upon them, the Popes inflicted crushing taxation on the subservient clergy, and distributed the best livings of the English Church amongst Italian favourites who never set foot in the country. Half-concealed, half-avowed, the great aim of the Popes—to establish an absolute despotism in the Papal Curia—was becoming plain to all men. The goods of the Church and the servants of the Church were to be as much at the disposal of the Pope as his own chattels and domestics. Of course they were to be used to further the ends of the Catholic Church; but of those ends the Papal Curia was to be the sole judge, and national and local wants and aspirations were to be as naught. The mass of the clergy, more and more removed from national and local sympathies, were inclined to side with the Pope; they trusted, in spite of the heavy demands on their purses, to be recompensed by the growing power of the Church. But even among the clergy there were not wanting men, like the good Bishop of Lincoln, Robert Greathead, who nobly championed the cause of national justice. And fierce was the opposition to the Papal policy

by the kings, whose laws and whose law courts were defied by the emissaries of the Curia, and whose revenues were endangered by the claims of Papal taxation; by the baronage, who grudged the Papal interference with their patronage, and who hated the Italian ecclesiastics at the King's side; and by the people, who were fleeced in the archdeacon's court and by the abbey's bailiff, that great sums might be sent to Rome for the war which Innocent IV. was carrying on, for purely Italian reasons, against his arch-enemy the Emperor
1243–1250. Frederick II. In a word, the policy of the Papal Curia was opposed by those very elements which were rapidly coalescing, as differences of speech and race were being forgotten, into the mighty English nation. No one of the follies and crimes committed by the wretched Lackland had raised against him a bitterer feeling than the sale of his kingdom to Pope Innocent III. As we shall
A.D. 1212. see, half the troubles of his worthless son and successor were due to his fatal weakness for Papal absolution and Papal friendship.

But no account of the religious side of the thirteenth century would be remotely just, if it did not al-
The Monasteries. lude to one great reforming agency which had manifested itself within the pale of the Church. The older monastic Orders were well
Benedictines. represented in England. To take one small district of the west alone, the great Benedictine abbeys of Evesham, Pershore, Gloucester, Shrewsbury, Leominster, Malvern, Tewkesbury, and Winchcomb, will recall to the mind

stately buildings which speak of wealth and splendour in days gone by. The names of Crowland, Thorney, and Peterborough in the east, and of St. Mary's at York, are sufficient to shew that the Benedictine influence was not confined to one quarter of the land. Before the triumphant march of Latin monasticism the older Celtic foundations had finally given way. In the evil days of Stephen the reformed Orders had spread widely through the land. Cluniacs and Carthusians were not so numerously represented, though the names of Northampton, Pontefract, Lenton, and Thetford show that they were not without success. But the Cistercians, after some struggles, had taken firm hold on the native land of their founder. Waverley, Tintern, Rievaulx, Fountains, Furness, Kirkstall, Buildwas, Jervaulx, Rufford, and Woburn, are but a few of their houses. Plunging into the wild valleys of the Yorkshire moors, where the harrying of the Conqueror still left its awful mark, or into the fastnesses of the Welsh forests, they settled down in their solitude to meditation and prayer. But wealth gathered round them in the shape of flocks of sheep, whose wool was in demand for the looms of Italy and southern France, where skilful workmen wove cloth which could not be produced by English fingers. The wool of the Cistercians soon became a tempting prize for King and Pope alike; and the port dues levied upon the export of sacks and fleeces were destined to be the pivot on which great questions of constitutional freedom were to turn.

Cluniacs.
Carthusians.

Cistercians.

Still, it was not from the great abbeys that the real religious fervour of the thirteenth century proceeded. Success had brought with it luxury and idleness; and before long the voice of Wicklif was to rise in denunciation of monastic sloth. The monastic Orders had never professed to be missionaries. Seclusion had been their aim, and the conduct of solitary meditation, undisturbed by the din of the world's cries and tumult. It was no part of the business of the monk to plunge into the arena, and rescue, by force if necessary, the souls which were perishing for lack of help. He mortified the flesh by fasting and by prayer, not by toiling for the sick and needy. Even the Cistercians, stern and self-sacrificing as they were at first, never thought of turning their energy outwards. The business of their famous General Chapters is concisely summed up by St. Stephen himself in his Charter. There is no word of missionary effort. The three subjects which the brethren meet to discuss are (1) the safety of their own souls, (2) the observation of the Rule, (3) the good of peace and charity among themselves. The world and the monastery were separated by an impassable gulf.

The Mendicant Orders.

But the needs of the times at last called other forces into existence. Eastern mysticism had shaken the foundations of the Christian faith; Eastern subtlety had led to questioning of things established. An earlier outbreak of heresy in Hungary had alarmed the orthodox; and the name of the Cathari was of evil sound in the ears of authority. But Hungary was

The Dominicans.

far off, and of recent conversion. The heresy of the twelfth and thirteenth centuries sprang up in the heart of Christendom, in the valleys of the Languedoc, where the Albigenses, the Waldenses, and other reformers made an effective, if silent, protest against the corruptions of the Church. Thoroughly alarmed, the Pope (Innocent III.) sent legates to suppress the evil; but they failed in their mission, and there was nothing for it, according to the ideas of the time, but to call in the aid of the secular arm. Edicts against heresy were hastily announced in Germany, France, and England; Spain had always been prompt to suppress the stirrings of free thought. But all was in vain; and the Pope found himself reduced to preaching a Crusade, not now against the Saracens of the East, but
against the heretics of the West. The A.D. 1207.
crusade against the Albigenses is of interest to English readers, as the scene of the exploits of Simon, the father of the man 1209–1224.
who was to play so large a part in English politics for a quarter of a century, and the founder of the great house of Montfort. But of far greater importance to England than the crusade of Simon was the other great agency which rapidly grew up to combat the evils of heresy, the Orders of the Preaching Friars. The Order of St. Dominic, the stern Castilian champion of orthodoxy, the very type of the rigid theologian, the organiser of the terrible Inquisition, seems never to have gained a very deep hold upon England, though the "Black Friars" have left their name indelibly engraved upon quarters of

English towns. But the followers of the gentle St. Francis of Assisi were gladly welcomed by the wretched dwellers in the rapidly growing slums, which they came to colonise and to civilise; and the Advent of the Friars is a real landmark in English history.

The Franciscans.

Born at Assisi, in green Umbria, in the closing years of the twelfth century, the son of a simple trader, St. Francis is one of the greatest, as well as the most lovable, of the Makers of the Middle Ages. At the age of twenty-five, he threw himself with ardour into a life of self-sacrifice, not with a view of stamping out heresy, but with a noble longing to bear the burden of care and suffering which bowed the heads of men and women around him. Poverty and asceticism were to him, not ends to be striven for as the highest glory of humanity, but simply means to reach the hearts of mourners. He would not spend, in the winning of earthly comforts, that time which might be devoted to the nursing of the sick, and the ministering of peace to the broken-hearted. No worldly ties should hinder him from going whither the call of duty led. No service was too small, no office too loathsome, for his cheerful spirit. Like a ray of sunlight he came into the prison, the hospital, and the lazar-house. His example spread like wildfire; and men and women hastened to place their lives and fortunes at his feet. The magic of his voice and look disarmed the hostility and the fear, not only of human beings, but, as his companions loved to tell, also of birds and

St. Francis. 1182-1226.

beasts. It was the inevitable triumph of perfect sincerity and absolute self-devotion, combined with the charm of a naturally winning temper. But the organising power which sent out his missionary followers two by two to carry on his work, which established a "province" in each State, and subdivided each "province" into "wardenships," were additional revelations of the genius of the Saint. The last item of perfection did not reveal itself till his death in 1226. Then, so the story ran, his body was found to be scarred with marks exactly corresponding with the wounds inflicted on the sacred body of Christ at his crucifixion; and the Christian world of the day was thrilled to the heart by the description of the *stigmata* of St. Francis. His canonisation followed, almost as a matter of course, in 1228.

Rule of St. Francis.

Strangely enough, St. Francis founded his Order in the teeth of œcumenical prohibition. The Lateran Council of 1215 had expressly forbidden the creation of new Orders; but the claims of the Grey Friars were overwhelming, and their association was verbally sanctioned by Innocent III. in that very year. The famous Rule of St. Francis * breathes the very spirit of charity and humility. The brethren themselves are strictly bound to vows of poverty; they may not acquire land or houses; they may not even receive money for services rendered. Their dress is to be of the simplest and coarsest. They may have "one coat

* An English translation is to be seen in *Monumenta Franciscana*, vol. ii., p. 65. (Rolls Series.)

with a hood, and one coat without a hood, and such as have need or are constrained may have shoes." But they are not "to despise nor judge those men which they see clothed with delicate and soft clothing, or with coloured and costly array, use delicious meats and drinks, but much more rather each of them should judge and despise himself." They are to keep themselves so clear from suspicion of worldly motives, that they may not even distribute the goods of those who join the Order. Their bodily wants they are to provide for by "faithfully, boldly, and surely and meekly asking for alms without fear or shame," "for our Lord made himself poor in this world." Yet there is to be no ostentatious fasting or asceticism; and, if a brother find himself a guest in a strange house, he may "eat of all manner of meats which be set before him." Strangely enough, as it would seem to us, no express mention is made, in the Rule, of attendance on the poor and sick; but the duty of preaching the gospel is contemplated, provided that the consent of the bishop of the diocese be obtained. And the sermons are to be brief and pithy, showing the people "vices and virtues, pain and joy, with a few words."

The English Mission.

The Franciscans came to England in 1224, nine years after the founding of their Order. They were a little band, half cleric, half lay. According to their Rule, they begged a passage from Fécamp, and, landing on the Kentish coast, set up their first "house" at Canterbury, in a little chamber allotted them in the "scholar's house." Here they made a fire on

Canterbury.

the earthen floor, and, putting on it a pot of ale-dregs, drank about, with cheerfulness and pleasant talk. They had a horror of debt; and one day, when the sudden appearance of two brethren compelled them to borrow a gallon of ale, the residents only pretended to drink, that the supply might last longer. In the same year, four brethren came to London, where they hired a piece of land in Cornhill, and built cells, stuffing the walls with grass. For a whole year they had no chapel; but the people hastened to offer them help, and in 1226 they migrated to Newgate, in the extreme north of the city, a neighbourhood whose charms may be guessed from the fact that it comprised the alley known as "Stinking Lane." Here church, chapter-house, vestibule, dormitory, refectory, infirmary, water conduit, hospital, and schools, appeared in rapid succession. In 1306, a church of noble proportions began to arise on the site of the ancient building, helped by the generosity of Margaret, second queen of Edward I., by John of Brittany, a neighbouring landowner,* and by Gilbert of Gloucester, who sent twenty great beams from his woods at Tonbridge. We even know the names of the benefactors who gave the thirty-six great windows which adorned the new church. In 1360 the brethren, by this time increased to a hundred, began once more to rebuild. In the autumn of 1226, two of them started for Oxford, where they were hospitably

London.

Oxford.

* His title survives in the district of "Little Britain," celebrated by Washington Irving, and still extant behind St. Martin's le Grand.

received by the Dominicans, and, hiring a house in St. Ebbe's, began to exercise a potent effect on the growing fortunes of the university. By their influence with Bishop Greathead of Lincoln, one of their earliest and staunchest champions, by their foundation of student houses which, no doubt, powerfully forwarded the nascent collegiate movement,* and by their establishment of readerships, they, though strictly outside the university scheme, really formed an important part of university life. From Oxford they sent out colonists to Northampton, where they hired a house in St. Giles' parish, and set up a wardenship under Peter the Spaniard, who wore an iron shirt next his skin. Settlements followed at Cambridge (where the brethren lived for awhile in a disused gaol), and at Lincoln, doubtless under the patronage of the bishop. By the year 1256, they numbered 1242 brethren in 49 convents.

North-ampton.

Cambridge.
Lincoln.

It is sad to have to relate, that this prosperity was soon marred by jealousies and quarrels, in which, apparently, the Grey Friars were not entirely free from blame. At any rate it is clear that they departed from the simplicity of the apostolic model. The older Orders, and even the Dominicans, accused them of poaching sites for churches, and of indirectly violating their profession of poverty. It is generally now accepted, that the famous practice of conveying lands "to uses," *i. e.*, for the real benefit of a person other than the nominal recipient, originated with the Franciscans. The

Jealousy of the older Orders.

* They had a large share in the foundation of Balliol College.

brethren became absorbed in worldly business; some of them acted as ambassadors and secret agents. In 1290 they had a furious quarrel with the Benedictines of Westminster, whom they accused of harbouring a relapsed Franciscan. In accordance with the practice of the times, they placed themselves under a Cardinal Protector at the Papal Curia. Famous scholars, like Adam Marsh and Alexander of Hales, issued from their midst; and before long they secured the highest dignities of the Church. Certainly as a force, both social and political, they are one of the most striking features of the thirteenth century in England.

CHAPTER IV

BIRTH AND EARLY YEARS

1239–1257

KING HENRY III. was married in January, 1236, to Eleanor, the second of the four famous daughters of Count Raymond Berenger of Provence. It was a natural thing for

Parents.

Henry of Winchester to do; for the lady was beautiful, she brought with her a possibility of a share in the romantic county of Provence, and Henry was not the man to let prudent considerations stand in the way of his impulses. But it was a disastrous marriage for England. Eleanor's sister Margaret was already the wife of Louis

A.D. 1234.

IX. of France (Saint Louis), Henry's most dangerous rival; and her sister Sanchia was destined to marry Henry's own brother

A.D. 1243.

Richard, afterwards King of the Romans, while the fourth sister, Beatrix, the ultimate heiress of the county, eventually married

A.D. 1246.

Charles of Anjou, the brother of the French King. Such a curious set of marriages—four sisters marrying two pairs of brothers,

PEASANT WOMAN CHURNING.

(*From Fairholt's "Costumes."*)

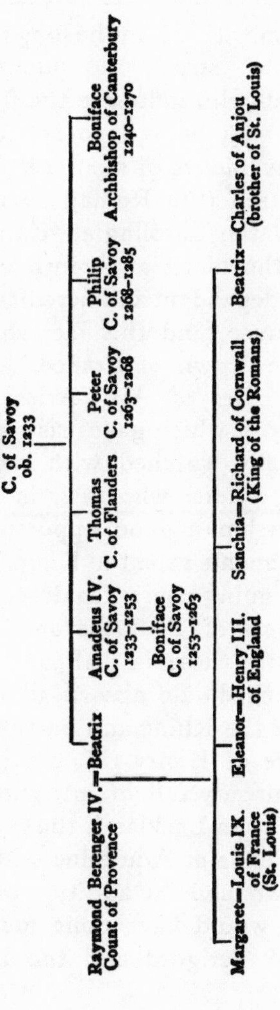

Thomas
C. of Savoy
ob. 1233
Raymond Berenger IV.—Beatrix
Count of Provence
Amadeus IV.
C. of Savoy
1233–1253
Boniface
C. of Savoy
1253–1263
Thomas
C. of Flanders
Peter
C. of Savoy
1263–1268
Philip
C. of Savoy
1268–1285
Boniface
Archbishop of Canterbury
1240–1270
Margaret—Louis IX.
of France
(St. Louis)
Eleanor—Henry III.
of England
Sanchia—Richard of Cornwall
(King of the Romans)
Beatrix—Charles of Anjou
(brother of St. Louis)

and all of them entitled, in the long run, to call themselves Queens — struck the popular imagination. And, as it really did influence the foreign politics of the time, it may be well to set it out in tabular form, for convenience of memory. (*See* p. 71.)

Provence itself (the Roman *Provincia*) had once been a fief of the Carolingian Empire; but, in the break-up of the ninth and tenth centuries, it had become an independent and hereditary county, owning no allegiance (and this fact should be remembered) to the Crown of France. As it contained the wealthy cities of Aix, Arles, and Marseilles, the two latter of which gave easy access to the sea, it was naturally watched with eager eyes by the neighbouring rulers, who saw, in the prospect of female succession, a good opportunity of plunder. The chief claimants were the Kings of Aragon, from whom the reigning court was descended, the neighbouring Counts of Toulouse and Savoy, and the Kings at Paris, these last already scheming for a kingdom which should absorb all the petty princedoms west of the Rhine and north of the Pyrenees. The marriage of Henry III. brought another rival on a scene already full of intrigue; for, in spite of the losses of John Lackland, the great neighbouring duchy of Guienne or Aquitaine still belonged to the English Crown, and the addition of the rich county of Provence would have done much to atone for the losses of Perigord and the Limousin in the north.

For reasons best known to himself, Amadeus of Savoy, the uncle of Eleanor, had favoured his

GREAT SEAL OF HENRY III.

(*From Hewitt's "Ancient Armour."*)

niece's marriage with Henry. But he expected to be well paid for his services. He had a quartette of greedy brothers, Thomas and Peter, Philip and Boniface; and these fixed their eyes longingly upon England, where rich benefices and grants of land seemed to them naturally to await a queen's relatives. England was already groaning under utterly unreasonable claims of a similar kind, for the King's widowed mother, Isabella of Angoulême, had married Hugh of Lusignan, Count of La Marche; and Henry, with his usual readiness to sacrifice his country to his personal feelings, was scheming to provide one of his half-brothers with a rich bishopric, while for another was destined the splendid earldom of Pembroke, recently vacated by the death of the younger Marshal. The evil influence of Peter des Roches, the Poitevin favourite of Isabella, was still remembered, though the King had been forced to dismiss him from office. Nevertheless, Henry persisted in his marriage plans; and Peter of Savoy received the earldom of Richmond in 1241, while his younger brother, Boniface, reached the great prize of ecclesiastical ambition in England, being made Archbishop of Canterbury, in spite of strenuous opposition, in 1245. These will be names of evil omen in England during the next quarter of a century.

Savoyards.

1234. Peter of Savoy.

Boniface.

To add to its other evils, the marriage of Henry and Eleanor threatened to be childless. But this last blow was averted by the birth of a son at Westminster, on the 17th–18th of

Birth of Edward.

June, 1239. The child was called after an English King whose name dwelt fondly in the memories of the people, and whose body, after resting for nearly a century, had been translated by another English saint, Thomas of Canterbury, to a more splendid tomb in that abbey of St. Peter at Westminster, on which the Confessor himself had lavished such tender care, and which Henry was now rebuilding with great magnificence. Three days after his birth the little prince was baptised in the abbey, amongst his sponsors being his uncle Richard, the future King of the Romans, and his uncle by marriage, the great Simon of Montfort. On the same day he was also confirmed by the saintly Archbishop of Canterbury, Edmund Rich.

London and the King.

The times were unhappy. The King had a fatal knack of becoming involved in petty quarrels, which led to no decisive results, except that they gradually embittered against him one section after another of his subjects. At this time he was engaged in a standing feud with the citizens of London, then rapidly rising in wealth and power, and perfectly willing to act as loyal subjects of the King, if he would but let them. On Henry's part there seems to have been little cause for quarrel, except an unworthy jealousy of the growing importance of the city, and a fear for his own dignity. The citizens had gained an important step just half a century before, when, at the coronation of Richard Cœur de Lion, who was anxious to get money for his Crusade, they had obtained leave to elect their own mayor and sheriffs, a privilege

WESTMINSTER ABBEY.

(*From Crull's "Antiquities of St. Peter's."*)

confirmed by John and by Henry of Winchester himself. The practice had wavered a good deal since the days of Richard Fitzaylwin, the first mayor, who dwelt in a very fair house on the north side of St. Swithin's Church, in Cannon or Candlewick Street, near the ancient London Stone. He had held the mayoralty till his death, in the year 1212. But, by the year of the little Edward's birth, it had come to be accepted as the proper thing, that mayor and sheriffs should be elected annually on the feast of St. Simon and St. Jude, and presented to the King for approval as soon as might be. Henry, however, could not bring himself to accept, fairly and fully, the new order of things. He hankered after the days when the King's bailiff and the Bishop's portreeve held the city in check, and when the citizens in their Guildhall might protest, but could not carry their protests into effect. On the slightest pretext, the liberties of the city were seized into the King's hand, and a warden and bailiff, appointed by the King, replaced the elected mayor and sheriffs. When, in 1240, Gerard Bat, the choice of the citizens, went to Woodstock to obtain the royal approval, the King, who had no pretext for refusal ready, made him swear to return everything received during his previous tenure of office, and not to accept the usual forty pounds' allowance for expenses. Bat gave way; but as he withdrew he could not help a regretful murmur—"Alas, my lord, with them I might have married my daughter." Whereupon the King, adding

Richard Fitzaylwin.

28th October.

Gerard Bat.

insult to injury, swore by the bones of St. Edward, and stammered out: "Thou shalt not be mayor this year, and for a trifle I would say, never. Away with thee!" The King and the citizens were always quarrelling over the coinage, which the King apparently desired to regulate by principles of artistic beauty, while the citizens, naturally, preferred to consider practical needs. In the year 1258, a battle royal took place over a mysterious roll, sealed with green wax, alleged to have been found in the King's wardrobe at Windsor. This precious document, probably the work of some partisan in the internal struggle between the Court and the popular parties in the Guildhall, was supposed to contain a list of oppressions committed by the mayor and aldermen in the collection of the royal taxes. John Mansel, the famous clerical pluralist and confidential adviser of the King, came down into the city, and insisted on an inquest, with great show of fair play, but very little reality. The inquisitors pleaded the privilege of the city, that no inquest should be held within its limits, and urged that the accused should be allowed to clear themselves in the accustomed way, by the oaths of their witnesses. The King's messengers, however, called a folkmoot at the Guildhall, and, by the use of wily words, persuaded the populace to shout "Ya, ya," in answer to a proposal of condemnation. Once more the victims pleaded the customs of the city; but the royalists, now thoroughly convinced of their power, summoned another folkmoot at St. Paul's, and asked

Coinage.

Charges of oppression.

whether people accused of bringing all sorts of evil on their fellow-citizens ought to be allowed to defend themselves by mere oath. Thereupon, without any decent discussion, and "by the mouths of the scum of the people, sons of strange mothers, and some of servile rank," the crowd answered, "Nay, nay, nay"; and the accused were deprived of their offices, fined, arrested, and forbidden to seek any office again without the King's leave. Equally petulant and unjust was the behaviour of the King over the great reconsecration of the shrine of the Confessor in 1269. The citizens were genuinely anxious to do honour to the proceedings, and had gone to great expense in the preparation of scarlet cloth "and other decent garments." But, at the last moment, Henry refused to wear his crown, and insolently said, that those who liked might come to dinner, but they should not take any part in the ceremony. It is not surprising to find London steadily against the King all through the Barons' War; and it is not difficult to understand how a ruler, who could treat a rising interest in such a way, should fail to secure the respect of his subjects. Unhappily, the dislike which he naturally felt towards the city which he had injured extended itself to his son Edward, who never forgave the citizens for an attack made on his mother's barge as it passed under London Bridge in the year 1263. The cause alleged by the citizens for the outrage was palpably false, being an absurd revival of the story of Eleanor of Aquitaine and Fair Rosamond. But that it should have been

Translation of the Confessor.

believed, shews the bad odour into which the Court of Henry III. had fallen.

In the year 1240 died Llywelyn ab Jorwerth, the last, or last but one, of the independent princes of

Wales.

North Wales. His two sons, Gruffyth the older, and David "the more legitimate," quarrelled over the succession, and agreed to submit their differences to the arbitration of the Bishop of Bangor. David, however, seized his brother by treachery, and imprisoned him at Criccieth. Regardless of consequences, Gruffyth appealed for help to Henry, and the latter's vanity would not permit him to withhold his interference. As a matter of fact, the expedition which followed was one of the very few successful achievements of Henry's reign. The King invaded Wales with a large army, and impressed David so much, that he agreed to come to London to discuss his claims,

29th August, 1241.

while Gruffyth was removed to the custody of the Tower of London. Ultimately, a treaty was signed, which professed to recognise the

Treaty of Rhuddlan.

legal suzerainty of the English Crown over the princes of Wales, to restore the lands alleged to have been filched from the earldom of Chester, and to secure compensation for the expenses of the war. But the treaty did not settle the dispute. David obtained of the Pope absolu-

1244.

tion from his allegiance, and though this was revoked, the death of Gruffyth in an attempt to escape from the Tower, and the failure of an unprovoked attack on Scotland in which Henry indulged in the same year, led to a renewal of the Welsh war. An expedition in 1245 was considered, at least by the Welsh chroniclers, as a disastrous failure; and only the death of David in the following year, along with that of Ralph Mortimer, the Marcher Earl, who had married David's sister, Gladys the Dark, gave Henry a respite from a troublesome foe. With characteristic cowardice, Henry, on his son's marriage, handed over Wales to his care, refusing thenceforward to own any responsibility in the matter. About the dealings of Edward with Wales something must hereafter be said.

As has been before hinted, Henry's conduct with regard to Scotland was equally open to criticism. The Scottish throne was at this time occupied by Alexander II., who had married Henry's sister Joanna. Notwithstanding the close tie thus existing, Henry protected the murderer of the young Earl of Athol, who fled south in 1242, and he chose to be offended because, on the death of Joanna, whose marriage had been childless, the Scottish King ventured to marry the daughter of Engilramm of Coucy. Summoning to his aid his brother in-law, the Savoyard Count of Flanders, who came with a hundred knights and sixty sergeants, and joined later by the future Archbishop of Canterbury, Boniface of Savoy, the King marched north on a plundering expedition. But at Newcastle a peace was patched up by Richard of Cornwall, on the basis of a marriage between Alexander, the infant son of the Scottish King and Mary

Scotland.

Threatened invasion.

Treaty of Newcastle, July, 1244.

of Coucy, with Henry's little daughter Margaret, a child of two years old. The marriage was actually solemnised in 1251; and it was probably the first public function since his baptism in which Prince Edward played a prominent part. It may therefore be of some interest to know that his costume on the occasion comprised a tabard of scarlet cloth, embroidered with leopards and furred with miniver, a supertunic parted with cloth of gold and furred, and a tunic of sendal or striped silk. Presumably there were hose and hat to match. Unhappily, details of the bride's costume do not survive, though we know that it was to cost the respectable sum of two hundred marks. Full particulars, however, of the plate, jewellery, and saddlery ordered for the occasion are preserved in the official documents, which are careful also to inform us of the gifts of rich robes to various ecclesiastical persons. Huge preparations of food and drink were made, and there was much feasting in York at the Christmas of 1251. It was on occasions like this that Henry was seen at his best. His love of display, his real affection for his children, his reverence for the externals of religion, his impulsive and somewhat superficial charity, united to make him an excellent master of ceremonies. The young prince seems to have made a good impression; and his tall, slender figure, which afterwards earned for him the nickname of Longshanks, his fair hair and ruddy cheeks, which reminded men of that Saxon descent which his name also pointedly recalled, combined to win him pop-

Marriage of the Princess Margaret.

ular favour. He seems to have passed a delicate childhood; but, as often happens, the delicate child grew up into a vigorous manhood, capable of endless fatigue and work, delighting in martial exercises and the chase, and finally into a green and vigorous old age, which did not shrink from undertakings that might have overtasked the strength of a man in his prime.

The serious duties of life now began to thicken around the young prince. His father's folly had embroiled England with the growing power of France, and had endangered the rich province of Guienne, or Aquitaine, which, with its dependent lordship of Gascony,* was all that survived to Henry of the once magnificent Continental domains of his Angevin grandfather, who had ruled from the Cheviots to the Pyrenees. In the reign of Philip Augustus, the great Norman inheritance of the Conqueror's descendants, as well as the hereditary domains of Henry of Anjou, had been wrested, bit by bit, from the feeble John; and although, during the reign of his son, Louis VIII., and the minority of St. Louis, Henry had made at least one foolish attempt to recover his lost dominions, he had merely wasted money without good results. In the year 1242, he allowed himself to be drawn into a feudal quarrel of the worst type between his step-father,

Gascony.

1179-1223.

* The names are used indiscriminately in the documents of the period. Gascony, the country of the Wasques or Basques, really was only an appendage of the great feudal duchy of Aquitaine, to whose ruler it had passed on the extinction of the native line of Gascon dukes, in 1054.

Hugh of La Marche, and Alfonso of Poitou,* Hugh's liege lord, and brother of St. Louis, who, by his marriage with Jeanne, daughter of Raymond of Toulouse, was scheming to attach that great county also to the throne of France. This latter power was now very different from what it had been in the days of Henry of Anjou, when, whatever his shadowy claims to overlordship of the Western feudatories, the actual domains of the French King consisted only of a narrow strip of land running from Arras in the north to Bourges in the south,—very little more, in fact, than the fiefs of the old Counts of Paris. The conquests of Philip Augustus had added Normandy, Maine, Anjou, and Auvergne to the direct domains of the Crown, while the great provinces of Brittany, Champagne, Burgundy, and Toulouse acknowledged themselves to depend directly on the kings of France. The rich county of Artois had been acquired by the
1180. marriage of Philip Augustus with Isabella of Hainault, and though it, like the county of Poitou, was held, as appanage, by a brother of the reigning monarch, such alienation was only temporary, and, as a fact, the "appanages" seldom long remained separated from the Crown. It will thus be seen, that the poor remainder of the great possessions of Henry of Anjou was hemmed in on two sides by the lands of Henry's most formidable rival, now fully conscious, saint

* Poitou had just assumed a new political existence as an appanage, created for the second son of Louis VIII, mostly out of the conquests effected by Philip Augustus at the expense of John of England.

FRENCH LADY.

(THIRTEENTH CENTURY.)

(*From Viollet le Duc's "Dict. du Mobilier Français."*)

though he was, of the great political mission which lay before the Kings at Paris.

If anything could have taught Henry wisdom, it was surely such a position as this. Nevertheless, he plunged rashly into the quarrel, and, having failed to obtain a grant of money from his Council, extorted sufficient for his immediate needs in what is significantly called "the Roman fashion," and set sail, in mid-May, with his queen and 1242.
brother Richard, for Bordeaux, the capital of Aquitaine. Louis at first offered peace, but, this being scornfully refused by Henry, he unfurled the oriflamme and marched on Poitou. The Kings met at Taillebourg on the Taillebourg,
Charente,* and Henry sustained a dis- July, 1242.
graceful defeat, which he tried to explain away by unworthy accusations against his allies. These were, no doubt, worthless enough; but Henry's flight to Saintes and subsequent second Saintes.
defeat ill accorded with the boastful professions of a few weeks before. The English army was really saved from destruction only by a mysterious sickness which appeared in the French camp, causing Louis to offer a truce for five years, which was eagerly accepted, and which at any rate released Henry from his stupid promise to pay seven thousand marks a year to the Poitevin rebels. Henry retired to Bordeaux, where a daughter (Beatrice, the future wife of John of Brittany, Edward's trusted ally) had been born to him in June.

* See an excellent account of this battle in Professor Oman's *History of the Art of War*, vol. ii., pp. 413–414.

Here he wasted the autumn, some accounts say also the winter, in foolish extravagance. When the truce expired, Louis was absorbed in his preparations for the Eighth Crusade, and Gascony was left unmolested by the French.

Simon of Montfort.

The interval was occupied by a series of events which must have brought the young prince into closest contact with a man who was destined to exercise, perhaps more than anyone else, an abiding influence on his mind and character. Simon of Montfort was the youngest son of Simon, conqueror of the Albigenses, who could boast descent not only from the Counts of Evreux, through whom he claimed the constableship of France, but, with the help of the bend sinister, from the royal house of Paris itself. The
1165. elder Simon had married Amicia, daughter of Robert, Earl of Leicester, who claimed the high office of Steward of England, through his marriage with Petronilia, a descendant of the ancient house of Grantesmenil. On the elder
1218. Simon's death, his great possessions were divided between his three sons—Aymer or Amauri, who succeeded to the office of Constable of France and to the ancient domains of the house of Montfort in Normandy, Guy, Count of Bigorre, who took such of the Albigensian conquests of his father as the ingratitude of Philip Augustus had left to him, and Simon, who, in the year 1229, came to England to claim his mother's inheritance. The young man was successful in his quest, through the favour of the King, notwithstanding that the hand

of Ranulph of Chester was already on the Leicester earldom. His mother's sister, Margaret, who had married Saer of Quency, seems to have made no claim to the title, though she obtained her share of the lands; and Simon became Earl of Leicester. By his descent from illustrious houses on both sides of the Channel, he was already entitled to rank among the proudest of the English aristocracy; and, in spite of the opposition of Bigod, Earl of Norfolk, he seems to have officiated as High Steward at the Queen's coronation. But he made a bid for yet higher place, and incurred the fierce resentment of the Court, by his secret marriage with the King's sister, Eleanor, the widow of William Marshal (the son of the famous Regent), who had died in 1231. It was evident now, that Simon's ambition went beyond that of an ordinary feudal baron; and Richard of Cornwall, the King's brother, openly quarrelled with Henry on his account. There were ugly scandals concerning the manner in which Simon had won his bride; but he probably owed his success, partly to his own character and position, partly to the friendship of the King. The latter, however, he soon lost; and a quarrel with Henry was followed by a voluntary exile to the Holy Land, whence Simon returned to France at the beginning of the year 1241. He served with the English army in the disastrous campaign of Poitou; but, before reconciling himself with Henry, he exacted from him a bond for the payment of sums which he alleged to be due

1236.

Marriage with Henry's sister, 1238.

Quarrel with Henry.

In the French war.

from the King. He spent the following winter in Gascony with his royal brother-in-law, and there, no doubt, formed those plans for the government of the province which were to excite such a storm when put into practice. He could hardly feel himself to be amongst strangers in the country of the Languedoc, where the fame of his father's exploits was still fresh. The county of Bigorre was still in his brother's family; and a cousin had married the famous Gaston of Béarn, one of the most powerful lords of Gascony. On the other hand, the King of Aragon and the Count of Toulouse had no kindly feelings towards the son of the northern interloper.

In Gascony, 1242-43.

Returned to England, Simon seems to have passed an uneventful period of five years, occupied, no doubt, in studying the political horizon, and, it may be, in impressing on the youthful Edward those lessons of wisdom and skill which he afterwards claimed as his own work. One significant incident suggests, that he was already inclined towards that opposition to royal misdeeds which was to bring him so much renown in after years. On his return from Gascony, the King found himself miserably in debt; and a personal demand for money made to the Council, which met at Westminster in February, 1244, produced the first of the long series of political experiments which are such a striking feature of the reign of Henry III. The demand was met by the appointment, by the Council, of a Committee of Twelve, upon whose report the King was invited

In England, 1243-1248.

The Committee of Twelve.

to place the choice of his chief ministers in the hands of the Council, as the price of a subsidy. The scheme came to naught; but it is interesting to find that the name of Simon appears among the baronial representatives. He could not, however, have acted very decidedly against his royal brother-in-law; for we find the latter employing him, at the second session of the Council in the same year, as his messenger in a last despairing appeal for funds. Moreover, a committee which comprised also Richard of Cornwall and Peter of Savoy can hardly have been violently hostile to Henry.

The government of Gascony.

The way was thus prepared for the step which was to prove, in many ways, the turning-point in Simon's career—his appointment to the lieutenancy of Gascony. The difficulties of this post, and Henry's lack of judgment in filling it, may be gathered from the fact, that no less than twenty-eight changes were made in it during the reign. There had been no resident ruler since the marriage of Eleanor of Aquitaine with Louis VII. of France; and the Gascon nobles,—the Counts of Bigorre and Perigord, the Vis- 1137.
counts of Béarn, Grammont, and Fronsac, the Lords of Albret and Bergerac,— secretly helped by the neighbouring Kings of Navarre, Aragon, and Castile, plundered the royal domains, under pretence of exercising the cherished feudal privilege of private war. The rich cities, on the other hand, secure within their walls, had wrested one privilege after another from the wretched seneschals at Bordeaux; and the consuls and commune of Limoges,

the mayor and jurats of Dax, and the good men of Bayonne, looked upon the distant king in London rather as an easy customer for their wines than as a ruler to be feared and obeyed.

Simon was in no hurry to accept the position. He seems to have foreseen that Henry would be likely to use him as a scapegoat if things went wrong, while anxious enough to exact the last penny to be raised from a successful administration of the province. He insisted on a seven years' tenure of office; he was to be no seneschal, but a vicegerent with royal powers; all the revenues of the province were to be placed at his disposal, and, if these were insufficient, the King was to recoup him his further expenses; if he were attacked by any of the hostile forces on his border, the King was to send him aid. All these demands were solemnly granted.

Simon appointed.

It was a great opportunity for a ruler of genius; but Simon was deficient in the higher qualities of statesmanship. He had courage, perseverance, vigour, and uprightness; he soon made a great impression on the province. At the end of three months he returned to England in triumph, and this triumph was repeated in the two following years. But, although the conflicting reports of the time render the details obscure, it is not difficult to see, that Simon's haughty manners, his hasty brushing aside of privileges which stood in his way, his avowed partialities, and his headstrong self-will, were bringing a terrible tempest upon his head. Louder and louder grew

Simon sets out.

Jan., 1249.

GASCON PEASANT WOMAN.

(THIRTEENTH CENTURY.)

(*From Viollet le Duc's "Dict. du Mobilier Français."*)

the complaints from Gascony. The King began to believe them. The Council of May, 1252, was occupied in hearing the impassioned addresses of the Gascon deputies, who represented almost all classes of the discontented subjects of Simon—nobles, merchants, peasants. Even churchmen, usually Simon's staunch allies, had their complaints to make against the viceroy. But the most singular feature of the petitions of complaint is, that more than one of them demand, not merely the recall of Simon, but the substitution of Edward, the King's son, in his place. We cannot suppose that Edward's personal qualities were yet known to the citizens of Bazas or Bayonne; probably they thought that a lad of thirteen would prove an easier ruler than the stern Earl of Leicester. But Henry, perplexed and impetuous, caught at the suggestion, and, without going fairly into Simon's defence, presented the young prince to an assembly of Gascons in London, as their ruler. He was received with huge delight, for the act virtually meant the condemnation of the hated viceroy.

Complaints reach England.

It is possible that Simon never quite forgave the young prince for the turn which affairs had taken. He angrily repudiated the charges which had been brought against him, and with such success, that the balance of opinion in England turned in his favour. The aged Bishop of Lincoln, Robert Greathead, remained his friend to the last; Adam of Marsh, the "Illustrious Doctor," was wholly in his favour. Men of affairs like Richard of Cornwall and Gilbert of Gloucester,

Prince Edward appointed.

none too favourable towards Simon, took his part. The Earl, after the first outburst of indignation, was not unreasonable. He offered either (1) to make his own terms with his accusers and to return and govern his province in peace, or (2) to carry on a vigorous war against those who were, as he alleged, disturbers of the peace, or (3) to resign his government on being indemnified for the expenses incurred. The King virtually accepted the third alternative; but forgot its condition. The prince received from Simon a formal surrender of the government, and the castles which he had fortified, on a promise to pay seven thousand marks, and an undertaking to hold Simon harmless from the debts incurred by him. The earl was allowed to retain the prisoners, whom he had captured outside the limits of Gascony. Simon withdrew to France, where he was received with open arms, and where the most brilliant offers of service were made to him. Henry set out in the summer of 1253, with a well-found army, to reduce the Gascons to submission; but the task proved harder than he had anticipated. Alfonso of Castile began to revive ancient claims; many of the Gascon nobles inclined to side with him. With incredible meanness, Henry summoned to his help the man whom he had just disgraced; but Simon refused to come. In the end, Henry determined to follow the Welsh precedent, and hand over to his youthful son a matter too hard for himself to manage.

Simon resigns.

The opportunity was taken to establish Edward in a definite position. According to the ideas of the time he, as the heir to the throne (and Henry had but one other son), was of an age when marriage was a duty. There had already been one scheme in connection with a daughter of the Duke of Brabant. But now the pressing needs of Gascony were foremost, and the young prince was betrothed and quickly married to Eleanor, daughter of Ferdinand III. of Castile, and half-sister of the reigning monarch, Alfonso X., who, in consideration of the marriage, transferred to Edward all his claims on Gascony. The marriage is the best proof that Edward's prospects, despite the disastrous half-century of English history which was just closing, were deemed of high value in the political market. For Eleanor was a beauty and an heiress, heiress in her mother's right to the counties of Ponthieu and Montreuil,* while her brother Alfonso was one of the most aspiring princes in Europe. On the other hand, Edward only settled upon his bride the modest dowry of £1000 a year, to be increased to £1500 on his father's death. But his own provision was splendid, and raised him at once to a position of independence. Henry conferred on his son not only the duchy of Aquitaine and Gascony, but the earldom of Chester, the lordships of Wales and Ireland, and the cities of Bristol, Stamford, and Grantham. The marriage was happy and fruitful; Edward and his wife lived together in peace till her death in 1290, and the series of crosses erected by Edward on each spot where her corpse rested on

Edward's marriage.

* These counties, on the channel coast, were highly valuable to any rival of the French king.

its way from Lincolnshire to Westminster, is one of the best-known memorials of royal affection. If Henry of Winchester really did arrange his son's marriage, he is entitled to the credit of at least one thoroughly successful act.

Of the other foreign politics of this period, there is not much of direct interest for Edward's career.

Germany and the Pope.

His birth had been almost coincident with the excommunication of the Emperor Frederick by Gregory IX., and the renewal of a long and bitter warfare which convulsed
1239. Europe. The death of Gregory made
1241. little difference to the struggle; Innocent IV. (Sinibaldo Fieschi) took up the task with ardour, and, hard pressed by the Emperor, looked about him for allies. He soon secured the Landgrave of Thuringia, formerly a candidate for the Empire, (who inflicted a severe defeat on the Emperor's son,
1246. Conrad,) and William, Count of Holland,
1247. whom, on the Landgrave's death, he set up as a rival Emperor. The death of Frederick in 1250 did not bring peace, for the Pope pursued the campaign against his children with unrelenting violence.

During Frederick's lifetime, Henry could not well move against him, for Frederick had married, as his third wife, Isabella of England, Henry's own sister.

Henry accepts Sicily for his second son.

But, on Conrad's death, Henry felt no scruples in accepting, on behalf of his second son, Edmund,
1254. the crown of Sicily, in opposition to Conradin, the Emperor Conrad's son by Elizabeth of Bavaria. It was, perhaps, the wildest act of folly

ELEANOR OF CASTILE.

(WIFE OF EDWARD I.)

(*From Stothard's "Monumental Effigies."*)

committed, even by Henry of Winchester. His brother, Richard of Cornwall, despite his enormous wealth and his hankering after titles, had refused the treacherous gift. For the next few years the Popes simply carried on the war against the Hohenstaufen in their own way, and for their own ends, and sent in the bills to Henry. Frederick II.'s descendants determined to fight for the remnants of their predecessor's territory; and the crown of Sicily had to be won from them. A demand of four thousand livres from the Abbot of Westminster for the expenses of the Sicilian war was
but the beginning of new troubles. In 1255.
the following year came fresh demands from Italy: in 1257 there was already talk of resigning the costly bauble; in 1258 the talk was stimulated by a further demand of four thousand five hundred marks. Meanwhile, Manfred, an illegitimate son of Frederick, had crushed the Papal army at Nocera, established himself as ruler of Sicily, and
carried the war on to the mainland. 1255.
Finally the Pope, having drained Henry's coffers dry, handed over the lands of Apulia and Sicily to
Charles of Anjou, who, in the two battles 1266.
of Benevento and Tagliacozzo, crushed 1268.
the last remnants of the house of Hohenstaufen.

In the year 1256, the vanity of Richard of Cornwall had succumbed to the charms of an Imperial
title, and he allowed himself to be **The King of**
elected, by a narrow majority, King of **the Romans,**
the Romans, and Emperor in prospect. **1256.**
The occasion is interesting, for it was the first on

which the exclusive claim of the college of seven Electoral Princes was definitely recognised. But the Holy Roman Empire had long ceased to have much territorial existence, and, as a fact, Richard had some difficulty in procuring admission to his coronation city of Aachen. He was never crowned at Rome, and so is generally spoken of in contemporary documents as King of the Romans only, not as Emperor. But, with the accession of Charles of Anjou to the throne of Sicily, the social success of Raymond Berenger's daughters was complete; the four sisters were now four queens. Also Richard's election is supposed to have opened up German trade with England, and certainly we find Henry, at his request, conferring privileges on

1260. the Teutonic Hanse in London. To offer any effectual resistance to the Mongol war-storm, now apparently about to burst over Europe, was, of course, far beyond Richard's powers.

Of the personal doings of Edward, we still hear but little. He returned to London with his bride in the year 1255, and was well re-

The Prince. ceived by the citizens, who had not at this time given him any cause of offence. His Welsh territories brought him a good deal of trouble, and he had to appeal to his father for aid. His Irish administration seems to have been a reality; and of this something must be said in another chapter. On the election of his uncle Richard as King of the Romans, he received from the newly elected potentate a letter containing a full account of the proceedings, together with moral

reflections on the conduct of turbulent German archbishops. In the following year he sustained from his father a very just rebuke for be-
stowing upon his uncle, Guy of Lusignan, 1257.
the valuable island of Oléron, part of his Gascon province. The King, in fact, quashed the gift, and Edward had to submit.

But the evils of the reign of Henry of Winchester were now approaching their climax in England, and to home affairs we must again turn our eyes.

CHAPTER V

THE GATHERING STORM

1258–1261

FROM the general mass of folly and incapacity which drove the subjects of Henry into revolt, three chief grievances are revealed to us beyond mistake by the records of the times.

The foreigners.

First and foremost was the favour shown to the hated foreigners. It may seem, at first sight, odd, that a country whose nobles were almost all of French descent, whose courtiers and scribes spoke the French tongue, and whose official affairs were conducted, either in that Latin, which was the universal language of educated Europe for a thousand years, or in the French imported by the clerks of the kings of the Angevin line, should display any strong feeling of nationality. Among the thousands of documents which contain the official history of the period, there is but one which betrays any acquaintance with the Saxon speech of England. The few technical terms which survived from the legal system of Edward the

Confessor had become mere gibberish, even to skilled clerks. Even the records of the growing towns are written in Latin or in French, though an occasional survival of "Ya, ya," and "Nay, nay," reveals the fact that, in moments of excitement or of popular action, the citizen relapsed into his mother speech. But the truth is, that the alien race, which had come with William of Normandy, was fast losing its separate existence in the mass of the people which it ruled and plundered. The boundary between State and Folk was being rapidly broken down; and a new Nation, which comprised both, was coming into existence. Doubtless, the feelings with which the great English barons regarded the Savoyards and the Poitevins were, mainly, personal feelings of rivalry and jealousy. They dreaded to see these new-comers invested with the fiefs and offices which they desired for themselves. But their hostility was backed by the growing strength of the shiremoot and the town's meeting, where men spoke the native English speech, and had a genuine fear and hatred of the foreign noble whose aim was to bring back the evil days of Stephen, when peasant and burgher lived in daily terror of their lives. The strong hand of Henry of Anjou had done far more than build up a central government firm enough to hold the barons in check. It had taught the mass of Englishmen what good rule meant, and rendered them unwilling to brook the lawless oppression either of king or baron. It was this that had given force to the movement which had wrung the Great Charter from

John, and, for the first time in English history, ranged the people against the Crown. The lesson might have appealed, even to such a man as Henry of Winchester. It was a sign of his incurable folly, that he thought lightly of provoking again the combined hostility of nobles and people. The will of the nation had been shown clearly in the choice of Hubert Burgh as Regent on the death of Henry's father, and the exploits of Falkes of Breauté had

Falkes of Breauté.

surely been an ample warning of the danger to be expected from entrusting office to foreign adventurers. Yet, on the fall of the Regent, Henry had not shrunk from recalling to his

Peter of Roches.

1231.

counsels Peter des Roches, the Poitevin Bishop of Winchester, who had caused so much trouble, in the early years of the reign, by his steady opposition to the great Regent. Peter's object was so very clearly to govern the land by Poitevin methods, and he brought over so many of his countrymen, that a storm arose, which drove him into retirement. On his death, Henry strove to continue the foreign succession in the rich see of Winchester by claiming it for his half-brother, Aymer of Valence, a son of his

Aymer of Valence.

mother's scandalous second marriage with Hugh of Lusignan; and, though it took him twenty years to accomplish his project, he succeeded in the end. Meanwhile, William of Valence,

William of Valence.

another of the King's half-brothers, had received in marriage Joan of Munchensey, one of the co-heiresses of the great Marshal inheritance, and with her the lordships of Pembroke

WILLIAM OF VALENCE.

(From Stothard's "Monumental Effigies.")

and Wexford ; and his secretary, Peter of Aigueblanche, had been rewarded with the see of Hereford. The eldest half-brother, Hugh of La Marche, had, as we have seen, lured Henry into an absurd and costly war, which had disgraced the English arms. Finally, Guy, the second brother, had persuaded the young Edward to make him a life grant of the island of Oléron, the key of the approaches to Bordeaux.

Peter of Aigue-blanche.

Hugh of La Marche.

Guy of Lusignan.

But Henry's choicest gifts were reserved for his Savoyard uncles. Peter of Savoy arrived in England in 1241, and was immediately knighted by the King, who also conferred upon him, amongst many rich gifts, that earldom of Richmond which, since the Conquest, had been in the family of Alan of Brittany. He became practically the chief adviser of the King, and the head of the Savoyard party in England. To these advantages he afterwards added the wardenships of the castles of Rochester and Dover, and of the Cinque Ports, a position which, combined with his other office of sheriff of Kent, virtually made him master of the approaches to England from the Continent. The profits of the great fair of St. Botolph at Lincoln were given to him, with towns and manors in Yorkshire, Norfolk, Cambridge, Suffolk, and Hertford. And when, in 1262, a prospect of his death without issue seemed likely to bring these vast estates back into the King's hands, Henry put the crowning touch to his mad extravagance, by solemnly granting him leave to devise his lands to his

Peter of Savoy.

collateral relations. Nor did Peter's greed stop at his own purse. A few years after his arrival he imported a troop of Savoyard damsels, whom he forthwith began marrying to the richest English youths—to Edmund Lacy, Earl of Lincoln, and to Richard, son of Hubert Burgh, the great Earl of Kent. He also dabbled freely in that very favourite but most mischievous form of medieval speculation, the guardianship of rich wards; and we may be fairly sure that, in disposing of their marriages, he did not forget his own kindred. His name has survived to modern times only in the great Palace of the Savoy, which long formed a little oasis of feudal anarchy in the growing order and good rule of Westminster; but, to the men of his own day, it was the embodiment of greed and cruelty. His brother Boniface, who, as we have said, obtained the primacy after the death of Edmund Rich, was comparatively popular, for he managed to quarrel with the Poitevins, and the Poitevins were, if anything, more hated than the Savoyards. At one time, too, it almost seemed as though he were going to reproduce Stephen Langton, and head the national opposition to the misgovernment of the King. But the true nature of the man came out in the extortions which he levied, with the sanction of the Pope, from the benefices in his diocese, and in the sham visitations which, in travesty of the reforming zeal of Greathead, he undertook for the purpose of exacting fines.

Peter's foreign damsels.

The Savoy.

Boniface of Savoy.

The second great grievance which fed the flame

of discontent was the King's own extravagance. The foolish expedition to Poitou had involved him in debt. The equally foolish and still more extravagant expedition to Gascony was said to have cost £2,700,000, and, with all the usual allowance for medieval figures, there can be little doubt that it permanently crippled the King's resources. Nevertheless, Henry took the opportunity of his return to bestow 31,000 marks on his half-brothers, and to spend a sum of £1000 in entertaining the "four queens" on his journey through Paris. No doubt it was a tempting occasion for the wiping out of his disgrace, and he must have been pleased to find the scholars of the "English nation" of the University of Paris willing to treat him as a hero. But all this was as nothing compared with the sums squandered over the harebrained Apulian business. The first demand made by the Pope, and this only two years after the acceptance of the Sicilian crown, was for 150,000 marks; the King was already in debt to the extent of three times that sum. The most desperate means were resorted to. The King borrowed freely from all who would lend; no opportunity for extortion of fines was omitted. The Jews, the citizens of London, the monasteries, even the parochial clergy, were in turn victimised. In 1254 a writ issued for an enquiry into the lands of the monasteries, and this "unheard-of" proceeding (as it is described by a chronicler) may shew that the King, in his despair, was turning his eyes upon the rich fields afterwards so thoroughly gleaned by his

The royal extravagance.

1254.

successor, Henry VIII. Year after year, with wearisome monotony, he unfolded before his indignant Council the tale of bankruptcy. Year after year the feeling against him grew. The blame was not all his. The old idea of kingship was changing; it had ceased to be merely the military leadership of an army of feudal barons, who rendered their dues by fighting in the field. A huge staff of officials was growing up round the Exchequer. England had almost inevitably become involved in the meshes of Continental politics, and wars and diplomacy were a constant drain on the revenue. The old feudal services were quite insufficient to provide for the new wants of the kingdom, and the occasional "scutages" for which they were commuted were equally inadequate. As we shall see, even the successful reign of Edward I. involved greatly increased taxation, and taxation, though naturally it is not popular, has never been really grudged in England when the necessity of it has been obvious. But the Council, quite apart from its own feelings, dared not grant the King aids to be spent on foreign favourites and unpopular expeditions.

Papal extortion.

Perhaps, however, the most crying of all the grievances of the time was the long series of Papal exactions which fill the records of the period. The gravity of the crisis produced by this cause is at first a little hard to understand. After all, the Papal demands only made direct appeals to a limited class of Englishmen; in the most desperate times of their need, Gregory and Innocent never ventured to address a direct demand to the English laity. Their agents collected the first-fruits of benefices, the tenths of episcopal revenues, and the proceeds of the wool of the monasteries. But, except in the way of mere alms and the ancient hearth penny, they had no claim on the goods or lands of the laity. And, moreover, the clergy were very unwilling to appear in opposition to the Papal Court; the whole course of ecclesiastical policy, during the last two hundred years, had been directed towards drawing close the ties, which bound the clergy throughout Christendom to the Chair of St. Peter. Yet it is undoubtedly true, that the patience of the clergy gave way at last before the steady pressure of the demands from Rome, and that a feeling grew up, of the utmost importance to the understanding of the time. An enquiry in 1245 revealed the fact, that the Pope was regularly drawing sixty thousand marks a year from English benefices. The King, in hasty indignation, bade Martin, the Papal agent, who had arrived with fresh schemes of plunder, be quit of the kingdom in four days. At the Council of Lyons, held in the summer of the same year, the grievances of the English Church were solemnly laid before the Pope, to the great indignation of the latter, who is reported to have said: "We must come to terms with this prince [*i. e.*, the Emperor Frederick], that we may crush that kingling of England, our rebellious vassal." The covert allusion to the disgraceful surrender of John Lackland was not likely to soothe the feelings of Englishmen, and the protest was taken up by the Council at Westminster in the

following year. The Pope retaliated by sending agents "with legatine powers," who laid claim to the goods of intestates (hitherto a perquisite of the bishops), and to the lands of the deceased Welsh Prince. The King behaved with the most contemptible weakness. He first forbade the remittance of any money to Rome; but, on the representation of the bishops that it would be difficult to withhold certain customary dues, he gave way, and even allowed the bishops themselves to act as tax-gatherers. The rapacity of the Pope is shewn by the fact that, notwithstanding the scandal created by his unsuccessful attempt to poison the Emperor, the beneficed clergy were in the same
1245. year subjected to the enormous demand of one-third of their goods (one-half from non-residents); and, though the King did protest against this outrage, Innocent calculated shrewdly, that a man of Henry's character, weak, superstitious, sentimentally religious, would not venture any determined opposition to the Head of the Church. Notwithstanding the spirited remonstrance
1247. of the French nobles in the following year, who alleged boldly that their kingdom had been won, "neither by the *jus scriptum*, nor yet by clerical arrogance, but by warlike toil"; notwithstanding the repeated protests of the English clergy; notwithstanding the stern reproof by Bishop Greathead of the Minorite collectors, who, so soon forgetting their true duties, began at this time to appear as agents of the Papacy, the exorbitant demands of Rome never ceased during the lifetime of

CLERK OF THE THIRTEENTH CENTURY.

(*From Viollet le Duc's " Dict. du Mobilier Français."*)

Innocent. In 1252 there was an open rupture between the Papacy and the national Church. Bishop Greathead flatly refused to admit foreign ecclesiastics to benefices "provided" for them by the Pope; and he resisted, with equal success, an outrageous demand of three years' income of all the English benefices, under colour of a Crusade. Just before his death, he declined to be a party to a flagrant piece of ecclesiastical jobbery planned by the Pope in respect of a canonry in Lincoln Cathedral; and although his adversary heard with indecent joy the news of his decease, the triumph of the Pope was soon clouded by a terrible dream, which so unnerved him that he died in the following year.

Innocent was succeeded by Alexander IV. (*Hostiensis*), who, though a great Canonist, continued with ardour the struggle against Frederick, and, as we have seen, soon persuaded Henry to his crowning act of folly, the acceptance, on behalf of his son Edmund, of the Sicilian kingdom. This event practically left Henry helpless in the hands of the Pope, and, of course, redoubled the extortions of the Papal agents. There was no necessity now for them to incur the odium of direct demands, and thus to run the risk of throwing Henry into the arms of the national party. The wretched King himself became the mouthpiece of their rapacity, and the odium of the Pope's policy fell in full measure upon him. The forces were now ranged in open opposition: on the one side the English nobles, the English clergy, and the citizens; on the other, the King, the foreign

1254.

favourites and ecclesiastics, the personal friends of the King, and, above all, the power of the Papacy.

Matters came to a crisis in the spring of 1258. Over and over again, Henry had sworn to observe

The crisis of 1258.

the Great Charter, granted by his father, and the Charter of the Forest, granted by himself. So late as the year 1253, a solemn sentence of excommunication had been published, threatening with direst spiritual penalties any one who should act against the letter or the spirit of these famous documents. But now the national party was bent upon executing a more definite scheme, which had been slowly maturing for some years, and which, in one shape or another, was really to be the great object of constitutional reform during the next four centuries. The Reformers saw that it was useless to attempt to bind the King by mere words or writing, so long as he was surrounded by officials whose ideas and hopes were bent upon evading those ties. Over and over again it had been proved, that formal declarations of rights were powerless to bind men who were determined to disregard them. It must be a poor ingenuity that cannot find a loophole of escape from a written document, especially when there is no independent tribunal to pronounce upon its meaning. It is an apparently curious, but perfectly well-established fact, that the personal safety of the average man, and his chances of obtaining even-handed justice, are greater in those countries in which these elementary rights are taken for granted, than in those in which they are guaranteed by solemn constitutional documents. No doubt it is well to have the written word on one's side. The most unscrupulous tyrant will hesitate to violate the express terms of a charter. Popular opinion, which may, and generally does, in the long run, decide between oppressor and oppressed, is apt to shrink from opposing authority, unless it can shelter itself behind a formal document. But the parchment scroll is not enough. It may be an excellent rallying-point in time of revolution: it will not prevent a steady oppression being exercised in quieter days. The real weakness of the Charters of John and Henry lay in the fact, that they were regarded by the King and by those who carried on the daily business of government, not as venerable monuments of antiquity, containing fundamental principles of justice, but as disgraceful infringements of the inherent rights of rulers, wrung by rebellious subjects from the misfortunes of their kings, and worthy only of being evaded by loyal ministers, or, if it might be, repealed once and for ever.

Objects of the Reformers.

It was felt, then, by the national party, that the only real safeguard against a repetition of the folly and extravagance of the past twenty-five years, was a change in the actual holders of office. We need not enquire too closely into their motives, nor speculate minutely as to how far jealousy of the foreigner and a hope of personal gain, how far a genuine desire to reform abuses, weighed in their plans. Then, no doubt, as now, a government office was looked upon as a "good thing," not merely as a position involving arduous duty and grave responsibility. It was inherent in the traditions of the monarchy that it should be so. William of Normandy and his followers did not invade England with the purely missionary object of reforming the abuses of Anglo-Saxon administration. Their primary purpose was to gain lands and riches, and it was the happiness of England that William was no mere plunderer, but a great organiser and administrator, who saw that a well-governed kingdom, in the long run, yielded more profit to its ruler than a plundered province. But the ideal of a ruler's duty had widened since the days of William the Bastard, and if the study of Roman Law was begetting a dangerous conception of the sovereign omnipotent ruler, whose word was law, and to whose authority there were no limits, the whole scheme of the *Corpus Juris* was opposed to the Oriental idea of government, as a machinery devised for the extraction of wealth to be spent on the private pleasures of the monarch. In other words, the conception of a King and his officials as owing duties to the community which they governed, as bound to care for the good of their people, —the conception of public spirit—was certainly acknowledged by the Reformers of the thirteenth century.

These suggestions may help us to understand the famous proceedings of the year 1258. At the meeting of the Council, held at Easter, the King, overawed by the stern demeanour of the barons under Bigod, Earl of Norfolk, with whom he had quarrelled in the previous year, con-

The Easter Parliament.

sented to put the reformation of the kingdom, subject to the approval of the Pope, into the hands of a Commission of twenty-four, half of them "councillors" nominated by the King, half of them "loyal men" chosen by the magnates. The Commissioners were to meet at Oxford in June, and to draw up a scheme for the government of the kingdom.

The Mad Parliament.

The so-called Mad Parliament of Oxford was thus nothing in the least like a national assembly, at any rate in point of form. But the novelty and the importance of the project made the gathering the centre of national life, during the summer months of 1258.

Oxford.

Oxford had by this time become one of the great centres of the new national spirit. The *studium generale*, which had, by insensible steps, grown together out of the schools belonging to the great monastic foundations at Oseney and St. Frideswide's, and to the settlements of the Franciscans and the Dominicans, had attracted to itself the acutest intellects of the country. One of the most striking proofs of the thoroughly national character of the educational movement is to be found in the existence of a very early statute, providing for the compulsory use of French as well as English in the grammar schools attached to the university, "lest French should be forgotten." In the new domestic foundations, or "halls," for the residence of students, which the liberality of pious benefactors was just bringing into existence, lived groups of eager men, young and middle-aged, who discussed in the familiar mother-tongue, not merely the Seven

Liberal Arts and the Three Philosophies, but, we may be quite sure, the burning political questions of the day. The "superior" faculties of theology, law, and medicine trained men for practical life, and gave a professional and substantial character to the studies of the place; while even the more academic Faculty of Arts, as the great mother of the teaching profession in England, had a practical side which bulked largely in the view of its members. One of the most striking features of this early time is the poverty of the students. Many of them begged their way to Oxford, and, when there, would probably have perished of hunger but for the system of charitable pawnbroking which was one of the most popular forms of medieval piety. The universities of the Middle Ages were rapidly taking the places of the monasteries, as the golden ladders by which the poor man's son, conscious of great gifts, but with no other prospect of employing them, might hope to rise to fame and fortune. So eager was the rush to the schools, so keen the life among the students, that it was then no idle boast to claim, that what Oxford thought one day, England would think the next. Needless to say, the aspirations of the university had expressed themselves, as always in the Middle Ages, in the many "franchises," or exemptions from ordinary jurisdiction, obtained from King, Pope, and Archbishop. Gradually freed from the control of mayor and sheriff, even of its own diocesan, the Bishop of Lincoln, the community led an eager and, it is to be feared, sometimes rather irregular life of its own. With its own Chancellor, whose court jealously resented all attempts to bring its clerks or scholars under the jurisdiction of the ordinary tribunals, with its own congregation, or legislative body, and its own elected agents or Proctors, the university proved itself a thorn in the side of the ordinary authorities. Only three years before the meeting of the Mad Parliament, the Council of the Realm had been compelled to issue an Ordinance for the government of Oxford city, in which the municipal authority of mayor and bailiffs had been strengthened by a Council of four aldermen and eight discreet and loyal men, and the rival jurisdictions of university and town carefully regulated. There can be little doubt, that the mass of public opinion at Oxford, in the summer of 1258, was warmly on the side of the national party; and it may well have been, that the labours of the Commission were informally assisted by the suggestions of the leading spirits in the university.

The Provisions of Oxford.

At any rate, the result of their session was a scheme so thorough and so startling, that nothing but a complete conviction of his own helplessness could have induced the King to accept it. The "special councillors" of the King, as they were then called, to distinguish them from the magnates who assembled annually in the Great Council or Parliament, were to be replaced by an elective body of fifteen, chosen by a Commission of four persons, themselves named by the Commission of twenty-four. This elective council was to

The Council of Fifteen.

constitute the permanent government; and the King was to undertake no act of importance without its advice. "Parliament," as the Great Council of the Magnates was now beginning to be called, was to meet no less than three times a year, not necessarily in full, but by a representative body of twelve of its members, something like the later "Lords of the Articles" in the Scottish Parliament. The appointment of the great officers of State, the Justitiar, the Chancellor, and the Treasurer, was to be in the hands of the elective Council,* and every year these officers were to render to the Council a strict account of their doings. The whole of the royal revenue was to be paid into the Exchequer, and the staff of the Exchequer was to be remodelled. The Chancellor was to seal no grants, especially of escheats and wardships, without the assent of the elective Council of Fifteen. The sheriffs nominated by the Crown were to be substantial landowners, and at each county court an elective body of four knights was to hold a general enquiry as to grievances and oppressions alleged to have been committed by royal officials. The wardens of the royal castles were to be replaced by men who could be thoroughly trusted by the Reformers, and the extravagance of the royal household was to be cut down.†

Parliament.

The great officials.

The revenue.

The sheriffs.

The royal castles.

---

* This point is not stated in so many words; but it was clearly the intention of the Reformers.

† This brief analysis only brings out the leading features of the

These "Provisions" were sweeping enough, but they would have been of little value without a corresponding change of *personnel* in the offices of government. This need, however, was not likely to be forgotten. The Reformers believed themselves, perhaps wished others to believe, that they were fighting against a bad system. They were really fighting against a set of men whom they hated. Hugh Bigod, a brother of the Earl Marshal, was made Justitiar, in the place of Stephen Segrave, and to him was committed the custody of the Tower; the Great Seal was taken away from John Mansel and given to Henry of Wengham; John of Crakehall was made Treasurer. But the greatest security for the future lay in the composition of the Council of Fifteen, and in this the Reformers managed to secure a decided majority. The Primate (Boniface of Savoy), though he affected opposition to the King, must be reckoned as a royalist, so also John Mansel, Peter of Savoy, the Earl of Warwick, the Earl of Albemarle, and, possibly, James Audley. But the remaining members of the Council, Bishop Cantilupe of Worcester, the Earls of Leicester (Montfort), Gloucester (Clare), Hereford (Bohun), and Norfolk (Bigod), Roger Mortimer, John Fitz-Geoffrey, Richard Gray, and Peter of Montfort,

Change of officials.

The Justitiar.

The Chancellor.

The Treasurer.

The members of Council.

Provisions of Oxford. The scheme, as drawn up, is very complicated; and the reader would probably be confused by a repetition of details. The whole of the documents can be seen in Stubbs, *Select Charters*, pp. 378–409.

were all, nominally at least, in the interests of reform.

So hopeless were the prospects if the scheme succeeded, that, for a moment, the King's party refused to submit. But the feeling in the country was too strong. Pleading the excuse of war on the Welsh borders, the Reformers had come armed and attended to Oxford; the city swarmed with their supporters. Earl Simon took the lead at once, and singled out for attack William, the Poitevin Lord of Pembroke, whose pride towered above that of the others. "You may take your choice," said Simon, "between giving up the royal castles which you hold, and losing your head." There was no mistaking the position. The King's advisers sought the protection of Aymer of Valence, the Bishop of Winchester, and shut themselves up in his castle. They were pursued by the Reformers, and fled to the Bishop's house in Southwark. But London was hostile to the foreigners, and they were glad enough to escape with a safe-conduct, and a part of their ill-gotten treasure. Of this, however, they were relieved by the vigilance of Richard Gray, the new baronial warden of Dover Castle, and they with difficulty reached Boulogne. Here fresh evils awaited them, for Louis of France, annoyed by the hostility displayed towards his sister-in-law, Henry's queen, by Henry's Poitevin half-brothers, refused them a safe-conduct through his territory. Seizing his opportunity, the fiery young Henry of Montfort, unknown to the

Struggle of the King's party.

Flight of the foreigners.

leaders of the baronial party, crossed the sea to avenge the insult of "old traitor" hurled by William of Valence at his father, and kept the fugitives strictly shut up in Boulogne.

Success of the Reformers.

Thus the Reformers appeared to be completely successful. Delighted to have got rid of the hated foreigners, they composed a long and careful letter to the Pope (Alexander IV.), justifying their proceedings, and begging him to keep the "elect of Winchester" (they would not admit the validity of the appointment of Aymer of Valence *) out of harm's way. The real fear of the Reformers seems to have been lest the young Edward, whose abilities they already recognised, should be won over to hostility by his foreign relations, and thus we may take it that the prince, though not officially appointed one of his father's representatives, was inclined (very naturally) to side with him. This view is confirmed by the existence of a contemporary writ, addressed to Alan Zouche, the Justitiar of Ireland, bidding him take no notice of Edward's orders unless they were confirmed by letters-patent of the King, issued with the assent of the Council. It perhaps also accounts for the revocation of the grant to Guy of Lusignan of the island of Oléron. Thus encouraged, the Reformers proceeded to hold a searching inquisition into local abuses. The Londoners joyfully accepted the Provisions of Oxford, as the new scheme of government was called; even Prince Edward was at last

* As a matter of fact, he was not consecrated until 1260; and so could not be full bishop.

induced to give in his adhesion, and finally, on October 18th, the new system was solemnly proclaimed *urbi et orbi*, the occasion being marked by the appearance of the one formal document of the period which condescends to use the speech of the common Englishman.

But dangers were at hand. Henry was not the man to submit honestly to a reform which placed galling fetters upon his liberty. Already he was scheming to obtain from the Pope an absolution from his solemn oath of adherence to the Provisions. Elements of discord began to appear among the Reformers, and we cannot entirely acquit the young prince of seizing on these for his own ends. In February of the year 1259, Richard of Cornwall, the King's brother, returned from abroad, and this fact boded no good to the Reformers. In the Parliament held during the same month, a violent quarrel, the true origin of which has never been ascertained, broke out between Earl Simon and the Earl of Gloucester. Perhaps it was personal jealousy, perhaps a genuine difference of policy. At any rate, Simon was provoked beyond measure, and burst out with the hasty words: "I care naught to live and walk with men so fickle and false. These things, which you now dispute, have we agreed on and sworn to observe. And you, my lord of Gloucester, as you are greater than all, so are you more bound to a wise policy." And he left the kingdom in wrath.

Dangers.

Quarrel between Montfort and Gloucester.

Two facts seem to throw light on this mysterious affair, which, in a sense, was the turning-point of the Reform movement. One is, that the rank and file of the party, during Simon's absence, put such strong pressure upon Gloucester, that he **Merits of the** gave way and professed an anxiety to be **quarrel.** reconciled with his rival. This looks as though the fault were Gloucester's. On the other hand, it seems quite certain that the peace negotiations with France, which were proceeding in the spring of the same year, were delayed by the refusal of Simon, acting on behalf of his wife, the daughter **1259.** of King John, to give up her hereditary claims on Normandy. This looks as though Simon could be unreasonable too, and could find leisure, in times of national crisis, to urge his own private interests.

Be this as it may, the French treaty proceeded, and was definitely concluded in May, 1259, Henry undertaking to be personally responsible **Treaty of** to his sister, Simon's wife, for her claims. **Paris.** The English King finally renounced the ancient title of his house to the provinces of Normandy, Anjou, Maine, Poitou, and Touraine, save that he retained the bishoprics and cities of Limoges, Cahors, and Perigord, and the Agenais.* A question of the dowry lands of the Countess Jeanne of Poitiers, the granddaughter of Joanna, sister of Richard Cœur de Lion,† was left open for settle-

* The Agenais was not handed over for some years to come; but its annual value was paid in cash.

† Joanna had married Count Raymond of Toulouse, and Richard had given her southern Querci as dower. The county of Toulouse had passed to the French Crown by the marriage of Jeanne with Alfonso of Poitiers, brother of Louis IX. The dower of Joanna had not been returned on her death.

ment. Henry received from Louis a sum of money which the French King intended to be used for the approaching Crusade, but for which Henry found, doubtless, a more pressing use. The terms of the treaty were distinctly favourable to England; the Norman and the Angevin inheritances were gone beyond hope, northern Gascony was really in French hands. But Louis had suffered severely at the disastrous battle of Mansourah, and in his subsequent captivity;
1250. he was by nature and family ties friendly towards Henry; he had views of the sacredness of hereditary titles, which made him uneasy even in retaining the conquests of Philip Augustus and Louis VIII. The treaty was solemnised by magnificent fêtes held in Paris at the conclusion of the year.
1259. Henry in person did homage for his French fiefs.

Edward's move.

Meantime, Prince Edward had taken at home a very significant step. In the October Parliament of 1259, "the community of the bachelors of England," *i. e.*, the smaller landowners, or knights, presented a petition to the heir-apparent, urging that the baronial party, having got the power into its own hands, was neglecting the reforms which it professed to advocate. These reforms had been specified in detail in the petition of 1258, on which the Provisions of Oxford were founded. There could therefore be no dispute about their terms. There can be also little doubt that the "bachelors" felt sure of a favourable answer, but it is difficult to be certain whether the move had been prompted by Earl Simon from abroad, or whether the young Edward had himself conceived the idea of organising a new and independent interest, to play off against the great feudal barons. The knights were a rising, but as yet unorganised class, the natural leaders, in the shiremoot, of the wealthy farming interest, which the rapid development of capitalist agriculture was bringing into existence. As their name implies, they, or some of them, had originally been the "knights" or servitors of the great landowners, enfeoffed by them with lands to hold on feudal service. But the growing practice of commutation, both of military and agricultural services, was, as we have seen, producing in the country a great middle class of small landowners, really compounded of various elements, but alike in boasting a security of tenure protected by the royal courts, and a growing interest in agriculture as the chief pursuit of their lives. In 1259 their normal sphere of political action was, as we have said, the shiremoot; but already, on more than one occasion, deputies from the shiremoot had been summoned, for various purposes, to a central assembly. Edward, or his advisers, were, therefore, working on thoroughly sound lines, when they gave the hint to the "bachelors" to intervene in the struggle. The baronial leaders were completely checked. They could hardly refuse such a petition, backed, as it was, by such a hand. But their disgust may be imagined, when it is realised, that the Provisions of Westminster, which they issued in response to the appeal, and which were

The Provisions of Westminster.

solemnly published on the Feast of St. Edward, were directed chiefly at abolishing abuses of feudal jurisdiction, such as the distraint of free tenants to attend at the manorial courts, the plunder of the lands of their wards by feudal guardians, the seizure of goods for default of service outside the limits of the manor, and the attempt to compel freeholders to sit on juries in the feudal courts—a privilege belonging strictly to the royal jurisdiction. There are even traces of still further reforms, but the document in which they are embodied was not enrolled, and was probably put aside by the baronial leaders.

5 Jan., 1260.

The result of this move was, for the moment, a bewildering change of parties. The King seems to have quarrelled with his son, and to have thrown himself into the arms of Gloucester. At any rate, the two are found together at London at the close of April, 1260. Apparently, the prince and Gloucester were on bad terms, for the prudent citizens of London would not allow both to lodge within the walls. Edward, accordingly, took up his quarters in Southwark, where he was joined by Earl Simon, who had just landed from abroad, having been preceded by rumours which accused him of intending an armed invasion. Richard of Cornwall tried to play the part of peacemaker from his lodgings at Westminster, but his efforts only led to a hollow truce. Elated by the split in the Reforming party, the King was actually in correspondence with the Pope for a release from his oath, and, with incredible folly,

Results of the step.

24 April, 1261.

shewed his hand, by removing the newly appointed baronial Justitiar, putting in his place a creature of his own. This step was followed by the triumphant production of a Papal bull, which solemnly absolved Henry from his oath to observe the Pro- 12 June,
visions of Oxford, and threatened excom- 1261.
munication against all who should question it. A gleam of hope appeared, in the steady refusal of the young prince to be a party to his father's act of treachery, and in the opportune death of the hated bishop of Winchester. But the latter good fortune was more than outweighed by the return Dec., 1260.
of the late prelate's brother, William of Easter, 1261.
Valence, and by the determination of the new Pope (Urban IV.) to adhere to his predecessor's policy. Disturbances at the universities heralded the approach of a storm; a secession of the February,
Oxford scholars to Northampton was 1261.
known to have been favoured by the King, in his hatred of the forward policy of the university. In defiance of the Provisions, the King attempted to send an "eyre," or general commission of financial enquiry, throughout the kingdom. The last warning was the arrival of troops under the Count of St. Pol and Gerard of Ross, sent by Saint Louis to the help of his brother-in-law. Simon and Gloucester buried their feud in the face of the common danger. Richard of Cornwall and the prince professed hesitation, but it was not difficult to foresee that the tie of blood would prove too strong for the triumph of justice. The King sent the Crown jewels for safety to Paris. It was clear that war was at hand.

CHAPTER VI

THE BARONS' WAR

1261–1267

IT is not surprising that, even at this crisis, the rival parties hesitated to light the flame of civil war. Although it was nearly a hundred years since the days of Stephen and the Empress Maud, the tradition of those evil times, when people said openly that "God and His saints slept," was strong in the land. On both sides the leaders were really humane men. With all his follies, Henry of Winchester was personally kind and affectionate, loving to see happy faces around him. The young prince, whose influence was daily increasing, could not be blind to the evils of domestic war; and his whole conduct shews that he was no advocate of rash measures. Earl Simon, and even the rough old Earl of Gloucester, were no brutal plunderers. The real danger, so far as the characters of the rivals were concerned, lay in the foreign element, in the Queen, with her passionate southern blood, and her utter indifference to popular feelings, and in the newly returned William of Valence, whose seneschal, rebuked for a wanton outrage, is reported to have said: "If I do you a wrong, who will right you? Our Lord the King wishes whatever my master wishes, but my master does not wish whatever our Lord the King wishes or orders." There spoke the true spirit of feudal turbulence, and nothing could have been better calculated to stir up in England that lurid hatred of oppression, which is slow to burst into flame, but which, when it once breaks out, is apt, like a devouring fire, to lick up everything that crosses its path.

And so we are prepared to find the next eighteen months occupied with fruitless negotiations and manifestos. In July, 1261, the many personal questions, most of them relating to money, outstanding between Henry and Simon, were referred to the nominal decision of Queen Margaret of France, really to a board of arbitrators presided over by the Duke of Burgundy (Hugh IV.) and Peter, the Chamberlain of France. Such a tribunal was not calculated to produce a decisive result, and we hear little more of it. Henry then issued a long manifesto, which he distributed throughout the country by the hands of the newly appointed sheriffs. So far as it is anything more than a vague protest against the policy of the Reform party, it is an appeal to the country to trust the King's foreign favourites rather than its hereditary oppressors. The Reformers retaliated by refusing to give up any castles without the express orders of the Council, and by replacing the newly appointed sheriffs by "wardens of the

Diplomacy.

16 August, 1261.

counties," chosen by themselves. Herein they were clearly going beyond the bounds of legality, and Richard of Cornwall, to whom the question was referred, was justified in pronouncing in favour of the King. Meanwhile, an assembly of three knights from each shire, summoned by the Reform leaders to St. Alban's, had been adjourned by the King to Windsor; but nothing came of its deliberations. The year 1261 closed without bloodshed, but without any real hopes of peace. The troubles in the kingdom were inviting the very real danger of a war on the Welsh border, which had for two or three years been subject to invasion by David and Llywelyn, the sons of that Gruffyth who had met his end in 1244, trying to escape from the Tower.

29th Jan., 1262.

It is a high tribute to the character of St. Louis that both parties should have persistently looked toward him as the arbiter of peace. It is true that the family of Montfort might naturally turn to the throne of France for guidance, while it is not surprising that Henry should put faith in his royal brother-in-law, with whose piety he had so much sympathy. But it was a distinct recognition of Louis's virtues, that Simon's confederates, the other leaders of the Reform party, who professed to regard all foreigners with suspicion, should not have shrunk from appealing to a foreign king, so closely connected with the ruler whose policy they opposed. The whole of the year 1262 seems to have been occupied with French negotiations. Henry, Prince Edward, and Simon him-

French arbitration.

self, all visited Paris, and, doubtless, argued their troubles at length in the presence of St. Louis. Two events of the year are of real importance for the history of the struggle. In the summer, the old Earl of Gloucester died; and the armed neutrality which existed between him and Simon was replaced by the warm friendship of his son and successor, the young Gilbert Clare. But this gain to the baronial cause was far outweighed by the final decision of the Prince, formed, doubtless, upon the advice of St. Louis, to throw in his lot with his father. The King returned to England at Christmas, ill and disheartened; a great invasion of the Welsh border at the beginning of the new year, and a terrible fire which destroyed part of the Palace at Westminster, added to his depression. Seeing himself apparently helpless, he once more confirmed the Provisions of Oxford.

The death of Gloucester.

1262.

But his luck seemed to turn. At the darkest point of the Welsh war, when Edward, who had been hastily summoned by his father from France, found himself helpless before the combined forces of the Welsh princes, there was a split in the invaders' councils. "At the instigation of the devil" (as the Welsh chronicle puts it), David deserted his brother and fled to the English camp. Disheartened by this defection, Llywelyn accepted a truce, and Edward was free to return to London. The King had also received advices from Paris, which encouraged him to hope that Simon's real feelings were with him against his professed

Split among the Welsh.

supporters. In his excitement, Henry required that all loyal subjects should take the oath of allegiance to his son. The barons, naturally suspicious, demanded, as a return, that the Provisions of Oxford should form part of the bargain. The King refused, and the barons, no longer in doubt as to his real intentions, took up arms. Marching on Hereford, they attacked and secured Peter of Aigueblanche, the Poitevin Bishop, and his foreign canons, and soon followed up their success by capturing the towns of Gloucester, Worcester, Bridgenorth, and Shrewsbury. There followed a general massacre of people who could not speak the "English idiom"; and the King's supporters, conspicuous among them Henry of Almaine, son of Richard of Cornwall, and John Mansel, the "hatcher out" (*incubator*) of English livings, fled over sea. Edward was besieged in Windsor, and, when the barons marched on London, the King withdrew to Westminster and thence issued promises of submission. Disheartened by his father's cowardice, Edward surrendered Windsor on the 26th July, but, finding things not so bad as they seemed, he slipped away to his own city of Bristol, and, persuaded by Bishop Cantelupe of Worcester to surrender the castle, he then turned his steps towards the north, where, with Roger of Leyburn, John Vaux, Ralph Basset, and the Lowland nobles, he undertook to guard the line of the Trent against the Reformers.

Outbreak of the war.

May, 1263.

But Henry was in no mood to continue the struggle at the moment. He saw, in fact, that the

violence of the baronial party in the field was winning adherents to his side, and he preferred to try
the effect of negotiations. A great Parliament of magnates met at London in the Negotiations.
early autumn, and there the King's party
laid much stress upon the personal losses Sept., 1263.
suffered by loyal subjects in the military operations
in the West, and urged the appointment of a commission to assess compensation. It was difficult for
the Reformers to deny the justice of the claim; no
doubt there had been much indiscriminate bloodshed. Henry took advantage of the turn of affairs
to slip away to France for a short visit, nominally
on the business of the approaching Crusade; really,
no doubt, to take the advice of Louis upon his domestic troubles. He returned to Lon-
don on October 7th, with a proposal to 1263
submit all matters in dispute to the arbitration of
the French King. With (as it seems to us) incredible folly, the baronial party consented, and in
Christmas week the King and his son once more
set off for Amiens, where the enquiry was to be
held. Simon himself was unable to plead his cause
in person; he was represented by his cousin Peter.

The truth seems to be, that the baronial party
was hopelessly divided in its councils, and that Earl
Simon had ceased to lead more than a
section. As a result, the royal party, now Split in the baronial party.
purged by the flight of the foreigners, was
growing daily in strength. It is very instructive
to compare the names of 1258 (ante p. 113) with the
signatures to the documents of submission forwarded

to Saint Louis. The King's submission is signed, not only by his son and his nephew, but by the Earl Marshal, the Earl of Hereford, Roger Mortimer, and Hugh Bigod, four of the most conspicuous of the baronial party of 1258, as well as by the Lowland nobles Balliol and Bruce. On the other hand, Simon's letter is signed only by Hugh Despenser, Richard Gray, and the younger Bohun, together with his relatives and personal dependants. The names of the young Earl of Gloucester and the Bishop of Worcester are significantly absent from both documents.

The Mise of Amiens.

The award of Saint Louis, commonly known as the "Mise of Amiens," was published, with praiseworthy promptness, on the 23rd January, 1264. It was a complete destruction of the Reformers' hopes. The scheme of the Provisions was not likely to find much favour with Saint Louis, or with the jurists, trained in the principles of the law of Imperial Rome, who surrounded him. Still, the French King might have been expected to pay some regard to the circumstances which had provoked the proceedings at Oxford, or, at least, to the repeated solemn oaths of Henry. But the Mise simply annulled the whole of the objects for which the Reformers had been striving. The Provisions themselves were quashed, and all proceedings taken in pursuance of them set aside. The castles were to be returned to the King, and the appointment of all officials was to be left absolutely in his hands. Even the exclusion of foreigners from office was prohibited; and any attempt to limit the royal power was formally

FRENCH MAGISTRATE.

(THIRTEENTH CENTURY.)

(*From Viollet le Duc's "Dict. du Mobilier Français."*)

forbidden. A vague exhortation to forgiveness by Henry, and a general saving of ancient privileges, as they stood before 1258, are the sole evidences that Louis recognised the existence of a constitutional struggle. The whole of the hard-won achievements of the past five years are treated as childish theories. The Mise was formally confirmed by the Pope in the following March.

Received with anger.

The evil counsellors of the King, Boniface of Savoy, the Bishop of Hereford, and John Mansel, were present at the proclamation of the award; and their faces must have shone as they heard the words which seemed to open before them a renewal of their former prosperity. But they misjudged the temper of the people whom they presumed to govern. The Mise of Amiens was received in England with fierce protest; and the prospect of return to the evil days before 1258 drew together the wavering ranks of the Reformers. The citizens of London prepared to resist the foreigners. They appointed a Constable and a Marshal of their own, at whose summons, sounded on the great bell of St. Paul's, they pledged themselves to attend in arms. They imprisoned the King's clerks, the barons of the Exchequer, and the justices of the Bench; and, sallying out in the direction of Isleworth, attacked and burnt a house belonging to Richard of Cornwall. "And this was the beginning of griefs, and the origin of that mortal war, in which so many houses were burnt, and so many men, rich and poor, were plundered, and so many thousands of men perished." In Passion Week

London.

(13th–19th April) a fierce outbreak in the city resulted in the massacre of five hundred Jews. The Jewry was sacked, and its goods and writings carried off. With difficulty the Mayor restored order. The money of the Italian and "Caursine" bankers, the agents of the royal finance, was "extracted" from the abbeys round London, and removed to the city.

The country. But, though the Londoners might flatter themselves that they were the centre of the opposition movement (and, doubtless, their adherence to Simon's party was most important), the Mise was received with equal indignation throughout the country. Simon and the young Earl of Gloucester, now reconciled, flew to attack Roger Mortimer, who, in conjunction with Edward, was rousing the Welsh border for the King. Defeating this project by a bold though dangerous step, Simon made a league with Llywelyn, the Welsh Prince, to whom he promised his daughter in marriage. The campaign in the West, however, went decidedly in favour of the King. The Earl of Derby, a supporter of Simon, captured Worcester; but Edward secured the castle of Brecknock, the seat of the Bohun power in South Wales, and drove the barons out of Gloucester. More important still was the surrender of Northampton, with Peter of Montfort and the younger Simon. The arrival of John Balliol and the northern barons, at Easter, still further strengthened the King's hands; and Edward moved off towards Derbyshire and Staffordshire, where he ravaged the Ferrers estates, in revenge for the sack of Worcester. Leicester and Nottingham fell into the King's hands. Thereupon Simon directed his steps toward London, where he was heartily welcomed by the citizens.

It is at this point, in the opinion of military critics, that the King's advisers made a fatal mistake in not marching on London. The desultory capture of towns which, in theory, still owed allegiance to the Crown, could not end the war. It was necessary to capture the leaders of the opposition. But Henry contented himself with relieving Rochester castle, besieged by the Londoners, and then he attacked and captured the ancient castle of the Clares (Earls of Gloucester), Tonbridge in Kent. At this point his plans seem to have come to an end. At any rate, he drifted aimlessly into Sussex, threatening, but not attacking, the Cinque Ports, and, at the beginning of May, found himself at Lewes, where he settled down in the Cluniac Priory of St. Pancras. On May 6th, Simon and the Londoners set out to attack him; and a long and tedious interchange of documents failed to produce an agreement. In spite of the ample warning conveyed by these attempts, the royal forces seem to have been taken by surprise on the morning of May 14th. Simon, marching from Fletching, had carefully disposed his forces, which were much smaller than those of the King, in three "battles," with a reserve. On his left were the Londoners under Hastings, and these, marching along the Pevensey road, approached the King's right, which, under Prince Edward, was resting on Lewes castle. Roused to fury by the sight of the

The King's mistake.

Battle of Lewes, 1264.

citizens, whose insult to his mother in the previous year the prince had never forgotten, Edward charged with reckless force, swept his opponents back into the river Ouse, which skirts the town on the east, and followed them up the steep slopes of Mount Cabourn. There his quick eye caught sight of Earl Simon's chariot and standard, left on the Downs when the Earl mounted his horse in the morning. Believing the chariot to contain the baronial leader, the prince charged the little group which surrounded it, only to find, when too late, that he had killed his own hostages. Returning towards the main battle, he soon saw that things had gone badly with the royal forces. The baronial centre, under Gloucester, charging down the steep slopes of the Combe, had broken up the King's forces under Richard of Cornwall, who was quickly obliged to seek shelter in a mill, while Simon and his sons defeated the King, who commanded the left wing of his own army. Edward succeeded in cutting his way through to his father; but the royalists were utterly routed. Balliol, Bruce, Comyn, and the northern barons were captured; the Earl of Hereford, Arundel, Percy, William of Valence, and Guy of Lusignan fled. The slaughter was terrific. Hemmed in between the river and the marsh which skirts (or skirted) the Priory on the south, the royalists fell an easy prey. One estimate puts the loss at 12,000; another, more moderate, makes it 5000. The monks buried 600 corpses, which they collected in the streets. The King and Richard only obtained their personal liberty by surrendering their sons,

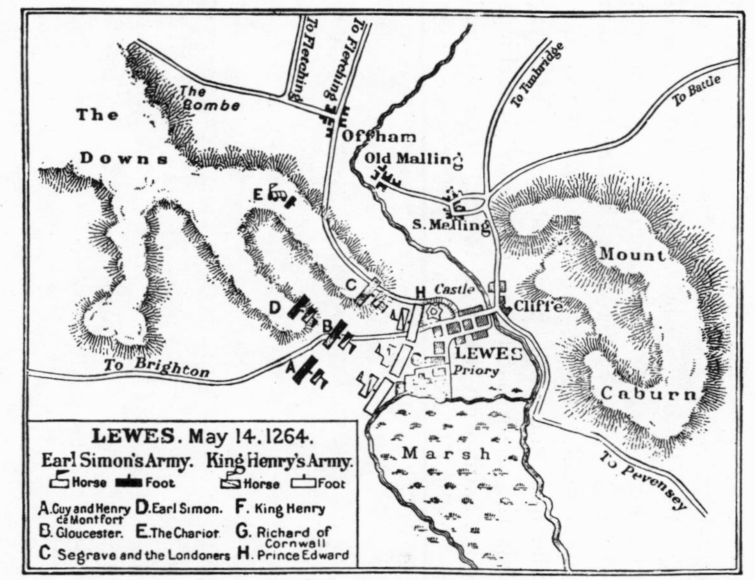

PLAN OF THE BATTLE OF LEWES.

(*From Oman's "History of the Art of War."*)

Edward and Henry of Almaine, as hostages. The whole of the machinery of government passed into Simon's hands; and for the next twelve months, all acts of State, though done in the King's name, were really the work of Simon.

It would not be fair to say that Edward lost the battle. The King's failure was inevitable, from the moment that the barons' army caught him unawares in a death-trap like Lewes. But the prince's conduct had turned a defeat into a hopeless surrender. He had allowed himself to commit a grave military fault, in the heat of his personal resentment. The man who stood shouting "Come out, Simon, thou devil," before a chariot which contained two or three of his own supporters, while the great Earl was dealing death amongst his father's army below, must have cut a sorry figure in the eyes of his followers. Moreover, though he was not in supreme command of his father's troops, Edward could and should have insisted on a proper watch being kept after the close of the negotiations. No excuse for his conduct has been seriously offered; probably none could be sustained. Edward was no longer a boy, nor was he a novice in practical warfare. The real value to him of the defeat of Lewes was, that it proved to be the turning-point of his life. It changed him from a reckless youth of promise into a sober, capable man. As we follow his career, we shall not see repeated the reckless charge up Cabourn, nor the still more reckless swoop on the Downs. What we shall see is, that Edward has thoroughly learned the lesson of

Edward's share in the defeat.

Lewes, and that he has the supreme quality of greatness, the power of learning from his own misfortunes.

The Parliament which followed the battle restored the scheme laid down by the Provisions of Oxford, and left the execution of it in Simon's hands. The committee of four, which had nominated the Council of Fifteen, had disappeared; its place was taken by Simon himself, Gloucester, and Bishop Berksted, of Chichester. These were instructed to nominate a Council of Nine, "from the loyal, wise, and useful men of the kingdom"; and the King bound himself to act by the advice of this Council, of whom three, at least, were always to be present in his "Curia." The Church was to be reformed, and compensated for the losses of the war; the councillors, the royal officials, and especially the wardens of the royal castles, were to be chosen from the native-born; but peaceable foreigners, cleric and lay, were to have liberty to go about their business. The Provisions of Westminster were to be faithfully kept. It was, however, understood that the arrangements for arbitration made immediately after the battle, in a lost document known as the "Mise of Lewes," would in due time be carried out.

The Mise of Lewes.

Meanwhile, imminent danger threatened the country. The King's party, headed by the Queen, were straining every nerve to collect an army of invasion. They were the old crew—Peter of Savoy, William of Valence, and John Mansel, reinforced by the Earl of Warenne

Threat of invasion.

ISABELLA OF ANGOULÊME.

(WIFE OF KING JOHN.)

(*From Stothard's "Monumental Effigies.*")

(doubtless influenced by his foreign wife), and the renegade Hugh Bigod. A great national army was summoned to London for August 3rd. Not only were all feudal tenants, with their whole power, to attend, but each township was to send four, six, or eight men, according to its size, with expenses for forty days provided; and the cities and boroughs as many men as possible. The clergy gave a tenth of their rents; the income of benefices held by aliens was confiscated. The army assembled on Harbledown,* near Canterbury, and marched coastwards. The Cinque Ports collected a fleet. So brave was the display, that the invaders hesitated, and, on August 15th, agents of both parties met at Dover, and agreed once more to submit their differences to arbitration. Again, however, the attempt came to nothing; the Papal legate thundered anathemas against the baronial party from the safe distance of Boulogne, and the Reformers determined to refer all questions in dispute to a great national assembly, to be held at London in January, 1265.

The Parliament of 1265.

The plan of this assembly has long been Simon's great title to fame; but it is doubtful whether it came to him as an inspiration. The events of the war had been steadily throwing him back for support on the middle classes, the knights and freeholders of the shires, and the citizens of the boroughs. He was engaged in a

* The village of Harbledown is said to be Chaucer's
"little town
Which that ycleped is 'Bob up and down,'
Under the Blee, in Canterbury way."

life-and-death struggle with unscrupulous foes. He determined to summon all his adherents together; and the fact that his choice was so wide, so confidently made, and so cordially responded to, shews that he really then had the nation at his back. On the 14th December, 1264, he issued, of course in the King's name, writs of summons to the Archbishop of York and twelve bishops, to five deans, to ten abbots, and to nine priors. On the 24th December, he followed these with writs to eighty-four abbots, priors, and heads of religious Orders, and twenty-three earls and barons. Up to this point he was merely following long-established precedents. These persons were, in fact, the magnates who formed the ordinary annual Parliaments, the "community of the realm," as the barons called them at Oxford. But Simon went a step farther. Repeating his own precedent of 1261, he bade the sheriffs to send from each shiremoot two knights, and York, Lincoln, and "the rest of the boroughs of England" each to send two wise, loyal, and upright citizens or burgesses.

Terms of settlement.

The Parliament met, and, by the middle of February, terms had been agreed upon. The King took the baronial leaders into his peace, and swore yet again to observe the Charters, the Provisions of Oxford, and the added articles of Westminster. A solemn record of the peace, under the royal seal, was sent into every county; and the King bade proclamation of it be made twice every year in the full shiremoot. Before he was released from strict custody, Edward, who had been made to swear to his father's charter, was compelled to promise, by separate sworn deed, to place three of his Welsh castles in the hands of impartial wardens for three years, to keep the Marcher Earls in order, not to leave England for three years, not to introduce any foreigners, and to oppose actively any who should come. The young Henry of Almaine became surety for Edward, and placed himself as hostage in the hands of Henry of Montfort. Edward's earldom of Chester, and his castle of Bristol, were handed over to Simon, as well as the lands of Richard, the King's brother, in Devon, the castles of the Marchers, and the castles of the Peak, and Newcastle-under-Lyme. In the middle of April Simon seems also to have been appointed Justitiar. To other members of the baronial party were confided the castles of Dover, Scarborough, Bamborough, Nottingham, Corfe, and Montgomery. Even then, the prince was not given his full freedom; but was carried about, with his father, in Simon's train.

Reaction against Simon.

But Simon was now going too far, even for his own supporters. So long as the country was threatened with foreign invasion, men were willing to trust to his ability, and to leave him a free hand. But they were not prepared to see him permanently installed as virtual ruler of the kingdom. Before Whitsuntide, a violent quarrel broke out between him and the younger Gloucester, who, by this time, shared his dead father's jealousy of Simon's power. The fleet, which had been collected by the Cinque Ports to repel the invasion, disgraced itself by wholesale plundering in the Channel—men said

Quarrel with Gloucester.

Piracy in the Channel.

with the tacit connivance of Simon and his sons. The citizens of London, determined to put down anarchy, at least in their own neighbourhood, proclaimed the King's peace, with a promise of summary execution on breach of obedience, in the four adjacent counties, and in all hundreds and townships within twenty-five miles of the city—an interesting forecast of Greater London. Several ruffians captured in open robbery at Stepney and Hackney on June 29th proved to be followers of the younger Simon. The same hot-headed youth disgraced himself by a barbarous attack on Winchester, on the morrow of the patron saint of its cathedral, Saint Swithun. Such events were not likely to increase Simon's popularity.

Ruffianism in London.

July 15th.

It hardly needed Edward's keen eye to see, that there was a chance for one who, representing the old order of things, would repeat neither the follies of Henry nor the innovations of Simon. He had shrewdness enough to realise that Simon's real strength lay, not in his constitutional machinery, for which the country as yet cared little, but in his national opposition to foreign adventurers. Escaping, by a clever trick, from his guards at Hereford, Edward was joined, first, by Roger Mortimer, and afterwards by Warenne and William of Valence, who had just landed in his wife's city of Pembroke. But Edward shewed real genius when he flung himself into Gloucester's arms at Ludlow, and offered, as his father's trusted adviser, to persuade the King to

Escape of Edward, May 28th.

Treaty of Ludlow.

adopt, of his own accord, the principles of government which Simon was endeavouring to force upon him through an elected Council. The foreigners were to be removed from the government, and the ancient laws restored. That was all the barons wanted; and Edward was the one person who could promise it to them. They distrusted Henry, but they trusted his son. From that moment Simon's cause was hopeless.

The Earl realised in a flash what the escape of Edward meant. The feudal array was summoned on May 30th. The sheriffs of the counties, who had been reinforced in the previous year by "guardians of the peace," were ordered to arrest Edward and his following. The bishops of the province of Canterbury, in the absence of their metropolitan, Boniface of Savoy, were invited to excommunicate him. With doubtful wisdom, Simon, in the King's name, bought the support of the Welsh Prince, Llywelyn, the natural enemy of the Marcher Earls who were supporting Edward, by the gift of the castles of Mold and Hawarden, and the Hundred of Ellesmere, together with a promise of help in Llywelyn's standing claims against the Marchers.

Dismay of Simon.

League with Llywelyn.

But all was vain. Edward had learned thoroughly the lesson of Lewes, and was determined to repeat upon Simon the tactics which had proved so fatal against the King. The Earl's headquarters were at Hereford; and Edward saw that the broad stream of the Severn, crossed only at rare intervals by bridges, was

Edward's strategy.

The line of the Severn.

a natural barrier which might serve to shut Simon up in a corner of England, where he would be harmless. Accordingly, he bent every energy to block the river at its vulnerable points. In spite of the resistance of Ross, Simon's captain, Edward took

Capture of Gloucester.

Gloucester on the 14th June, broke down the bridge, and destroyed the ford. Simon, driven south, and unwilling to sever himself from his Welsh allies, attacked and captured Monmouth;

Monmouth.

but was again blocked at the passage of the Wye by Giffard, acting under Edward's orders. Thoroughly frightened, the Earl urged the Bristol citizens to send boats to Newport, a little

Newport.

town at the mouth of the river Usk, whence he hoped to be able to transport his army across the Bristol Channel, and so open the road to London. The citizens complied, though their minds must have wavered between their rival

Abergavenny. Usk.

lords, and Simon captured Abergavenny, Usk, and Newport, in preparation for the great move. He also indulged himself in the pleasure of harrying Gloucester's Welsh lands. But Edward's forces made a successful attack on the boats at Newport, in galleys brought from the captured city of Gloucester; and Simon saw his last chance disappear. Slowly and wearily he turned north, and plunged into the wild country of Brecon, where, though the Welsh were friendly, his followers

Leominster.

suffered from hunger and lack of shelter, at last (July 20th) reaching Hereford, no whit the better for their long march. He captured Leominster on the Wye; but the royalists, now

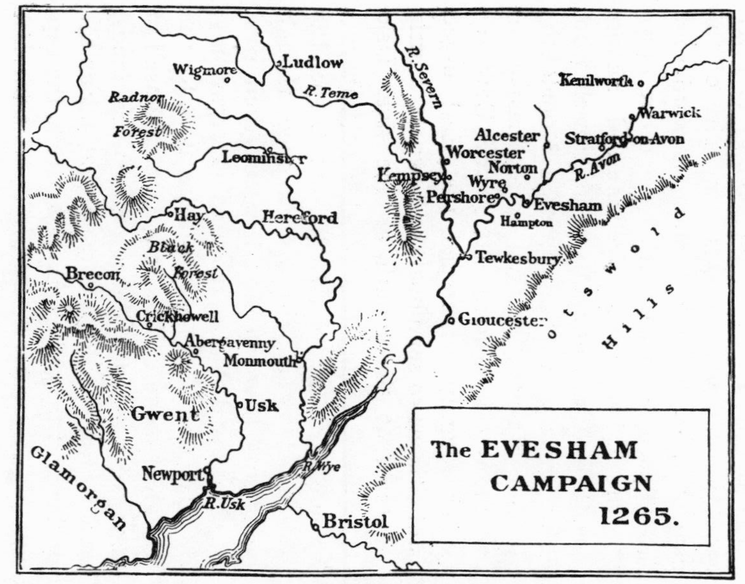

PLAN OF THE EVESHAM CAMPAIGN.

(*From Oman's "History of the Art of War."*)

back at Worcester, still barred inexorably the passage across the Severn.

At this point, a grave danger threatened Edward's army. The younger Simon, at his father's urgent call, had hurried up from Pevensey, where he was besieging the castle, and reached Kenilworth, the great stronghold of the Montfort power in the west, on July 31st. Edward, kept well informed of his movements, saw that his only chance was to prevent a meeting of father and son. Sallying out of Worcester on the evening of August 1st (Saturday), he covered the thirty miles of road by a dashing night march, and appeared before Kenilworth early on the Sunday morning (August 2nd). Young Simon's forces were completely surprised, with most of his chief followers, the Earl of Oxford (Vere), William Munchensy, Adam Newmarch, Baldwin Wake, and Hugh Nevill. But Simon himself managed to escape into the castle; and Edward dared not wait to besiege him. Marching his triumphant followers back to Worcester, he learned that the old Earl had at last succeeded in forcing the passage of the Severn, having employed the Sunday in throwing his troops across the river at Kempsey, at the junction of the Severn and the Teme, four miles below Worcester. There, for the first time, Simon learnt of his son's arrival at Kenilworth, but not, apparently, of his defeat. He pushed on (August 3rd) to effect a junction; but, not daring to take the direct road, for fear of the royalist army, marched by Pershore to

The younger Simon.

Attack on Kenilworth.

Simon crosses the Severn.

Evesham.

Evesham, where he took up his quarters in the ancient Benedictine abbey which lies to the south-east of the little town, overlooking the river Avon. Here the tactics of Lewes were almost exactly repeated, the parts of the combatants alone being changed. Just as the King had been shut up between the river, the marsh, and the Downs at Lewes, so at Evesham the Earl was hemmed in on three sides by the loop of the river, which almost encircles the town. Just as, at Lewes, the attack of the barons had been made in three divisions, so, at Evesham, Edward divided his army into three "battles." The great glory of the royalists is that, after their night march of Saturday to Kenilworth, followed by the battle on Sunday morning, and the return to Worcester on the same day, they were prepared, on the Monday evening, to undertake another march of fifteen miles to Evesham. The three divisions, moreover, marched by different routes, two at least of which must have been roundabout. On the morning of August 4th, the Earl's followers saw a host approaching from the north, the direction of Kenilworth; and this they fondly hoped was the troops of the younger Simon. Apparently, the prince had forseen this mistake, and, to profit by it, had displayed in the van the captured standards of Kenilworth. But the sharper eyes of one of Earl Simon's men soon descried the royal banner over the main host; and then it was clear, that the approaching army was that of the prince, and, moreover, attacking on the one undefended side of the town. This was bad enough, but a shout from the west revealed the fact that a second host, under

RUINS OF EVESHAM ABBEY.

(*From Dugdale's "Monasticon.*")

the banner of Gloucester, was marching in from Wyre to join the prince. And, to crown all despair, the horrified leaders of the baronial host caught sight of yet a third attack, under command of Roger Mortimer, which approached their rear along the road from Pershore, by which they themselves had marched on the previous day. They were in a hopeless trap. Even if they could have beaten off the double attack from the north and west, they would have been taken in the rear by the approach of the army of Mortimer, which would have forced the bridge at Bengeworth while the fight was going on across the river. If they attempted to fly from the prince, they fell into the arms of the same troops, who would wait for them to cross the bridge. A noble death was the one alternative of disgrace; and it speaks well for the good faith of Simon's followers, that not a single man of note accepted his generous offer of release. The Earl himself, with gentle scorn, refused to provide for his own safety; he was too old, he said, to learn how to fly from battle. Forming up steadily in column, the baronial army charged grandly up the hill, down which the prince's troops were pouring. But the numbers, the weight, the confidence of victory which cheered Edward's troops, were all against Simon's men; and they were soon surrounded. Fighting bravely to the last, there perished the Earl himself, his son Henry, his cousin Peter, and all the leaders of the baronial host, save the young Bohun and Simon's second son, Guy, who were wounded and left for dead, but afterwards recovered. It was

Complete defeat of Simon.

rather a massacre than a battle. A disgraceful story which, if true, reveals the depths of barbarity to which even a well-ordered host could in those days descend, tells how the body of the great Earl was mutilated, and dispersed throughout the land.

The Reforming party, though it still held out in isolated fragments, was wholly crushed. All royal charters granted since the day of Lewes were formally annulled. The lands and houses of Earl Simon were given to the King's second son, Edmund, to console him for the loss of Sicily. London surrendered, after a brief resistance. The younger Simon, after a stubborn defence of Kenilworth, surrendered at Northampton in the following year, but, not liking the prospects, soon fled with his brother Guy oversea. Guy was taken into the service of Charles of Anjou, who made him his vicar for Tuscany and the Romagna. But both the brothers disgraced themselves, and incurred the undying hatred of Edward, by the wanton murder of Henry of Almaine, Edward's favourite cousin, in the Church of St. Silvester at Viterbo, in the year 1271. Thenceforth they were outside practical politics. The only real danger to the King came from Gloucester, who, now that the royal cause proved successful, seemed inclined once more to favour the Reformers. But the year 1267 marked the final conclusion of peace. It was the most fertile within living memory, in woods, fields, gardens, and vineyards. Gloucester was formally reconciled, both to the prince and the Church. Peace was made with Llywelyn. In the flush of victory, the *Dictum of Kenilworth*

31st Oct., 1267.

had annulled all the Reformers' achievements of the previous seven years; but the reforms which did not seriously curtail the royal power were embodied in the permanent Statute of Marlborough in the autumn session of 1267. And so the land at last had peace.

Earl Simon.

This is not the place for an estimate of the character of Earl Simon. But we can hardly take leave of the Reformer without a brief word of farewell to one who played such a great part in the England of his day, and whose death must have so completely altered the world for his young nephew. There can be little doubt that he attracted to himself the best elements of the nation. The estimate of him to be found in the Chronicle of William of Rishanger very fairly represents Earl Simon as he appeared to the world. He was wise and prudent, skilled above all his contemporaries in the use of arms, nobly eminent in knowledge of letters, a diligent attendant on the offices of the Church, spare in diet and in drink, labouring in the night-watches, jovial and humorous of speech, steadfast to his plighted word even to death, respectful towards all Churchmen of honest lives, distinguished for his friendship with Greathead, who had destined him for the part which he afterwards played. It is the character of a great leader of men. To his inferiors, Simon seemed all that was good and gracious. They never questioned his wisdom, nor grudged his power. Where he failed always was with his equals in social position, the leaders of the baronial party in England, the feudal nobility of Gascony. They could not tolerate the pretensions which his undoubted ability claimed. They were jealous of him for his marriage with Henry's sister, still more for that (as it seemed to them) treasonable friendship with the lower ranks in the social hierarchy, to which he owed so much of his power. He could not stoop to the petty arts of conciliation which, odd as it may seem, yet do so much to ensure personal success. His statesmanship was a failure. If it had an object, it was to set up a king who reigned but did not govern, and a chief minister (by preference Simon himself) who governed but did not reign. As we know, the wheel of Time was to bring round this ideal also, in the ages to come. But, in the thirteenth century, men were not prepared for such an expedient. Edward read the times aright when he decided, that the country yet leaned towards a strong king, who should govern it sternly and justly, as Henry of Anjou had done, keeping the feudal nobles in check, and ruling his own conduct within the easy limits of established custom, as expressed in the Charters. He staked all on this view, and he won.

Edward himself came grandly out of the Barons' War. By the sheer force of his own character, he had built up again a royal party out of the wreck of Lewes, and, after waiting quietly till Simon had shown by experience the impossibility of his ideal, he had moved against him with steady resolve. After worsting him in two months of masterly strategy, during which the victor of Lewes had wandered wearily about the west country, vainly seeking an escape from the toils which were closing relentlessly around him, Edward,

The victor of Evesham.

by a series of forced marches so rapid that, even now, men can hardly bring themselves to credit the contemporary accounts,* defeated the Earl's long-awaited succours, and rushed to deal the final blow. In after years, the breath of scandal dared to assert, that Edward lost heart on the famous march to Kenilworth, and was only saved from the disgrace of falling back by the earnest remonstrances of Sir Roger Clifford. But there is no proof of the truth of the accusation; which, at most, would shew that, in a time of frightful anxiety, a man of twenty-six, confronted with a grave responsibility, hesitated for a moment. At any rate, Edward's plans were triumphantly successful; and the brilliant tactics which sent Simon's army to its doom were a worthy climax of the strategy of the campaign. When Simon fell at Evesham, there was left but one man fit to rule England; and that man, happily for her, was England's future king.

* The total distance covered in the two days and a half was, if our accounts are correct, about seventy-five miles. True, there were no hedges to prevent short cuts, and it was full summer. Moreover, the proportion of cavalry would be large. Still, the achievement is marvellous.

CHAPTER VII

THE COMING OF THE KING

1266–1278

THE battle of Evesham marks the attainment by Edward of the full vigour of his glorious manhood. From that day, until his death in harness at Burgh-on-Sands, forty-two long years, his life was full of strenuous action. Among his faults, and he had his share, none could accuse Edward of that sumptuous idleness which had been the curse of his father, and which was to be the curse of his son and grandson. Though his home life was pure and happy, though he loved sport and magnificence, Edward never forgot that his kingdom had the first claim on his life. That intense conviction of the importance of public affairs, which is the great safeguard of the statesman, and which is denied to the mere politician, was Edward's in abundant measure. And this, no doubt, is why, in all his troubles, the barons whom he kept in check, the clergy whose undue aspirations he controlled, the people whom he taxed so hardly for his grand schemes, never really doubted the greatness of their ruler. Fierce as might be the discussions of the moment, the King had but to appeal to the common bond of sympathy between himself and his people, and all was forgiven. In the King his people saw no idle voluptuary, but a great and commanding ruler, whose one object was to make his country also great. In him the budding consciousness of national existence found its one concrete expression; he stood, not for Normandy, nor for Anjou, nor for Gascony, but for England, in such wise as none of his predecessors since Hastings had done.

After Evesham.

The old King Henry could not but feel, that to his son he owed his escape from the galling fetters of Simon. The prince's lands were restored to him, as a matter of course, and a grant of the port dues to him for life shewed that Henry was not ungrateful. The need of money in which Edward stood, and the small beginning of English foreign trade, are both revealed in the fact that Edward farmed out this revenue to a firm of Italian merchants, for the modest return of 6000 marks a year; but this step, unwise in itself, became the happy occasion of at least a temporary friendship between the prince and the citizens of London, who complained of the violation of their privileges by the Italian collectors. Edward released them from their liability, and they made him a "courtesy" of two hundred marks. In his hatred of the Londoners, the King, at the close of the war, had made Edward a grant of all the goods of the citizens, alleging that they had been forfeited by the conduct of the

Grant of the "Customs."

The foreign merchants.

city. But this imprudent step had been subsequently revoked, and in exchange the King gave to his son that special jurisdiction over foreign merchants which was one of the most cherished prerogatives of the Crown. In these transactions, we see the germ of Edward's future policy regarding the "Great" and the "Little" custom, which was to excite so much jealousy in after years. The King, as usual, remained in a bankrupt condition; in the year 1267 he was obliged to pledge the jewels from the shrine of Saint Edward, and, two years later, a disgraceful repudiation by the King and his son, of all debts owing to the Jews, shews the straits to which the royal exchequer was put.

Meanwhile, the embers of the civil war were being slowly stamped out. In 1266, Edward undertook a vigorous campaign against the more desperate supporters of Simon, who held out in the Isle of Axholme, in Lincolnshire, and won knightly fame by his single-handed capture of Adam Gordon, a notorious outlaw, in the woods of Alton. In the same year, the Cinque Ports were received into favour, and their ancient privileges restored. At Michaelmas, a board of twelve elected commissioners, under the control of the legate Ottobon and Henry of Almaine, undertook a general enquiry into the circumstances of the "disinherited"—*i. e.*, those of Simon's followers who had been deprived of their lands by the *Dictum of Kenilworth;* and these were allowed (with one or two exceptions) to redeem their estates on payment

End of the war.

Lincolnshire.

Hampshire.

The Cinque Ports.

The "Disinherited."

of fines varying with their degrees of activity. Kenilworth was surrendered in December. A brush between Gloucester and the legate in the spring of 1267 interrupted but slightly the course of proceedings. In the following year, Ottobon held a general Council at St. Paul's, the coming national unity being foreshadowed by the presence of Irish, Scottish, and Welsh ecclesiastics, secular and monastic. Minor measures of peace were not wanting. Peter of Savoy was persuaded to accept an exchange for the Honour of Richmond, which at last returned to the House of Brittany. Henry of Almaine was married to a daughter of Gaston de Béarn, Edward's turbulent Gascon feudatory, who, for a time, at least, became a friend of the prince. Edward himself went into Wales, to settle the details of the treaty with Llywelyn. Reparation for the damages inflicted on the Church in the war was enforced, on pain of excommunication, at a solemn assembly of nine bishops at Paul's Cross; and the opportunity was taken to rehearse the Bull, issued by Innocent IV. in 1253, against the breakers of the Charters. By the good offices of the King of the Romans, the questions in dispute between Gloucester and Edward were finally settled; and, to crown all, the prince buried his long-standing grudge against the London citizens, and personally requested his father to grant a full renewal of their ancient privileges. It was a gracious and a wise act; and the gift of five hundred marks

Kenilworth.

Council at St. Paul's.

Peter of Savoy.

Gaston de Béarn.

Llywelyn.

The Church.

to Edward by the grateful citizens by no means represented the extent of its value.

The Crusade.

For Edward had now determined on a step which, rash as it seems at first sight, was really one of the wisest acts of his life. So long as his father lived, the prince's position was difficult. His own filial piety, and his father's somewhat peevish jealousy, rendered it impossible for him openly to assume the direction of affairs during that father's life. In his first gratitude after Evesham, Henry was, no doubt, willing to place himself in the hands of his son. But Edward knew well that this attitude would not last; and he did not care to have his father's acts attributed to his advice. He was now at the height of his popularity; he could withdraw for a space, in the full confidence that his memory, during his absence, would abide as a precious possession in the hearts of Englishmen. Inaction was hateful to him. An opportunity for distinction opened in the nick of time; and Edward seized it eagerly.

The Tartars.

In the battles of Benevento (1266) and Tagliacozzo (1268), the power of the Hohenstaufen had been finally crushed by Charles of Anjou; and the Papacy, issuing victorious from the deadly struggle, had once more eyes for the affairs of Christendom. The death of the Khan Ogodai had rolled back the tide of Tartar

1241.

invasion from Europe; and Ogodai's successors had turned their victorious armies towards the rich conquest of Persia. Saint Louis, in his sojourn at Cyprus, on his way to the Eighth Crusade,

had been cheered by the arrival of a Tartar embassy
with offers of help against the Saracens. The authority of the embassy was doubted at the
time; but a mission was sent to the Tartar 1248.
head camp, which, after adventures of a comic opera
character, met with a gracious reception, and returned with a friendly message from the Great
Khan. But by the time of its return, the
disasters of Mansourah and Damietta had 1250.
fallen upon the Crusaders; and the Tartars were left
to attack the Moslems alone. This they did so
effectually, that, in the year 1258, as has been said,
Baghdad was captured and destroyed by the Tartar
general Hulagu. It now seemed as if the Tartars
would save Europe the necessity of pursuing the Crusades; but their defeat at Ain 1260.
Galud, by the Mameluke Sultan, divided the East
between Mongol and Moslem, and left it open to a
third power to hold the balance between them.
Clement IV., stirred by the fall of
Antioch, preached a vigorous Crusade; 1267.
and, though he died in 1268, the vacancy in the
Papal Chair which followed was not entirely fatal to
the scheme. Once more the saintly King
of the French felt his crusading ardour **Saint Louis.**
burn; and his nephew Edward followed his example,
taking the cross at Northampton in June, 1268.
The great difficulty was money; but a conference at
Gravesend with his uncle Richard of Cornwall, in
August, 1269, seems to have suggested to Edward a
way out of the difficulty. Crossing with his cousin,
Henry of Almaine, and the latter's brother-in-law,

Gaston de Béarn, to France, he found the French King generously disposed, and a bargain was soon struck. Louis offered to lend Edward seventy thousand livres for his expedition, to be secured on the Customs of Bordeaux, and repaid by half-yearly instalments of five thousand livres. To this sum England generously added a twentieth of movables as a free gift. The now reconciled Earl of Gloucester, Roger of Leybourn, Robert Walerand, and many others of the prince's friends, joined in the scheme; and all preparations were made for a start. Louis himself, however, was ready long before his nephew, who did not actually leave England till the end of
1270. August, sailing direct for the Mediterranean, where Louis was besieging Tunis. Charles of Anjou ordered quarters to be prepared for the prince at Marsala; but Edward stopped short
Death of Saint Louis. at Sardinia, where he heard the terrible news of the death of Saint Louis before Tunis, amid the ruins of Carthage. Hastening with all speed to Tunis, Edward found, to his horror, that Philip, the successor of Louis, and Charles of Anjou his uncle, with the Kings of Navarre and Aragon, had made a disgraceful treaty with the Moslem ruler, who had agreed to pay tribute to Charles, as King of Sicily, on condition of being left in peace. Edward tried in vain to convince his allies of the enormity of this proceeding; they were anxious to reach home before the winter, promising to sail for Acre in the following spring. Finding his remonstrances useless, Edward reluctantly started for Sicily, and arrived at Trapani on the 26th October.

He would, however, touch no part of the hateful tribute; and the chroniclers of the day saw the reward of his piety, when a terrible storm broke over the open roadstead of Trapani, and the hundred and twenty ships of the other Crusaders, with the tribute money on board, perished utterly, while Edward's thirteen vessels escaped unhurt. In the morning, the bodies of fifteen hundred sailors, with animals innumerable, strewed the beach; and the kings, their whole resources wrecked, abandoned the Crusade.

1270.

But Edward was made of sterner stuff. Leaving Sicily at Easter of 1271, he sailed to Acre, which was still in the hands of the Christians, and, after there resting a month, marched out to attack Nazareth with an army of seven thousand men. He was completely successful, and, on his return, being followed by an army of Saracens, offered battle at Kerak, near the Dead Sea, where he inflicted a crushing defeat on the enemy. The titular King of Jerusalem (Hugh of Lusignan) had long urged his Cypriote subjects to take part in the Crusade; but they had refused until Edward's arrival, when they came to him with flattering offers of service and allegiance.

Reaches Acre.

Nazareth.

Kerak.

Edward's fame as a Crusader now became so great, that the Sultan was seriously alarmed, and, as the firm belief of the time held, determined to remove him by the hand of an assassin. The Admiral of Joppa feigned a desire for conversion to the Christian faith, and letters and

Escape from assassination.

messages passed between him and Edward. The Admiral employed a favourite messenger, whose conduct seemed so harmless, that the vigilance of Edward's guards relaxed, and, when he arrived for the fifth time, on the evening of Tuesday,
1271. June 2nd, he was allowed to pass, without a very severe search, into the royal presence. The day had been hot, and Edward leaned on a couch in a light tunic, with his head uncovered. Handing to the prince his letters, as was his wont, the messenger waited until Edward was deeply intent upon them, and then, softly stealing his hand to his belt as though to bring out another letter, he hastily drew a poisoned dagger, and made a lunge at Edward's breast. Quick as thought, the prince put up his arm and received the wound in its flesh, while, with a vigorous lunge, he kicked over the assassin as he leaned forward for a second blow. Then, snatching the dagger from the man's hand, he despatched him in an instant, while a horrified attendant rushed forward, and, seizing a stool, dashed out the brains of the dead man. Coolly rebuking him for striking a corpse, Edward drank off the antidote offered by the Master of the Templars, and, a few days later, seeing the flesh round his wound mortifying, insisted on a thorough cutting away of the diseased place, tenderly putting aside his wife, who clung to him with tears and groans. He then made his will, and quietly awaited the issue of events. The story is worth the detailed telling, for it reveals the high temper of the prince, his quick resource, coolness, vigour, and patient courage. He shewed the further quality of

dignity, when the Sultan, professing horror at the incident, sent three of his notables, who, with profound reverences, congratulated him on his escape. "You bow before me, but you love me not," was Edward's dignified rebuke; but he treated them nobly, and dismissed them in safety. Perhaps, too, it had been something more than mere courtly language which came from the lips of Edward's attendants as they led the weeping queen away: "Lady, it is better that you should shed tears, than that the whole of England should mourn."

News now came to Edward that his father's health was failing; and he accepted a ten years' truce from the Sultan, and set out on his way home, reaching Trapani once more about the end of September, 1273. There he heard of the deaths of his father and his infant son, John.

Returns to Europe.

It is a proof of Edward's conviction of his own strength, that, even now, he did not hurry his return to England. The Exchequer, the great centre of administration, had undergone a thorough reform shortly before he had started on the Crusade; his most dangerous rival, Gloucester, had sworn fealty to him just before the old King's death. His peace (as he doubtless learnt) had been proclaimed through all the counties immediately on his father's decease, by the most powerful men in the kingdom. Boniface of Savoy and Richard of Cornwall were dead. Every month was tending more and more to wipe out the bitter memories of the Barons' War. There were certain things to be done abroad. Journeying to Orvieto,

Leisurely Progress.

Orvieto

Edward procured from the new Pope the excommunication of Guy of Montfort for his share in the murder of Henry of Almaine. His deep resentment of the treacherous act is shewn by his stern conduct towards the new bishop of Chichester, who had ventured, on a visit to Rome, to consort with Aymer of Montfort, a brother of the murderers. The Constable of Dover was ordered to seize the bishop on the sea, and prevent his landing. His barony was to be confiscated by the justices. Edward had also to receive the homage of the Count of Savoy for his Gascon fiefs, and to render homage to the French King for his own possessions in the south. Scrupulous feudalist as he was, Edward did not hesitate to journey to Paris, where he was splendidly received by Philip, and where he shelved outstanding questions by a convenient phrase. He did homage to his suzerain for all the lands which he held "or claimed to hold" of him. On his way to Paris, he had indulged in two knightly adventures. He had broken the anarchic independence of a robber chief of Burgundy, and compelled him to become a vassal of the Count of Savoy. Not without some misgiving, he had accepted the challenge of the Count of Chalons to a tourney; and when, as he foresaw, the sham fight passed into real earnest, he and his followers gave such a good account of themselves, that much blood was shed, and the affair became known as the "little battle of Chalons."

Receives and pays homage.

Gascony.

From Paris Edward turned to Gascony, where Gaston de Béarn was again in revolt. He spent the winter of 1273–74 in a not very successful attempt to restore order, and, in the following May, patched up a peace with Gaston at Limoges, by the advice of a commission of jurists, at whose head was Francesco Accursius the younger, the famous Bolognese civilian. Meanwhile, Edward had been aiming to secure peace in the south by arranging marriages between his eldest surviving son, Henry, and the daughter and heiress presumptive of the King of Navarre, also between his eldest daughter, Eleanor, and a son of the Infanta of Aragon. Neither of these matches, however, was destined to be completed. Two daughters had been born to Edward in the Holy Land; a son (Alfonso) was born in Gascony in the autumn of 1273. The important Council of Lyons sat in the summer of 1274. A hollow union of the Greek and Latin churches was arranged, another Crusade planned, and a friendly deputation from the Tartars received. But Edward seems to have turned his back on Lyons and journeyed northward at last; for, at the end of July, we find him arranging at Montreuil, with the help of a deputation of London citizens, a peace with the Countess of Flanders, between whose subjects and the English merchants a bitter quarrel had long raged. His two years of pilgrimage had not been barren of results. But now he was to take up the real work of his life, the government of England. On August 6th the King landed at Dover; on the 16th he was crowned at Westminster. The character of a medieval feast may be gathered from the fact, that 440 oxen, 450 swine, 430 wethers, 14 boars, 22,460

Council of Lyons.

1274.

capons, and 278 "bacons," were considered to be requisite for the occasion. The conduit in Cheap ran with red and white wine, and London welcomed its new king right royally.

Edward's first great act of home policy is significant. Two months had not elapsed since his return, when he ordered a great enquiry into the feudal franchises. As has been explained (p. 12), one of the most striking features of feudalism was the conversion of powers, originally exercised as royal delegations, into proprietary rights attached to the tenure of land, or, a still more dangerous development, into personal privileges exercised irrespectively of landownership. In England, such claims were mostly without historical foundation. Feudalism had there shaped itself in conscious imitation of foreign models, and had aimed deliberately at reproducing the anarchic privileges of the Continental seigneur. As we have said, the ambitions of the feudal barons in England had been only partially realised; but enough had been done to hamper the work of the central government at every turn. The King's officials, traversing the land to exercise justice or to collect revenue, found themselves met by claims of feudal privileges which deprived them of the power to exercise their most important duties. From an enquiry, subsequently held before the King's justices in 1294, on the occasion of the great quarrel between the King and Antony Bek, the famous Bishop of Durham, it appeared that, even after Edward's rigorous action, the feudal privileges of the see practically

England at last.

The franchises.

Example of a franchise.

FURNESS ABBEY.

(*From Dugdale's "Monasticon."*)

reduced the royal power within its limits to a shadow. The bishop's officers used to meet the royal judges at the frontiers of his territory, and demand of them the Articles of the Eyre, a list of enquiries to be made on the King's behalf. Having obtained these, the bishop next proceeded to hold the Eyre himself by his own justices, merely returning to the Exchequer a brief report of the proceedings, with the net produce of the fines and assessments. The bishop had his own Chancery, his own justices and coroners, his gallows at Durham and at Norham, his markets and fairs at Durham, Darlington, and Norham. His peace was proclaimed throughout his bishopric; those who infringed it were outlawed or otherwise punished in his name. He afforested and disafforested lands, and granted the privileges of the chase. His bailiffs sat at the bridge head at Berwick, to seize all wool and hides not duly sealed with the "cocket" or weigh-mark, which was the receipt for customs duty. He claimed the proceeds of wrecks, and half the goods of felons; and he held the Assise of Bread and Ale, which regulated the prices and quantities of the prime necessaries of life. Even his tenants were great potentates. The future King of the Scots held Barnard Castle of him; the greatest nobles in the land were proud to accept his fiefs and render him fealty. The Bishop of Durham was, of course, no common feudatory. He held the Palatinate as freely by his crozier as the King held England by his crown. Luckily for England, there were but two or three other Palatinates; but there were the Marcher Earldoms on the Welsh border, which came very near them in feudal independence. And these great fiefs were continually before the lesser nobility, as examples to be imitated. It needed lynx eyes on the part of the royal officials, to detect the thousand gradual encroachments springing up on all sides. Under a weak king, the central government threatened to die of inanition, or to resolve itself into a mere overlordship, like the overlordship of the French king in respect of the great vassals of the south, or even like the shadowy headship of the Holy Roman Empire.

Edward determined to make a great effort to reassert the royal powers. Grouping the counties together, he started a systematic visitation, on a scale like that of Domesday itself, with a view to ascertain the exact boundaries of feudal and royal jurisdiction. The King's visitors were armed with a long series of articles of enquiry, the answers to which were to be ascertained in each district by sworn men of the neighbourhood. The ancient privilege of the Crown, already becoming so useful a part of ordinary legal machinery, the right to demand on oath an answer to a royal enquiry, was to be put once more to its original purpose. But, whereas Domesday Book was, primarily, as has been well said, a Geld Book, a record drawn up with a view to the assessment of taxation, the enquiry of 1274 was aimed at producing a Franchise Book, a list of those feudal privileges which, if they could be really proved to exist, were to mark forever the extreme limit of feudal independence. All claims to profits which normally should have

Articles of enquiry.

Juries.

reached the royal coffers, all assertions of privileges "which impede common justice and are subversive of royal power," all imitations of the jealously guarded prerogative of the chase, all claims of exemption from obedience to the orders of royal officials, all hereditary sheriffdoms, as well as such clear abuses of power as the acceptance of bribes, the connivance at escapes of prisoners, and the plundering of the royal domains, were to be carefully recorded, with a view to future action.

The labours of the commissioners resulted, in the following year, in the compilation of the Hundred Rolls, a record second only in importance **The Hundred**
to Domesday Book, as a picture of na- **Rolls.**
tional life in a remote age. They derive their name from the fact that they took, as the basis of their report, the Hundred, an ancient unit of
land settlement which still survives in 1275.
name, and which, in the thirteenth century, was not much less important than the county as an organ of local government. In many cases, the whole of the revenues which ought to have accrued to the Crown from one of these districts was being appropriated by private hands; and the Hundred itself, as was said, had become an appendage of a private manor. Other less glaring encroachments were numerous. Fiefs granted by the Crown on condition of military service had been so split up by their holders, that the difficulty of enforcing the service was enormous. Claims to monopolies of mill rights, fishing rights, ferry rights, and other valuable perquisites, were almost countless. The feudal landowners claimed

to hold courts of all kinds, and to retain the profits of justice. They demanded exemption, on the other hand, for themselves and their tenants, from the ordinary liabilities of Englishmen. We have not, in the Hundred Rolls, those details of economic conditions which make Domesday Book, if we could only be sure what it means, such an invaluable picture of medieval rural economy. But, as a picture of the diseases of government, as a study in political pathology, the Hundred Rolls are of priceless worth.

To Edward they seemed, of course, a challenge to vigorous action. For three years the King pondered over the tale which they told; and then his mind was made up. At a Great Council of the most discreet men of the realm, held at Gloucester on his return from a successful campaign in Wales, the King appeared with a brief notice or direction, which stands as the preamble of the so-called Statute of Gloucester. The magnates, whose claims to franchises were stated in the Hundred Rolls, might continue to exercise them until the approaching Eyre, or general visitation of the counties, which was due to take place in the following year. Then there would be a strict enquiry "by what warrant" (*Quo Warranto*) they exercised those rights which (in Edward's theory) naturally and properly belonged to the Crown. With that attention to detail, and knowledge of the value of forms, which are so marked a feature of Edward's work, the precise shape which the *Quo Warranto* writs of enquiry were to take

The "Quo Warranto" proceedings.

Aug., 1278.

was solemnly announced; so that the claimants might know what to expect.

Much displeasure, no doubt, was provoked by this announcement, and, doubtless, much muttering of discontent went on in that winter of 1278–79, following the Council of Gloucester. But the magnates soon found, that in Edward they had a king who kept his word. Armed with those sections of the Hundred Rolls which referred to the sphere of their labours, the Eyre justices set out, at the following Easter, on a prolonged visitation of the counties. The work before them may be guessed by the fact that, in the county of Gloucester alone, there were upwards of seventy persons claiming to exercise royal franchises. The vigour which Edward brought to the enquiry may also be gathered from a glance at a few of the names which appear in the records of the proceedings. The Master of the Templars, the heads of the religious houses of Llanthony, Chichester, Tewkesbury, Gloucester, Keynsham, Stanley, Great Malvern, Chester, Malmesbury, Abingdon, Bedford, Pershore, Winchcomb, and Evesham, were arraigned before the royal justices for usurping the rights of the Crown in that county. With them stood the archbishop of York, the bishops of Worcester and Hereford, and the great names of Gilbert of Gloucester, William of Valence (the titular Earl of Pembroke), the Earl of Warwick, Edmund the King's brother (now Earl of Cornwall), and William de Munchensy. The line taken up by the King's agents was bold, even to

The struggle.

1279.

The Eyre in Gloucester.

rashness. No plea of long-continued usage was admitted as a defence. The prosecution laid down the naked principle, that every claim to exercise a "franchise," or exceptional right of a quasi-public character,—a fair, a free warren, a park, the view of frank-pledge, exemption from toll, an exclusive fishery, the assise or regulation of the prices of bread and ale, a claim to wreck, strays, or the goods of convicted felons—must be fortified by proof of *express* royal grant. Let the claimant produce his charter, or pay his fine and for ever after hold his peace. Nay, it is not quite clear that the King did not assert the extreme view, that he was not bound by his ancestor's charters.

The compromise.

The claim was too severe to be enforced, even by such a king as Edward. Murmurings broke out; great nobles talked of the deeds of their ancestors, who helped William the Bastard to conquer England; they urged that their titles were as good as that of the King himself. The real truth of the matter was, that many of the rights in dispute were, in their origin, neither royal nor feudal, but customary exercises of authority, which had grown up by immemorial usage in the ancient assemblies of township, hundred, and shire. But, if Edward's history was weak, his politics were sound. It was far better for the country, that these vague popular rights should be vested in the central government, than in the hands of feudal landowners. The ancient popular organisation had been broken down by the growth of feudalism, and the establishment of a strong central rule under Henry of Anjou.

Much of the ancient jurisdiction had inevitably got into feudal hands. But it was of supreme importance that the line should be firmly drawn between the High, the Low, and the Middle Justice. Edward was inclined to draw it very sharply. But he was too wise to provoke a baronial rising. So a compromise was arrived at, a compromise which, if it did not give the King all he wanted, at least put a stop to future encroachments. The landowner who could prove that his ancestors or predecessors had exercised their franchises as of right since the accession of Richard I., was allowed to keep them. Any title arising since that date must be fortified by the production of a royal charter, of which there were, alas, too many in existence. The date chosen is significant. It suggests that the reign of Henry II. was recognised, even in the thirteenth century, as closing the period of feudal aggression. If the Crown, after the strong measures of Henry, had deliberately left franchises in the hands of a subject, it was a reasonable presumption that there had been some good cause for the step. At any rate, it was not wise to stir up ancient quarrels. So the accession of Richard I. has come down through the centuries as the "commencement of legal memory," "the time whereof the memory of man runneth not to the contrary." And it is strict law, even to this day, that a claim to the exercise of a royal franchise by a subject must, in the absence of express title, be supported, if questioned, by evidence of usage before the accession of Richard Lion Heart; for "time runs not against the King." The way in which to realise the great work of the *Quo Warranto* proceedings is to take the documents in strict chronological order (an order too often neglected):

1. The Articles of 1274. (Fœdera, I., 517.)
2. " Hundred Rolls, 1275. (Record edition.)
3. " Preamble to the Statute of Gloucester, 1278. (*Statutes of the Realm.* I. p. 45.)
4. " *Placita de Quo Warranto.** (Record edition.)

A single item chosen from the Rolls, and followed to its natural conclusion in the *Placita*, will help the reader, more than pages of explanation, to realise the heavy piece of work accomplished by Edward's ministers during the first ten years of his reign.

But there was another piece of retributive justice to be performed. It was useless for Edward to attack the abuses of feudalism, so long as the royal officers were not free from reproach. The great increase in the number of these agents, arising from the introduction of direct taxation in the reign of Richard, John, and Henry, had led to great abuses. King and people alike suffered. An useful reform in the system of presenting accounts at the Exchequer, established at the close of Henry III.'s reign, had probably checked the defalcations formerly made at the expense of the King. But from all parts of the country came complaints, loud and deep, of the oppressions and extortions of the local officers of the King—sheriffs, bailiffs, escheators, purveyors,

The royal officials.

1270.

* Some of these are dated before 1278. But the writ was, of course, not new. It was the wholesale application of it which startled people.

foresters, and the like. The real truth seems to have been, that, ever since the Conquest of England, a slow process of development had been going on, which was gradually converting what had originally been a mere body of domestics, into an elaborate machinery for the government of the kingdom. It is well known, that traces of this original simplicity survived until very recent times, that Wardrobe and Stable accounts, Bedchamber Ladies and Knights of the Bath, long remained mixed up in hopeless confusion with records and officials of State, and that, in the eighteenth century, as Burke picturesquely put it, "the scullion of the King's kitchen is a Peer of Parliament." The process of specialisation, by which the household of the Norman Duke, or the Angevin King, gradually surrounded itself with the vast network of public administration, is one of the most fascinating examples of political evolution; but it has not yet been thoroughly laid bare. All that we know is that, before the accession of Edward I., some substantial progress had been made.

The exchequer.

The "Tallies," or the "Exchequer," which had originally been simply the money department of the royal household, charged with receiving the revenue of the king and providing for the domestic expenses, had, under the fostering care of Roger, the great Bishop of Salisbury, and his nephews, become a vast financial organisation, with fixed rules and a staff of officials, still claiming the peculiar privileges attaching to the domestic surroundings of the king's person, still conscious of the fact that it was, primarily, the mere keeper of the king's purse, and bound to obey his orders, but gradually, through the stiffening bonds of official routine, beginning to realise its independence, as part of the regular machinery of State, which the mere personal caprice of the king could not be allowed to dislocate. Still, in the thirteenth century, the Exchequer, as we shall see, might be dragged about by the king in his campaigns, to Shrewsbury, or Gloucester, or York; but, gradually, the mere bulk of its belongings, its records and clerks, was compelling it to anchor at Westminster. A few years more, and its judicial staff, the "barons of the Exchequer," were to separate from the financial body, and set up a quasi-independent Court of their own, nominally concerned only with revenue questions, but really, under cover of obvious fictions, taking its part in the growing judicial business of the country. Meanwhile, the commission appointed by Henry II. to sit permanently as the "Chief Court of the King," had secured for itself a definite independence in the scheme of government, by the clause of the Great Charter which declared that Common Pleas should not follow the king, but be held "in some certain place." And so, the "Common Bench," or, more simply, "The Bench," in the thirteenth century, sat regularly at Westminster, except when its members were going circuit as the King's commissioners of assize; and writs intended to be heard before it bade the defendant come before "Our Justices at Westminster." The King's own personal tribunal of justice, vaguely alluded to in

1178.

1215.

The Common Pleas.

The King's Bench.

ROGER OF SALISBURY.

(ORGANIZER OF THE EXCHEQUER.)

(*From Stothard's "Monumental Effigies.*")

Henry II.'s creation of what afterwards became the Court of Common Pleas, was just now, in Edward I.'s reign, beginning to harden also into an independent body, the future "King's Bench," or "Upper Bench." It was very loyal to the king, always, in theory, sitting in the king's presence, its suitors bound to come "before Us, wherever We shall be in England," Nominally it was concerned only with pleas in which the Crown was specially interested; but really it soon also was to stand out as a great independent tribunal, administering that Common Law of which we shall have to speak farther on. The most dangerous element in the original domestic organisation, the feudal tendency to make the public offices hereditary, was, happily, already in Edward's time, on the wane. We see it very clearly in the ancient offices of the Marshal, the Constable, the Steward, and the Chamberlain; but these great functionaries became of less and less importance, seldom appearing in the Exchequer, though, in theory, entitled to do so, and restricting their energies to the management of the feudal army and the great Court ceremonials. The greatest office of all, the Justitiarship, was, happily, never hereditary in England; and it was therefore easy for an ambitious king, like Edward, to abolish it altogether. After the Barons' War we hear no more of it.* The place of the Justitiar as

The feudal offices.

The Justitiar.

* Its disappearance gave an obvious opening to the Chief Justice of the King's Bench, in Edward's reign a very modest person, to claim the great title of Lord Chief Justice of England. Historically, there is no foundation for the claim.

Minister of Justice was taken, without formal proclamation, by the Chancellor, who thereupon retired from his former position in the Exchequer, leaving that body to be managed by its natural working head, the Treasurer. The offices of Chancellor and Treasurer were long held by ecclesiastics, and could not, therefore, well become hereditary. Once and for all, Henry II. had decided against hereditary sheriffdoms; and the sheriffs were now annually appointed at the Michaelmas session of the Exchequer. The great question of the day in home politics was, whether the ordinary course of general administration, the thousand and one questions which daily arose for settlement, should, like the financial and judicial sides of State business, become vested in a permanent body, with independent traditions and a fixed routine, or should be carried out under the personal direction of the King, by the domestics of the royal household, and by those "special councillors," such as John Mansel, Adam of Stratton, and Peter Chacepore, whom the King retained in his "chamber." We have seen that Simon of Montfort took the former view; Edward steadily maintained the latter.

The Chancellor. **The Treasurer.** **The Sheriffs.**

But, while he confirmed all the privileges of the Exchequer, Edward determined to correct the abuses of royal administration. His first great statute, the famous Statute of Westminster the First, is mainly concerned with this question. At a great Parliament of the magnates held in April, 1275, he brought forward the measure;

Statute of Westminster I.

and it received the consent of the assembled body. The abuses of purveyance, claims of wreck, unjust fines, refusal of bail, are cut down to strict limits. Collectors of Crown debts are to give receipts for the money paid to them, and to produce their authority to demand the debts. The royal officers are to take no personal part in suits conducted in the royal courts, and to demand no fees for the performance of their duties. No royal clerks are to be presented to livings the titles to which are in dispute in the royal courts. The mere list of these provisions reveals the character of the abuses which had flourished in Henry's reign. But Edward did not stop with the reform of his own house. He went on to check the excesses of feudal jurisdiction, reserving the greater question of title for the pending enquiry about the franchises. Landlords distraining for lack of services are not to take the law into their own hands. The guardian of his tenant's heir is not to waste the land, nor to dispose of his wards in marriages unsuitable to their degree. Travellers are not to be stopped by feudal landowners through whose territories they may pass. Even the abuses of the merchant class are not forgotten. A foreigner* is not to be distrained for the debts of his fellow citizen or gildsman—a practice surviving from early communism, and dearly cherished by the municipal courts. Outrageous tolls are not to be demanded in the markets, nor claims for "murage" (repair of the city walls) to be unduly made. The most striking feature

* Probably the word here includes not merely aliens, but all persons not members of the merchant gild of the town in question.

of the long statute is its strict concern, for the most part, with administrative details. The student who looks for the enunciation of general principles will be disappointed; for these he must turn elsewhere. Edward was simply setting his house in order, after the anarchy and turbulence of his father's reign. The Statute of Westminster the First is not national legislation, but a sweeping Ordinance against Abuses, directed by the strong hand of a new ruler. Once, indeed Edward does lay down a really striking principle, destined to be the fruitful parent of English liberties. The legal official who abuses his trust not only incurs a forfeit of his office to the King, but is liable to pay threefold damages to the party injured. The privileges of the royal household are not to cover such a case. It was a great concession from a medieval king, and it marks a great advance in political thought. But, for the rest, the clauses of the Statute deal with matters, as it seems to us, almost wearisomely minute and technical—with the number of "essoins," or excuses, which litigants may urge, with the "strong and hard imprisonment" of felons who refuse to plead, with the precise scope of the Assize of Novel Disseisin, with the oath of the champion in trial by battle, and so on. Behind it all, however, are seen the clear determination of the King, that justice shall be done to the meanest of his subjects, and the full appreciation, by the King's advisers, of the real evils of everyday life. The men who drew up the Statute of Westminster the First were no theorists; they knew exactly where the shoe pinched. If Francesco Accursius sat by to suggest remedies, we may be fairly sure that Burnell and Hengham were there to report grievances. The Parliament of 1275, it is true, was not concerned only with the redress of grievances. The King's officials brought forward an elaborate scheme for the collection of the customs revenue, which put the "ancient" or "Great" Custom * on a statutory footing; and a later assembly at Michaelmas granted Edward a fifteenth of all movables. But the Ordinance concerning Coroners, and the Rageman Ordinance of enquiry into the arrears of business left over from the last reign, which were issued in the following year, shewed that the King realised his duties as well as his rights. The country felt that at last there was a man at the head of affairs.

* Oddly enough, in the record itself, the Custom is described as "New." But it became "ancient" when a new Custom was laid on the alien merchants in 1303.

CHAPTER VIII

WALES

MORE than once before in our story we have heard the name of Wales. Now we must try to gain some orderly idea of the part played by the Welsh question in the early years of Edward's reign.

It is but natural that Englishmen should speak of their western neighbours by the name conferred

The Cymry.

upon them by the English invaders of Britain. To these invaders, men of Teutonic speech and habits, the Romanised Britons were "Welsh" or "strangers" (*wealh*). But the Britons themselves, in their last great struggle against the Teutonic foe, adopted the name "Cymry," to signify the common bond which linked together the Britons of Strathclyde, the Wales of to-day, and Cornwall or "West Wales." This great border strip of Britain, the last refuge of the defeated Celt, was, however, even then split up into three severed districts; and the common name

A.D. 577.

of Cymry (the "men of the kingdom") stood for a dream rather than a reality. The great battle of Deorham (? Dyrham near Chipping Sodbury) had driven the Saxon wedge between the west and the north Welsh, and cut off Devon and Cornwall from the Cymric league. Thirty-six years later, the capture of the great British stronghold of Chester, on the Dee, had severed the Welsh of Strathclyde and the north from the middle Welsh of "Wales"; and this last name began to settle down on the mountainous land which stretches from Anglesea to the Bristol Channel. On all sides save one, the rugged coast and the wild seas combined to form strong barriers, behind which the defeated Welsh lay in safety. On the east, however, the absence of a natural bar was dangerous alike to friend and foe, till Offa, the Mercian King, built the great dyke or wall which runs due north and south, from the Dee to the Wye. Within these boundaries lies, for the most part, the present country of Wales; but the name of Cumberland in the north, and the popular "Cambrian" allusions of Wales itself, are strong reminders of the defeated hopes of the great British league.

A.D. 613.

Circ. 780.

Long before Edward's day, however, Offa's boundary had ceased to mark the territory of the independent Welsh. The great Palatine earldom of Chester, created by the Norman conquerors of England, had spread into the western lands. The Marcher earldom of Pembroke in the south, and the mighty lordship of Glamorgan, guarded the northern shore of the Bristol Channel from the Welsh. In his fear of a compact Welsh kingdom, Henry II. had encouraged his discontented barons, disgusted with the steady rule which had

The Lords Marcher.

put down the feudal anarchy of Stephen's day, to invade the eastern Welsh. It was pure freebooting. The King took no responsibility for the expeditions, furnished no supplies, asked no questions. On the other hand, the invading baron, if successful, carved out for himself a "Marcher" lordship, which he held by his sword as the King held England by his crown. Nominally, the Marcher Lords—the Mortimers of Chirk and Wigmore, the Bohuns of Brecon, the Hastings of Abergavenny, the Fitzalans of Oswestry—were vassals of the kings of England, just as William the Norman had been a vassal of the kings at Paris. In effect, the sound system of government which was being slowly built up in England no whit affected the Marcher lordships. The King's judges did not enter them on circuit. There were no shires or sheriffs. Somewhat later, indeed, the Customs dues were collected at the Welsh ports; but this result had only been achieved by the careful precautions of Edward at the Parliament of 1275; and the collection was made by local officials, who secured for their "franchises" the incidental profits of forfeitures and fees. It is significant that, in Edward's grant of the Customs dues to the Lucchese firm of collectors, no provision whatever is made for the Welsh ports.

Llywelyn the Great and John.

The iniquitous bargain made by Henry II. with his barons had recoiled on the head of his unfortunate and worthless son. John's distress was the opportunity of the Welsh, who did not scruple to join the discontented barons against the King. The combination might have been fatal to the nominal supremacy of England, had the Welsh themselves been able to rise to the conception of a united kingdom. But this was precisely what they were unable to do. Although there arose from time to time great rulers, who called themselves "princes of Wales," it is not difficult, looking closely at their claims, to see that they were merely patriarchal chieftains, whose special abilities had lifted them above the ordinary run of their fellows. They were not territorial rulers at the head of definite military and administrative systems. Over their own clans they wielded great power, a power founded on kinship and tradition. Over the other Welsh kindreds they had only the influence of a great name, seen in the halo of romance and myth. The Celt had a genius for hero-worship; he responded like a harp to the vibrations of popular sentiment. But he had no love for the weary drudgery by which a people makes its way to national independence. In a sudden foray, for a mighty effort, none so ready as he. But to labour long years in storing up the wealth necessary to support a great national rising; to submit patiently to training in arms and strategy; to play a waiting game; to retire before an invader in order to lure him to his destruction; to endure the wasting of his home and lands in the sure hope of a distant revenge—these things were not in the character of the Celt. He loved to sit in his chieftain's hall, listening to the song of the harper and the story of the bard, to wander on his native hills, musing over the legends of his race, and watching the mists glittering in the sunbeams. When, after Edward's conquest, the light is thrown upon Welsh social life, we see in a flash how it is that the first serious effort of English statesmanship proved fatal to Welsh independence. The real social unit of Welsh society in those days was not the compact household, working under the control of a single head, and owning direct allegiance to a central ruler, but the loosely connected *gwely*, or kindred, consisting of three generations, often living together in a common homestead, always claiming undivided rights over a tract of pasture land, and setting more store on the genealogy of its tribe than on the history of the nation. Its real occupations were the breeding of cattle, and the chase, pursuits which leave much leisure for patriotic aspirations, but which rarely tend to national greatness. Such agriculture as there was seems to have been left mainly to unfree, or at least inferior races, accorded no share in the privileges of the "free Cymry," and, in all probability, recruited largely from the old Iberian or pre-Celtic inhabitants of the land, whose small frames, dark hair, high cheekbones, and swarthy faces, still make such a striking contrast with the tall and ruddy Celt. The Cymro paid tribute in kind to his chief; but there was, virtually, no government beyond the frequent gatherings of the kindreds and tribes, in which the elders pronounced dooms and tendered counsel.

Llywelyn's defiance.

When Edward returned from the Holy Land, the greatest of the Welsh chieftains was Llywelyn ab Gruffyth, grandson of that Llywelyn who had wrested from King John the

recognition of his independence, and who had been such a thorn in the side of Edward's father in the early years of Henry's reign. Llywelyn's father
was that Gruffyth, the "stout man of mid- 1244.
dle age," who had been killed in trying
to escape from the Tower, whither he had been carried as a hostage. Llywelyn had two brothers, Owain Goch (or Red), the elder, with whom he had quarrelled, and whom he now held under lock and key, and David, with whom he was likewise on bad terms, but who had escaped from the power of his formidable brother, and was now enjoying Edward's hospitality at Westminster. The quarrels of Llywelyn and his brothers are only too typical of the weakness which prevented Wales rising spontaneously into a compact kingdom. One of Llywelyn's aunts had married Ralph Mortimer, and their son, Llywelyn's cousin, Roger, was the greatest of the Marcher Lords, save only the earls of Pembroke and Hereford. Another aunt had married John, Earl Huntingdon and Chester, first cousin of the Scottish King; and, on his death in 1237, had espoused Robert of Quency, the claimant to the earldom of Southampton or Winchester. To crown all, Llywelyn ab Gruffyth, as we have seen (p. 130), had followed the example of his grandfather in the days of King John; and, having betrothed himself to Eleanor, daughter of the great Earl of Leicester, had rendered substantial help to Simon in the days before Evesham. Altogether, a most formidable person, this Llywelyn. Perhaps a brief pedigree will help us to realise his position.

PEDIGREE OF THE WELSH PRINCES.

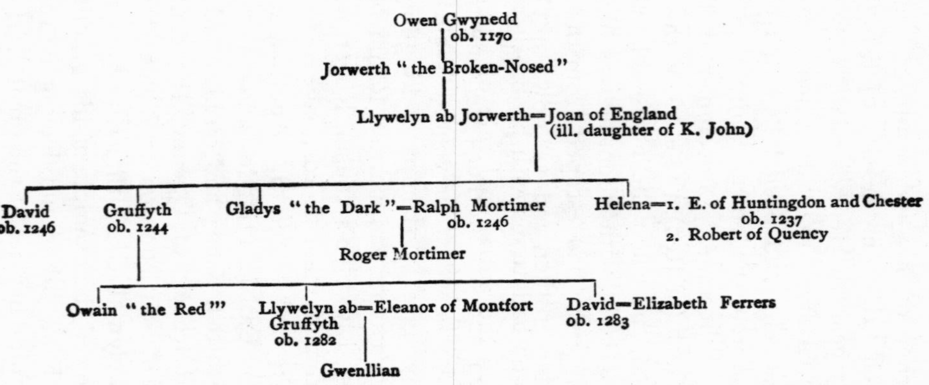

From the point of geography, the situation was curious. In theory, Llywelyn's dominions included two distinct districts: one in the north, comprising Anglesey, the lands about Snowdon, the hills of Arvon, and the lands of Merioneth; the other, in the south, including the ancient principality of Ceredigion (Cardigan) and the lands afterwards known as the county of Caermarthen. But, of these two districts, only the former was Llywelyn's hereditary domain; the other clung to him but feebly as the representative of Welsh independence.* Moreover, as we have said, he was for the time on bad terms with his brother David, who, relying on the patriarchal rule of equal division of lands, claimed also an equal division of the chiefship. But the strangest feature of all was, that between Llywelyn and the forces of Edward lay the broad belt of Marcher lordships, nominally subject to Edward and hostile to Llywelyn, in reality quite capable of blocking Edward's advance on Wales. The Mortimers had been on Edward's side in the Barons' War. But that would not, necessarily, prevent them adopting a different view when it came to a direct struggle with Llywelyn, with whom they were, as we have seen, closely allied by marriage.

Geography of Wales.

The note of defiance was struck by the Welsh prince. Relying on his position, he refused to take the oath of allegiance to Edward, founding himself upon the independence

The defiance.

* Its real affection was probably given to the line of Rhys ab Meredith, whose homage had been expressly reserved to the English Crown by the treaty of 1267.

recognised to his grandfather by the Great Charter. This proceeding was, of course, in direct violation of the treaty of Shrewsbury (p. 151), by which Llywelyn had undertaken to hold his principality as a vassal of the English Crown. At that time, such a refusal would, in whatever circumstances made, have been treated as a gross breach of loyalty. In the circumstances of the moment, it was an unmistakable defiance.

1267.

Edward did not act hastily. The first summons to Llywelyn had been issued by his ministers in his absence. In September, 1275, it was solemnly repeated by Edward himself, who bade the Welsh prince come to London for the purpose of rendering homage. Llywelyn refused, alleging that the King was harbouring his fugitives, *i. e.*, his brother David, who had fled to the English court.* Edward moved towards Caerleon, to give Llywelyn a chance of saving his dignity, or, possibly, to disabuse him of fear of personal danger. At this juncture, a great stroke of luck fell to the King. The Cinque Ports fleet captured Eleanor of Montfort, who, under the escort of her brother Aymer, was making for the Welsh coast, to join her affianced husband. Irritated by the loss of his bride, Llywelyn once more put himself in the wrong by declaring war. David, his vacillating brother, threw in his lot with the English, and Llywelyn found himself utterly unable to resist Edward's march. Careful, as always, of the legalities, the

Capture of Eleanor Montfort.

* Edward, in his formal statement of justification, alleges that he summoned Llywelyn no less than five times.

King obtained the formal condemnation of his rebellious vassal, by a Parliament which met at Westminster in November, 1276. At the same time, the whole feudal array was summoned to meet at Worcester on the following 24th June; and an elaborate plan of attack in three armies was planned against the Principality.

1277.

The campaign was won almost before it was commenced. In February, 1277, Edward procured the excommunication of Llywelyn by Archbishop Kilwardby, and the Welsh chieftains, shrinking from a foe armed with spiritual as well as material weapons, began slowly to desert their leader. In April, Edward moved the Exchequer and the Law Courts to Shrewsbury, that the ordinary business of government might not suffer by the campaign. When the host assembled, the Welsh withdrew to the fastnesses of Snowdon, and endeavoured to repeat the trap which had so often proved fatal to the feudal horseman. But Edward was no longer the rash youth who had fallen into the meshes of Llywelyn twenty years before. Deliberately laying waste the accessible valleys of North Wales, he calmly awaited the surrender of his foe. His plan was fully justified. Although he had to beg the feudal host for an extension of the forty days of service, he saw Llywelyn a suppliant for peace in the early autumn; and the treaty of Aberconway, signed on the 9th November, marks a distinct advance in the English conquest of Wales. Although Edward did not carry out his threat of dividing Llywelyn's

Edward's success.

1277.

hereditary domains between his two brothers, he deprived the Welsh prince of the homage of the chieftains (saving only those of some half-dozen personal followers); he took from him the four cantreds yielded by Henry in the treaty of Shrewsbury;

1267. he compelled him to release from prison his brother Owain, as well as those of the chiefs who had been imprisoned for adherence to the English Crown. The island of Anglesey was confirmed in heritage to Llywelyn; but, after his death, it was to be held by his heirs simply as an ordinary fief, at the heavy annual rent of a thousand marks. In other words, after the death of Llywelyn, the last vestige of Welsh independence was to cease. On the other hand, there was no attempt to assimilate Welsh and English institutions; Welsh custom and the barbarous usage of the Marches were still to be the standard of social life.

For a time, the treaty brought peace. Edward had taken care to extract both moral and material

Respite. pledges from Llywelyn. The Prince took the oath of allegiance at Rhuddlan, and, at the following Christmas, renewed the ceremony at Westminster. Some of the Welsh nobles were surrendered as hostages; and it is asserted by more than one chronicler, that Llywelyn paid a sum of no less than 50,000 marks as the price of peace. More probable is it, that the demand was held over him as security for his good behaviour. His bride was restored to him, Edward taking a cousinly interest in the details of the lady's dowry, and, according to some accounts, giving her a very handsome wedding. When the King left England for France, in the spring of 1279, he made Roger Mortimer special warden of "West Wales," a district which seems to have included Dorset, Gloucester, Hereford, Salop, and Somerset, as well as the Welsh districts of Cardigan and Caermarthen. But this was hardly an unreasonable precaution.

Renewal of war.

Llywelyn, however, soon became restless. His wife died within a year of the marriage, leaving a little daughter Gwenllian, who afterwards became a nun. There seems to have been an understanding (not expressed in the terms of the treaty) that Llywelyn should present himself in London every year, as a guarantee of his peaceful intentions. For two years he observed the agreement; in the third year (1280) he refused to come. Doubtless the demands of Edward's officials had been heavy on the land; and the Welsh nobles perhaps thought with regret of the easy-going days of the tribal chieftains. The *Quo Warranto* proceedings (p. 164), and a reform of the coinage, had produced discontent, even in England. A searching "distraint of knighthood" * had impoverished the smaller landowners. Some young nobles, with whom Edward was amiably chatting on the eve of the Michaelmas Parliament of 1279, somewhat startled the King by repeating to him a doggerel which was

* *I. e.*, a visitation made with the object of compelling all landholders of a certain value to take up the degree of knight, with its costly ceremonies, or pay fines for neglect. Owing to the fall in the value of money, the class liable to the feudal dignity of knighthood was becoming very large.

floating about the Court, and which was by no means complimentary to its ruler. The lines ran:

"The King grabs our pence,
The Queen grabs our lands,
And the Quo Warrantò
Shall cause blood to flow."

Still, no open disturbance followed. In the autumn of 1280, Edward and his wife paid a visit to the priory of Lanercost in Cumberland, and held a mighty hunting in the forest of Inglewood. The King had come into the Ponthieu inheritance by the death of his mother-in-law, Joanna of Castile, in the previous June. A visit to France had wound up the outstanding details left over from the last treaty. Edward's chief interest appears to have been in the active pursuit of Guy of Montfort, his cousin's murderer, whom he chased from Italy to Norway. He had wisely refused to quarrel with Pope Nicolas for refusing the primacy to his favourite minister, Robert Burnell; and had even borne with patience the daring exercise of the Papal prerogative which thrust upon him, as Primate, John Peckham, a Franciscan, who had been a Reader at Oxford and Paris. In June of 1281, there were disturbances in Wales, but Edward treated them lightly; and announced his intention of visiting Gascony in the autumn.

The outbreak.

It is difficult to avoid the suggestion, that Edward was waiting for Llywelyn to commit himself beyond forgiveness. He probably realised, that Welsh independence was inconsistent with peace on the Marches; and, though he was willing to wait, if need were, for Llywelyn's death in the course of nature, we can hardly blame him for not acting towards his vassal as an indulgent father, who watches to prevent a disobedience which he will be bound to punish. In the spring of 1282, the King learnt that David's patriotism had triumphed over his gratitude,* and that the two brothers had entered into a plot against him. On the eve of Palm Sunday (March 22nd) David made a sudden attack on Flint and Hawarden, and captured Roger Clifford, the King's lieutenant. Thence he started out on a lively foray, in which he was joined by his brother Llywelyn; the lands of Englishmen were harried, and their goods plundered and burned, without mercy. It was a racial war, pure and simple; and Edward resolved this time to make an end.

The Welsh campaign.

His measures were prompt. The rebels were excommunicated by the English bishops. Roger Mortimer was given command of the forces in North Wales, Reginald Grey in Chester and Flint, Robert Tiptoft in the south. The greater barons were summoned once more to meet at Worcester at Whitsuntide. But Edward knew that, in the mountain fastnesses, the Welsh were safe from the heavy-armed warrior; and, not daring to trust to the Welsh archers in his pay, sent to Gascony for a supply of the new arm. Even the

* Edward had given him rich estates after the Peace of Aberconway, and had married him to Elizabeth Ferrers, daughter of the Earl of Derby.

old crossbow was not neglected; for we find the Warden of the Royal Exchange in London ordered to furnish 4000 "quarrels," or bolts, to the men of the Cinque Ports, who were manning a fleet to attack Llywelyn by sea. The navy scored the first success, carrying the island of Anglesey by a brilliant assault, a success which drew from the King the joyful remark, "Our friend Llywelyn has lost the first feather of his tail." Prompt to follow up his victory, the King proceeded to throw a bridge of boats across the Menai Straits, with a view of attacking the mainland from the west. At this point, however, the English arms received a check, through the headlong haste of a band of knights. Burning to distinguish themselves, in the true spirit of knight-errantry, they collected a body of three hundred followers, many of them Gascons, and, dashing across the half-completed bridge, waded through the shallows to the mainland. Cut off from retreat by the rising tide, they were suddenly attacked by a body of Welsh who sallied from the woods, and fled in confusion, many perishing in the sea.

Capture of Anglesey.

The Menai Bridge.

Check.

Meanwhile, the King, who never underrated the difficulties of the campaign, had summoned the remainder of the feudal array to Rhuddlan for the beginning of August, and commenced a steady attack on Llywelyn from the east. In this he was greatly helped by a body of a thousand woodcutters, whom he had prudently collected from the midland and western counties, and who cleared away the dangerous coverts of the mountain passes.

The battle of the campaign was fought at Orewin Bridge in midwinter.* But it seems to have been entirely unpremeditated. Edward's plan was, clearly, to drive Llywelyn out of the country by sheer force of superior strategy. Llywelyn, however, had descended from the hills to take stock of his resources, leaving his army encamped on the Wye. His movement was perceived by some sharp eyes in the English camp; and the English leaders, Giffard and the younger Mortimer, were approached by one Hélie Walwyn, who offered to shew them a ford, by crossing which a few resolute men might take the Welsh in the rear, and effect a diversion. The advice was followed, and great confusion arose among the Welsh. Hearing the noise, Llywelyn and his son, who were not far off, returned cautiously to learn the truth, but were espied by an English knight, Stephen Frankton, and he, not knowing who they were, pursued them with a small body of followers, and thrust the Prince through with a spear, leaving him dead on the ground. Meanwhile, the Welsh, disheartened by the absence of their leader, remained standing on the high ground above the bridge, instead of charging down on the advancing English. The latter, adopting new and momentous tactics, mingled with the mounted knights a strong body of archers who, under cover of the horses, poured a deadly volley into the irresolute defenders

Orewin Bridge.

Death of Llywelyn.

* There is great dispute as to the geography of the campaign; but Orewin Bridge is generally considered to have been near Builth, in the modern shire of Brecknock.

of the position. The Welsh broke and fled; and then it was discovered, that the two fugitives slain by Stephen Frankton were Llywelyn and his son. Llywelyn's head was cut off and dispatched to London, where, to the huge delight of the citizens, it was paraded down Westcheap to the Tower, crowned with a silver circlet, in mock fulfilment of the prophecy known to have been made to Llywelyn by a Welsh soothsayer. David fled from the slaughter, and for the next six months led a miserable existence, concealed in swamps and caves, hopeless and helpless. The resistance of the Welsh was broken, and the thought of each was to make terms for himself. At last David was captured by treachery (June, 1283), and resistance was, for the present, at an end.

Capture of David.

Edward now determined to dispose of the Welsh question, once and for all; and he set about the task with a grim deliberation which boded ill for the prospects of his foes. Realising the importance of his presence on the scene of affairs, he summoned a great Parliament of earls, barons, knights of the shire, and burgesses to meet at Shrewsbury on Michaelmas Day, 1283, to discuss the whole settlement. Meanwhile, he retained the Exchequer and the Law Courts at Shrewsbury, and, as we shall hereafter see, found leisure, in the intervals of more urgent business, to attend to measures of great future importance for commerce and industry. But his first care was, of course, the completion of his conquest. He built the castles of Flint, Conway, and Caernarvon, to keep disaffection in check,

Settlement of Wales.

SERGEANT-AT-ARMS.

(THIRTEENTH CENTURY.)

(From Viollet le Duc's "Dict. du Mobilier Français.")

but, somewhat later, shewed his statesmanship by granting municipal charters to the boroughs which lay beneath the walls of his fortresses. He planted Anglesey with English farmers. Unwilling to leave a magnet to attract hopes of independence, he insisted on the seizure of the precious national relics, the "Crossneych," or fragment of the true cross, and the crown of Arthur; but he softened the blow by granting special privileges to the men who yielded them into his hands. He paid large sums by way of compensation to the Church, whose goods had been injured in the war. He proposed to move the see of St. Asaph, "which is situated in a certain solitary and rural place," to the then military centre of Rhuddlan; but, in deference to ecclesiastical prejudices, forebore. He insisted, however, on the inclusion of the Welsh bishoprics in the province of Canterbury — a decision which at last set at rest a long-agitated question of ecclesiastical administration, and dealt a shrewd blow at possibilities of Papal tampering with national aspirations. The daughters of Llywelyn and David were placed in the great Gilbertine Abbey of Sempringham, the special retreat of ladies of noble English birth. A terrible vengeance was taken on the traitor David, who, after being tried by a specially appointed judicial commission, was executed with the utmost barbarities of the horrible treason law. Two happy events, the discovery at Caernarvon of the alleged body of Constantius, the father of the great Constantine, and the birth, at the same place, of a son to the King, served to relieve the gloom which had gathered around the tragic fate of David; and the conquered Welsh, perhaps willingly deceived, allowed themselves to be tricked into acceptance, as their titular chief, of the infant Edward, "a prince who could not," as his father truly said, "speak a word of English." The death of the King's eldest son, Alfonso, in the following August (1284), made the infant prince the heir apparent to the English throne, and laid the basis of the tradition of six hundred years, by which the title of Prince of Wales has become the most popular of the many titles of the future kings of England.

The Statute of Rhuddlan.

But Edward had no intention of allowing Wales to remain a separate entity, even as an appanage of the Crown. He was bent on incorporation; and the title given to Edward of Caernarvon was not to be allowed to derogate seriously from the power of the central government.* The great Parliament had duly assembled at Michaelmas, and, by the following Lent, had thrashed out an elaborate scheme for the future government of Wales. The Statute of Rhuddlan, dated on Mid-Lent Sunday, declared, in its opening words, that Wales had ceased to be a mere fief of the English Crown, and had become "annexed and united . . . unto the Crown of the aforesaid

1284.

* The writer does not mean, of course, to assert that the princedom of Wales was a mere title. It carried substantial revenues, and a moderate amount of patronage. But it did not involve political power. For a description of the rights and privileges of the princedom, together with its congeners, the duchy of Cornwall and the earldom of Chester, the reader may consult the classical work of Sir John Dod(e)ridge.

GILBERTINE NUN.

(*From Dugdale's "Monasticon."*)

realm, as a member of the same body." Out of the hereditary domains of Llywelyn were constituted four new shires, to wit, Anglesey, Caernarvon, Merioneth, and Flint. For judicial purposes, the first three of these were grouped under a permanent "Justice of North Wales," or "Snowdon," with an Exchequer and Chancery at Caernarvon. Flint was annexed to the palatine earldom of Chester, which was committed, on the 14th September, to the capable hands of Reginald Grey, as "Justice," or, as he was more generally called, "Chief Justice," of Chester. Edward knew that much of his success in the late war had been due to his hold on the great city and its county; and he intended that the earldom, long in his own hands through the death of the last of the independent earls, should become a royal appanage. But Flint, like its neighbouring shires, was carefully organised on the English model, with a sheriff, coroner, and bailiffs of commotes or Hundreds; and the elaborate regulations laid down by the Statute for the conduct of shire business are, perhaps, a better picture of English county administration, as it was in the best years of Edward's reign, than of anything which actually took place in Wales. The conquered districts of the south appear, from the wording of the Statute, to have already been organised into the shires of Cardigan and Caermarthen; at any rate, the document treats these counties as in existence. But they were too far distant from the northern conquest to be safely

The new shires.

North Wales.

1284.

"West" or South Wales.

trusted to the same administration; and, accordingly, they were placed under the control of a "Justice of West Wales" or, as he later was called, of "South Wales," and a new Exchequer and Chancery created for them at Caermarthen. With great wisdom, Edward adopted the old patriarchal and feudal divisions as the basis of his new arrangement; but he took care to infuse into all his machinery that happy compromise between local independence and central control, which has been the great secret of the success of English politics. At every local moot, whether of shire or Hundred, the King's business was to come first; and the royal officials were, obviously, to stand as representatives of a power greater than that of any local magnate, whether feudal lord or clan chief. But all inhabitants of the land, from the great noble to the humble freeman, were bound actively to aid the royal officers in the performance of their tasks; and the conquered Welshman was to feel, every day of his life, that the King expected of him, not merely submission and orderly conduct, but an active share in the maintenance of peace and the punishment of evil doers. A prudent and skilful concession to the patriarchal system of the Welsh allowed the prosecution in cases of alleged murder to be commenced by the "Welshery," or kindred of the slain man; but the prosecution was to take the form of a decent and orderly accusation, or "presentment," before the sheriff at a monthly session of the shire court, not the wild disorder of a midnight foray. Under this wise system, the blood-

The blood feud.

SEAL OF THE CHANCERY AT CAERMARTHEN.

(TEMP. RIC. II.)

(*From Nicholas' "Annals of Wales."*)

feud of the ancient custom glided gradually into the "appeal of murder" of the English courts. But the prosecution of vengeance was not left entirely to the initiative of private persons. Twice every year, the sheriff was to hold his "Tourn" in every Hundred, and there conduct a rigorous enquiry concerning the behaviour of the neighbourhood during the last six months. It was there that it behoved the Welshman, if he would escape fine and imprisonment, to report to the King's official all rumours of misdeeds which had come to his ears; and these rumours, sifted by a sworn jury of twelve or more, became the basis of vigorous exactions and other punishments by the Exchequer officials. Thus, gradually, duty to the State took the place of duty to the kin, as the paramount obligation of conduct; and the country entered upon that slow process of assimilation, which was to convert the old patriarchal Wales of Llywelyn into the modern political Wales of to-day. But Edward was too wise to force the process. No provision was made for the appearance of knights of the Welsh shires in those Parliaments which were fast becoming the great events of the year in England. Though the procedure of the English law courts was introduced into Wales,* the law which they administered was to be, in all save a few cases,† the ancient customs of the

The sheriff's Tourn.

Legal procedure.

* The Welsh were, however, still allowed to use their ancient forms for suits of minor importance.

† The Statute introduced into Wales the English institution of the widow's dower, and admitted women to the inheritances on failure

Welsh. With characteristic care, Edward seized the opening to make a few needed amendments in the English forms. The unpopular Trial by Battle was abolished in land suits; the list of "essoins," or permissible delays, was rigidly cut down; the statute also abolished the ancient rule which demanded pedantic accuracy in pleading ("he who fails in a syllable, fails in the whole cause"), a rule perhaps necessary in the days when lawsuits were conducted entirely by word of mouth, and "record" was a matter of memory.

The Marcher lordships.

It must, of course, be carefully remembered, that the Wales of Edward's new system was very different in extent from the Wales of to-day. A glance at the map will show that it covered less than one-half of the modern Principality, which is itself smaller than the true area of the Welsh tongue. For two centuries and a half from Llywelyn's death, the Marcher lords continued their lawless careers, holding courts, creating officials, founding churches, granting municipal charters, setting their local customs above the common law of the realm. But the shadow of their coming doom began to fall upon them. More and more men felt that such doings had had their day. Their system (if system it could be called) was the system of the past; Edward's was the system of the future. Not for many a long day was

of males of the same degree. On the other hand, it expressly reserved the Welsh patriarchal custom of equal inheritance among males of the same degree, though it rigidly excluded from the inheritance of land the offspring of loose patriarchal marriages.

Wales to become a peaceable and orderly land ; Edward himself found that the conquest of Llywelyn
and David did not dispense him from the necessity
of teaching a stern lesson to the chieftains of Cardigan and Caermarthen. But 1287.
rarely again was England in serious danger from a
Welsh rising ; the stern measures of Henry VII.
and his son were directed quite as much against
their English rivals as against the native Welsh.
The work done by Edward in Wales was a work for
all time.

CHAPTER IX

THE ENGLISH JUSTINIAN

THE few years which followed the conquest of Wales have given Edward his title to immortal fame, a fame earned by that noblest of all royal virtues, a steadfast devotion to the happiness and prosperity of his subjects. Keeping a wary eye on the ominous prospects of the Scottish succession, never forgetting the possibility of a Welsh rising, taking a conspicuous part in the territorial and dynastic problems of the Continent,— the quarrels between France and Aragon in particular,—coquetting with successive Popes on the subject of the proposed Crusade, exacting from Philip of France a due fulfilment of the treaties of Paris and Amiens, his main strength was yet steadily spent in those great internal reforms which mark the change from feudal to industrial England, from the old divided England of the Barons' War to the united England of the end of the century, from the Middle Ages to modern history. In the winter of 1290, he lost his faithful and beloved wife, Eleanor of Castile; and the event seemed to close the chapter of his prosperity. From that time till his lonely death in 1307, the King was involved in unhappy quarrels — the interminable quarrel of the Scottish succession, the quarrel with France, the quarrel with his own nobles, the quarrel with the Church. In all these, the country never lost its faith in the King; Edward never sank in public esteem as his father and grandfather had sunk. He never lost the power to recall the affections of his subjects by a frank appeal to old memories. "Except in opinion, not disagreeing," might truly have been said, at any moment, of the King and his people. But that the firm trust of Englishmen in the nobleness of their ruler remained unshaken during those sixteen years of storm and stress, of taxation and war, of absence and seeming neglect, was surely due to the profound impression of justice, patience, honesty, wisdom, and self-denying toil, created by the two brilliant years of internal reform, whose course we now attempt to trace.

The Statute of Merchants.

First in point of date comes the famous Statute of Merchants, or Acton Burnell. As we have formerly seen (p. 38), the expansion of foreign commerce, brought about by the Crusades, had rendered the merchant a figure of new importance in the social system of the country. But he fitted badly into the established order of things. As often as not a "foreigner," * he had no native town in England, he was a member of no

* The word "foreigner" has various shades of meaning in the records of the time. Often it merely means a person not a member of the speaker's immediate locality. But, in these pages, it will be used in its modern sense of a political alien.

clan or blood-feud group, of no fief or monastery. He was a lost unit in a society which barely recognised individualism in its humbler ranks; which had a profound distrust of strangers; which looked on commerce mainly as an opportunity of cheating, and commercial profit as something nearly akin to usury. The safety of the stranger merchant, at first secured by placing him under the "mainpast," or guarantee, of his host, subsequently strengthened by his own spontaneous association into gilds or brotherhoods, was finally recognised, as a matter of national policy, by the express words of the Great Charter.

The merchant and his debtors.

But it was necessary to the welfare of the merchant, not only that he should be protected from bodily harm, but that he should be actively assisted in the enforcement of his rights. People were beginning to discover, that credit is the life-blood of commerce; and credit could not exist in a society which knew nothing of commercial honour, as we understand it, without an adequate machinery for the enforcement of commercial obligations. No man, in the England of the thirteenth century, would have thought a fraction the worse of himself for refusing to satisfy a commercial claim, however just, which could not be legally enforced against him. Scandalous as the position seems now to us, it had grown easily and naturally out of the history of the law of debt. The earliest "debts" did not arise out of voluntary transactions: they were bloodfines reluctantly offered by guilty men, robbers and murderers, to appease the just vengeance of the injured or their relatives. Quite naturally, these offenders resisted payment until the last possible moment. Nowhere are *a priori* conceptions more inadequate to explain facts, than in the discussions of legal morality. But a patient study of the history of legal ideas not only removes all difficulties: it leaves the student wondering at the simplicity of the explanation, so long sought in vain by the exalted methods of deductive speculation.

Thus it becomes clear, why the merchant of the thirteenth century, especially the foreign merchant, was helpless in the hands of his debtors. Three difficulties stood in his way. First, he could not, in all probability, appear as the ostensible plaintiff before a tribunal which did not recognise him as one of its proper "suitors" or constituents. He had to trust himself in the hands of a native agent, or "attorney," who might decamp with his money. Second, he would find his adversary resorting, perhaps with the secret goodwill of the tribunal, to every trick and delay that chicane could suggest—and no one who knows anything of legal history will believe that chicane is a modern vice—to postpone the evil day on which judgment should be pronounced against him. Finally, if the plaintiff were successful in procuring a judgment, he would find himself obstructed in enforcing it by a defective procedure which, once more, is intelligible only by a reference to the history of the action of debt. In the days when debts were, as we have said, mere alternatives of corporal vengeance, the

Imperfection of remedies.

man who could not satisfy them "paid with his body." In other words, if the avenger of blood did not get his money, he got his revenge, either in the form of imprisonment of his debtor, or even by exacting the extreme penalty. This is the simple explanation of the horrible system of debt-slavery, of which students of Roman history learn so much—and so little. Apparently, before Edward's day, the right of the judgment creditor to seize the chattels of his debtor, through the hands of the sheriff, had become generally recognised. But the strongest instincts of feudalism were opposed to the suggestion that a debtor's land might be sold for payment of his debts, and a new tenant thus imposed upon his lord. And feudal instincts were, in this respect, as in so many others, powerfully supported by still older social instincts, surviving from an age in which land was not the property of the individual, but of the clan or kindred, and when to admit that the sacredness of the kin group might be disturbed by the intrusion of the creditor of one of its members, would have been regarded as little short of blasphemy.

Change in social conditions.

But the rapid progress of industry, and the rapid decay of patriarchal and feudal institutions, in the twelfth and early thirteenth centuries, had really rendered this antiquated rule a relic of barbarism and a cloak of injustice. Now that the services of nearly all tenants, except those in the lowest ranks, had been commuted into money, now that the coheirs of a deceased landowner could obtain the assistance of the King's courts to effect a division of their inheritance, it was absurd to maintain the fiction of patriarchal and feudal connection. It was, clearly, the duty of the lawgiver to express in formal terms that revolution of social ideas which had actually taken place, and to carry the revolution to its legitimate issue.

This, in fact, is just what Edward did in his famous Statute (passed even before the death of Llywelyn at Orewin Bridge), at the manor of his Chancellor, Robert Burnell, Bishop of Bath and Wells, near Shrewsbury, on the 12th October, 1283. The so-called "Parliament of Acton Burnell" has no more claim to constitutional importance than the so-called Parliament House, which professes to be the very building in which it sat; for the body which best deserved the title of Parliament was then sitting at Shrewsbury, seven miles away, and the Statute was probably drawn up and promulgated, as it professes to be, by the King and his Council, *i. e.*, the small body of officials who accompanied him on his journeys. But its legal validity has never been questioned, and its importance is beyond dispute. A merchant who doubts the honesty of his would-be debtor may insist upon his "recognising" or admitting his liability in a formal document, sealed in the presence of the mayor of a chartered borough, and entered upon a roll which remains in the official custody, while a "bill" or "obligation," sealed by the debtor and authenticated by the royal seal, is handed over to the creditor. If the debtor fails to pay, at the appointed time, he may not only be imprisoned, but his

The remedy of the Statute.

chattels and "burgage" tenements (*i. e.*, lands in the borough) may be sold, without any preliminary proceedings, by the mayor to satisfy the debt, or, if there is any difficulty in effecting the sale, the debtor's chattels and *all* his lands may be handed over at a reasonable valuation to the creditor, until, out of the issues, the debt is liquidated. Even the death of the debtor will not destroy the creditor's remedy against his lands, which will remain liable in the hands of his heir, against whom, however, there will be no personal remedy.*

Importance of the Statute.

No apology is needed for the space which has been given to the Statute of Merchants. Under the cover of its technical phrases, the King dealt a death-blow at the still surviving forces of patriarchalism and feudalism, and recognised the new principles of individual responsibility and commercial probity which were to be watchwords of the political and social future. Like a wise legislator, he had merely interpreted and guided the overwhelming drift of evolution, and distinguished between obstruction and progress. He saw that the future greatness of England lay, not with the feudal landowner, but with the despised merchant. His enactment is admirable in its simplicity and effectiveness. It was freely used, not only by merchants, but by every class of society, until improvements in the procedure of the courts

---

* Legal readers will realise that I have combined into one the original Statute of 1283 and the amending ordinance of 1285. But it would have been pedantic, in a general work, to have separated the two.

had rendered it unnecessary. The still simpler machinery of "negotiable paper" (Bills of Exchange and Promissory Notes) ultimately superseded the machinery of Edward's enactment; but, at least until Elizabeth's day, capitalists lent their money on "statutes," no less than on mortgages. And if "statutes" were abused by a Sir Giles Overreach, we must not forget, that an institution is to be judged by its uses, not by its abuses. One injustice Edward's advisers unquestionably did, in making the entire inheritance of a wealthy landowner responsible for the debts and follies of his eldest son. But this was the inevitable consequence of the policy which, before Edward ascended the throne, had forced the feudal custom of primogeniture, in all its naked simplicity, upon an unwilling nation.

The Statute of Entails.

Nothing but an excusable dislike of the dry details of legal history can explain the failure of the many able historians who have treated of the reign of Edward, to detect the close connection between the Statute of Merchants and the yet more famous Statute of Entails, which so soon followed it. On the King's return from his Welsh campaign, he summoned a great Parliament to meet at Westminster at Easter of the year 1285. It was a very different body from the small Council of ministers which had drawn up the Statute of Merchants. Though the precise details of its composition are, unhappily, obscure, it is obvious that the reactionary feudal element was strong enough to deal a severe, though temporary, check to the policy of the latter statute.* Nor is it at all difficult to understand the motives which produced such an outbreak. If the lands of an improvident baron or knight were liable to be seized by his creditors, what was to become of the great feudal families whose pride of lineage was only equalled by their recklessness and extravagance? The feudal landowners were quite shrewd enough to see, that a long family pedigree is cold comfort unless accompanied by a substantial rent-roll — nay, that it is practically impossible for the pedigree to be maintained without the estate. And so, banding all their forces together, they refused to pass the long series of excellent minor reforms on which the King had set his heart, unless he first consented to the solemn promulgation of the legality of entails. It is impossible to look at the famous Statute of Westminster the Second with a trained eye, and not to see the inconsistency of its first chapter (the so-called Statute *De Donis*) with all its subsequent forty-nine clauses. The latter are the work of skilled officials, guided by a King of great ability and honesty, and aim at the minute reform of the machinery of an antiquated system. The former is a bold and defiant assertion of conservative prejudice, veiled by the King's advisers in specious language, which barely conceals the chagrin of the

* Mr. Pearson in his admirable *England in the Middle Ages* (vol. ii., p. 337) suggests, that the Parliament of Easter, 1285, consisted only of the King's officials. This is incredible in the face of the statement made by Walter of Hemingburgh, that "in that Parliament the King informed the *magnates* of his intention of visiting Gascony."

legislator in whose name it is produced. Broadly speaking, it authorised the creation of estates which should descend in unbroken succession down the line of inheritance prescribed in the original gift, so long as that line should last. The successive occupants of the land might pose as the owners, might draw the rents, and even cut down the timber; but instantly on the death of each, his heir would take possession of an unencumbered interest, unfettered by any liability for the debts of his ancestor, or by any disposition made by him during his lifetime. Even an attainder for treason or felony was not to work a forfeiture of the estate; for, immediately upon the attainder, the culprit became dead in law, if not in fact, and his heir succeeded, in defiance both of the Crown and the creditors of the deceased. As, by the rule of primogeniture, the great bulk of such inheritances would go to eldest sons, another obvious result (in the days in which wills of land were not recognised) would be, to starve the younger members of a landowner's family for the benefit of the eldest. By a refinement of perversity, the estate, on failure of the issue of the first acquirer, was to revert, not to his collaterals or his creditors, but to the original donor, who thus reaped an unexpected windfall from the misfortunes of the purchaser's family. The whole chapter is a monument of colossal family pride and feudal arrogance. Left to its natural results, it would have converted the English aristocracy into a close corporation of stupid and unprogressive grandees, filled with the pride of pedigree, starving on lands which they had neither the intelligence nor the legal power to develope, divided from their own kindred by feelings of injustice and oppression, and especially at daggers drawn with their expectant heirs, whose utmost neglect and disobedience they would be powerless to correct by threats of disherison. To suggest that Edward was a willing party to such an act of folly, is a monstrous calumny on his fair fame, and a gross outrage on the probabilities.

Happily, the Statute *De Donis* was not destined to endure. Though, like much of Edward's legislation, it has never been formally repealed,* it has, unlike much of that legislation, long been rendered a dead letter by the more cruel process of contemptuous evasion. In spite of the solemn provisions of the Statute, the principle laid down by it was defeated by the use of a legal fiction so indecently transparent, that it proves conclusively the unpopularity of the rule which it so successfully destroyed.† Before the judges, without whose con-

Its failure.

* An impious Parliament, moved thereto by an impious committee, laid profane hands on the Ark of the Covenant in the year 1887. But it only ventured to remove the merest trappings, leaving the substance untouched—and meaningless.

† If A, the owner of an entailed estate, wished to sell it to B, he got B to bring an action against him (A), asserting that the land belonged already to him (B), and that A was an interloper. Thereupon A attempted no defence on the merits, but merely pleaded that the estate had been entailed upon him, or one of his ancestors, by C, who had then guaranteed, or "warranted", its title. This process, technically known as "vouching to warranty," was repeated as often as was necessary to maintain a decent appearance of truth, but was finally assumed by an impecunious person (usually the crier of the court) who, for the modest fee of fourpence, was willing to take

nivance such an evasion would have been impossible, allowed themselves to sanction it, we may be quite sure that they had satisfied themselves of the feebleness of the force behind the Statute. Unfortunately, it is at present quite impossible to say at what date the convenient fiction of the "Common Recovery" made good its footing in this connection. The classical instance occurred in the year 1472; but it is obvious, from the merely incidental way in which it is mentioned by the reporter, that the process was perfectly familiar at that time; and, as our knowledge of legal history increases, it may very well be discovered, that the Statute *De Donis* had even a shorter life than that usually attributed to it. At any rate, ever since the close of the fifteenth century, the unbreakable entail has ceased to exist, save in the few cases of land settled by Act of Parliament as the reward of public services, and—in the pages of the novelist.*

---

upon himself the responsibility of defending the case. A convenient adjournment allowed the fictitious claimant (B) to "imparl" (or talk) with the fictitious defendant (the crier), and, on the resumption of the trial, the latter failed to appear, having, in all probability, retired to spend his fourpence at the nearest alehouse. Thereupon, after solemn proclamation, he was pronounced in default, the claim of B was established by the judgement of the court (which, of course, no one could dispute), and the disappointed heirs of A were compensated, in theory, by a decree that the defaulting crier should give them lands of equal value. There were heavy fees all through this process, which may perhaps account for its success and complexity.

* Honorable exception from the criticism implied in this last sentence must always be made for the classical case of George Eliot, who, in the pages of *Felix Holt*, shewed that she was quite capable of grasping the subtleties of medieval conveyancing.

Only a very brief analysis can be attempted of the long and elaborately technical clauses which make up the rest of the great Statute of Westminster the Second. It was natural that an enactment avowedly based upon the evils brought to light by the Hundred Rolls, and the proceedings thereon, should contain a good deal about feudal abuses. The harsh proceedings of landlords who make use of the new legal procedure to extort their dues from their tenants, are checked; none but sworn bailiffs are to be employed in seizing goods for default of rent; and in such cases the tenants are to have full opportunity of testing the validity of the seizures in an independent court. The use of violence in the place of legal procedure is sternly prohibited. Further encroachments on the jurisdiction of the Crown are anticipated by the provision, that every judge who goes circuit is to be furnished by the Exchequer officials with a list of "franchises," lawfully claimable by subjects within the counties of his commission; and any tampering with the returns by which such lists are brought up to date is to be punished as treason. On the other hand, the Statute shews every disposition to protect the feudal landowners in the exercise of their admitted rights; and, in one particular case, we may well think that it assists them at the expense of a class far less able to make its claims heard. The 46th clause of the Statute expressly authorizes the manorial lords, in continuance of the policy of the older Statute of Merton, to "approvē," *i. e.*, bring under cultivation, any part of the common wastes which then formed such a valuable

Feudal abuses.

preserve for the humbler members of the villages. The established rights of the "commoners" are, of course, theoretically safeguarded; but there is no provision for the growth of population; and a lurid light is thrown on an otherwise obscure economic struggle, by the provision, that if hedges or dykes, erected in the course of approvement, are secretly destroyed, the adjoining townships are to be distrained, without proof of complicity, to make good the damage.

The royal officials.

But Edward was not the man to reform his neighbour's household while he left his own in disorder; and one of the most conspicuous features of the Statute of Westminster the Second is its elaborate provision against abuses by royal officials. Not only are the circuits of the judges carefully regulated, to prevent, on the one hand, oppressive multiplication of public burdens by too frequent sessions, and on the other, delay and injustice arising from insufficient attendance, but the more glaring abuses of official power are treated with a frankness which must have convinced the culprits that the King, at least, had his eyes open to their misdeeds. Sheriffs and bailiffs who start bogus prosecutions, with the object of extorting money, are to suffer imprisonment. Petty officials of local tribunals, who connive with feudal landowners to withdraw suits from the circuit courts, in order that they may oppress the poor in private, are to make fine to the King, and to pay threefold damages to the party injured. Whilst the duty of service on juries is asserted, the obvious danger of persecution and extortion, by the officials charged with the preparation of the lists, is carefully guarded against. A very significant clause requires the sheriffs to give sealed receipts for all writs delivered to them for execution. The fees of the hierarchy of royal officials, from the Marshal and the Chamberlain, down to the porters, cyrographers, and clerks, are carefully regulated. And, finally, a most wholesome clause lays it down emphatically, that no royal official may accept a share of, or purchase any interest in, property which is the subject-matter of dispute in the royal courts.

The exchequer ordinances.

The Statute of Westminster the Second is, perhaps, mainly concerned with the conduct of the King's local representatives in the country districts; but an almost contemporary group of Exchequer Ordinances made strict and much-needed reforms in the machinery of the central government. The cherished abuse of all revenue officials, from the days of Falkes de Bréauté to the days of Marlborough and Stephen Fox, viz., the retention of heavy balances in their private pockets, was sternly, though, it is to be feared, ineffectually forbidden by Edward's rules. The employment of irresponsible private agents in the King's business is strictly prohibited. Alleged deductions on account of expenses are to be carefully scrutinised by independent surveyors. Oppressive exaction, even of the King's debts, is deprecated. And it is twice laid down, but, alas! ineffectually, that the special royal privileges of the Exchequer process, which were intended for the benefit of the

King only, are not to be made use of by private persons.* Leaving, for the moment, the eloquent comment on these regulations furnished by the proceedings of the year 1290, we return to our analysis of the Statute of Westminster the Second.

Reform of legal process.

The third and last great object of this Statute may be said to have been, to apply to ordinary litigants the same rules of justice and moderation which, as we have seen, the King had imposed on the feudal nobility and his own officials. The farther back we go in legal history, the more clear does it become, that the abuse of legal process, by litigants and officials alike, is no new thing, but, on the contrary, an ancient evil which steadily, if slowly, tends to diminish. Nor is there anything in this discovery that should surprise us. Legal procedure grew out of a gradual substitution of argument for violence, and it bears the marks of its origin at every turn. The doing of "abstract justice" is, no doubt, an unwise ideal for any human tribunal to cherish. But long before the far more modest ideal of "substantial justice" arises in the minds of judges and legislators, the most exalted aim of courts of justice is to secure a "fair fight", of a kind which shall not disturb public order. And a subtle or wealthy litigant no more refrains from profiting

Character of early legal process.

* This wholesome rule proved entirely unable to withstand the opposition of two powerful interests: (1) of the Exchequer judges, to whom increased business meant increased fees, and (2) of wealthy litigants, who coveted the special privileges exercisable by a royal litigant, and were willing to pay for them. It was evaded, as every student of our legal history knows, by the use of transparent fictions.

by tricks or bribery, than a modern general refrains from exercising his skill or resources because he knows that his adversary is a fool. Early reforms in the administration of justice are really made in the interests of sport, rather than in the interests of what we call justice. Even now, the fascination of a great lawsuit, for the mass of men, lies in the excitement of the duel between plaintiff and defendant, or between Crown and prisoner, rather than in any desire to see injustice reproved or wickedness punished. In early society, the Court Day is one of the few excitements in a monotonous existence; and unfair tricks and outrageous oppression are gradually prohibited, just as wide bats and "no balls" have been prohibited in cricket—because they spoil sport. The details of the Statute show that Edward's advisers thoroughly grasped this truth. They are far too technical to be set out here; but, broadly speaking, we may say, that they are aimed solely at preventing collusion, fraud, and delay, offences (as we should deem them) which are inconsistent with wholesome sport. The first obviously tends to deceive the spectators, and stands on the same footing as the "pulling" of a horse in the Derby. The second is always unpopular in a society which prefers the exercise of physical to mental force; and the third is obviously disappointing to people who have come a long way to see the performance, and are apt to lose the thread of the story if the intervals between the acts are too long. So the dowress, the life tenant, or other temporary occupant of land, who allows himself to be defeated in lawsuit by a collusive claimant, with a view to excluding his successor; the husband who surrenders his estate that it may not pay dower to his widow; the guardian who takes advantage of his ward's minority to allow a stranger to exercise rights which properly belong to his ward; the man who warrants title to land and then refuses to defend it; the man who shams illness and lies in bed to delay proceedings, are put under heavy penalties; and their acts are not allowed to prejudice their intended victims.

Finally, the Statute contains, in its twenty-fourth chapter, a clause of which lawyers have long recognised the importance, but which lay historians are too apt to regard as mere technical jargon. Carefully concealed under the guise of an administrative regulation, the Statute lays it down, that the chancery officials, through whose hands must pass every royal writ, which was then, and still is, the normal beginning of every action in the royal courts, need no longer be guided by a strict adherence to precedent in the issue of these documents. It is sufficient if the remedy sought and the circumstances of the case are *like* those for which writs have previously been issued. In other words, principle, not precedent, is henceforth to guide the Chancellor and his officials in the issue of writs.

The *consimilis casus* clause.

To a layman, impatient of the intricacies of legal history, such a direction may seem the most obvious piece of official platitude. In truth, it covered a daring attempt at completing, by a master stroke, a revolution which had been gradu-

Its importance.

ally proceeding during the twelfth and thirteenth centuries. Once more it is necessary to remind the reader, that the conception of the Crown, as the sole fountain of justice, is a very modern conception in legal history. The Crown in the later Middle Ages was but one of many competitors for the profitable business of judicature. The Church, the feudal nobles, the chartered boroughs, the merchant guilds, the shire and hundred moots, were all rivals, more or less formidable. And any premature attempt on the part of the Crown to claim universal and exclusive jurisdiction would assuredly have led to the fiercest opposition, even if it had not resulted in the dissolution of the State. Time was on the side of the Crown; but the King had to walk warily, and to be content for a long time with small things. Bit by bit, as chances offered, the royal officials filched the business of their rivals; and, as each claim was established, it was carefully enshrined as a precedent in that Register of Writs, which was one of the most precious possessions of the royal chancery. If an intending litigant could bring his case within the terms of a registered writ, well and good. If not, the King's courts could do nothing for him. He might have the best case in the world from a moral, or even from a legal point of view. But his remedy, if any, lay elsewhere. With sorrowful hearts, for they disliked "turning away business," the chancery officials regretted that they could not supply the desired article. The officials knew that their path was beset with dangers. The bold assertion of Henry II., that no lawsuit touching the title to freehold could be commenced without a royal writ,* had played no mean part in stirring the baronial rising under John; and the claim had been solemnly renounced in the Great Charter.† Now, perhaps, we are in a position to understand something of the audacity of the *consimilis casus* clause of the Statute of Westminster the Second, which, if acted upon to its full extent, would have left it open to ingenious chancery officials to discover analogies of existing precedents in the case of every intending litigant. But its comparative failure is another signal proof, that sound legislation is little more than the official consecration of enlightened public opinion, and that "fancy" or premature reforms are mere waste of words. The opposition to the full use of the clause came, not merely from feudal and clerical tribunals, but from the King's own judges, who refused to recognise as valid writs which, in their view, departed too widely from precedent, no less than from the Parliaments of the fourteenth century, profoundly jealous of a power which, under the form of mere official documents, was really a power to declare the law of the land. The final victory of the royal jurisdiction was won, by the skilful use of fictions, by the rise of the Court of Chancery, and, finally, by the Reformation, which crushed the independence of the Church courts. It could not be achieved by a

* Even Henry did not dare to say that it could only be *tried in a royal court*. But this was, of course, what he desired; and the barons knew it quite well.

† "The writ, which is called *præcipe*, shall no longer be issued to any one concerning any tenement, to the loss by any freeman of his jurisdiction."

single clause in the Statute of Westminster the Second.

To the same year (1285), but to the autumn Parliament, belongs the credit of another great statute.

Statute of Winchester.

The Statute of Westminster had been mainly concerned with the conduct of the ruling classes—the landowners and the royal officials. The Statute of Winchester is almost wholly occupied with the humbler ranks of the community. It is much shorter, far simpler, but even more comprehensive than its predecessor, and its purpose is clear as the day. It insists that every man, rich and poor alike, has active duties of citizenship to perform; that the good citizen is not merely to abstain from disorder and crime, sitting by with folded hands whilst others defy the law, but that he is bound to assist the forces of order and good government.

The hue and cry.

Three simple but comprehensive duties are imposed upon every citizen by the Statute. He is to report every felon whose offence he may witness or hear of, and take an active part in pursuit of him. He must personally assist in maintaining the police of the country, by serving in the Watch,* and by helping to clear the highways from the growth of underwood which affords such a convenient refuge for thieves and

The watch.

* The Watch is to be kept every night from Ascension Day to Michaelmas. The writer has never been able to understand why the winter nights were left unguarded. Was it because in the winter there was little to steal, or because thieves were too lazy to turn out, or because the health of the Watch would have been injured by the cold weather?

murderers. He must, at least so long as his years permit, provide and maintain himself with arms regulated according to his means, and, twice a year, present himself at the View of Armour held in his Hundred, that the King may know the condition of his militia forces. The Statute of Winchester is deeply interesting; it contains just that surviving fragment of the old Saxon system of local autonomy which was adopted by the strong central government of the Plantagenet Kings. It is silent, of course, as to the strictly popular elements in the old system; and it is probable that these disappeared rapidly before the increasing vigour of the central government. The two Constables of the Hundred mark the beginning of a new era in the history of English local government, in which local officials, though preserving a good deal of healthy independence, are brought into direct contact with the central administration. The genuineness of Edward's interest in the Statute is shewn by the frequent appointment, in the succeeding years, of "Conservators of the Peace," charged with enforcing the duties prescribed by the enactment; and this step seems to have been the direct forerunner of the great institution of the Justices of the Peace, which has a continuous history from the end of the fourteenth century.* Obedience to the Statute was ultimately enforced by the simple, but very effective expedient,

View of Armour.

Commission of the Peace.

* The "Conservators" were, like the later "Justices," local landowners of a certain estate. (See the case of Lawrence Basset, *Parl. Writs*, I, p. 389.)

of holding the local unit responsible as a whole for the neglect of any of its inhabitants.

The Church.

But the wondrous activity of the year 1285 did not end with the Statutes of Westminster and Winchester. In the same year, Edward defined, by the so-called Statute of *Circumspecte Agatis,* which is, in truth, nothing more than an official regulation, addressed to his judges respecting their behaviour in the diocese of Norwich, but which was accepted as a general declaration of royal policy, his attitude on the delicate question of ecclesiastical jurisdiction. The King had already taken up a decided position on the equally delicate subject of the acquisition of lands by the Church, when, in 1279, by the first Statute of Mortmain, he had announced his intention of rigidly enforcing the policy of the Great Charter. No person, cleric or lay, was, without royal license, to vest lands by way of perpetual succession in a monastery or other body not subject to the ordinary chances of death, upon pain of forfeiture of the land in question. This policy, commenced in the natural dislike of the feudal nobles to a practice which deprived them of the incidental windfalls of wardships, marriages, fines on admission of new tenants, and the like, was warmly seconded by the King, who saw the grave public danger of allowing land which represented a liability to military service to get into the hands of clerics who claimed exemption from such duties, and whose tenacious grip would effectually prevent its coming again into the market. For once, Edward and his barons were at one; and the

Mortmain.

Statute of 1279 was supplemented by certain useful clauses in the Statute of Westminster the Second. Moreover, this same enactment contained a salutary clause, compelling the clerical authority, which claimed a share in the goods of every man who died without making a will, to satisfy the debts of the deceased out of the assets coming to its hands. But the Statute *Circumspecte Agatis* makes no extreme claims. In all suits really spiritual, such as the enforcement of penances for deadly sin, the infliction of penalties for neglect of the fabric of a church or of a churchyard, the claim by a parson to tithes, mortuaries, oblations, or other customary dues, even claims to the proceeds of benefices (so long as the titles to the benefices themselves are not in dispute), and in actions for violence to a clerk, or for defamatory words, the King's judges are not to interfere by the issue of a Prohibition. On the other hand, the King provides the judges with a list of matters properly belonging to the royal jurisdiction, and the list, long as it is, amply establishes the position so frequently insisted upon in these pages, that the jurisdiction of the royal tribunals was, even in Edward's reign, a jurisdiction which was being slowly built up, bit by bit, in the struggle of many rivals. A truly liberal regulation, variously attributed to the years 1286, 1290, and 1296, but probably belonging to the year 1290, provided for the contingency of a Prohibition being issued in a case in which the King's courts did not provide a remedy. In such a case, the King's official (the Chancellor or Chief

Circumspecte Agatis.

Statute of Consultation.

Justice), having satisfied himself of the possibility of a failure of justice, is to write to the ecclesiastical judge, bidding him to proceed notwithstanding the Prohibition.

The Ordinance for London.

The last piece of legislation to be noticed, in this fruitful year (1285), is an Ordinance for the government of London, which seems to have been published just before its close. Evidently, Edward could not bring himself to forgive entirely the great city which had taken up arms against his father, and insulted his mother. He steadily refuses to recognise the Mayor as an essential feature of municipal existence. There may be a Mayor, but if the city is in the King's hand there will be, instead, a Warden nominated by the King, who will care little for the views of the citizens.

Taverns. **Fencing.** **Wardmotes.** **Brokers.**

Taverns are only to be kept by fully qualified citizens, and are to be closed rigidly at curfew. No one is to teach fencing within the limits of the city. Each alderman is to hold frequent enquiries as to the presence of malefactors within his ward, and to send all whom he may discover, in safe custody, to the "Warden or Mayor." No roysterer or other serious disturber of the peace is to be let out on bail, without the express warrant of the "Warden or Mayor"; and no broker is to carry on business until he has been presented and sworn before the "Warden or Mayor" to exercise his craft honestly. Incidentally, the ordinance is of interest, as revealing the fact that London, even in 1285, was already a cosmopolitan city, which attracted wanderers from all lands, some of whom " nothing do but run up and down through the streets, more by night than by day, and are well attired in clothing and array, and have their food of delicate meats and costly."

Summary.

The three glorious years, 1283–85, have only twice been rivalled for honourable activity in the annals of English statesmanship. Once in the sixteenth century, when the Reformation Parliament of Henry VIII. set itself, under the guidance of the King and his ministers, to the reconstruction of the national Church, and once in the nineteenth, when a spontaneous outburst of epoch-making legislation followed on the assembly of the first reformed Parliament, has the history of English law a parallel to offer. Had those three years been the utmost limits of Edward's reign, he must have come down to us as one of the greatest and wisest of rulers, who surveyed the body politic in all its members, and laid his healing hand on every sore. But when we reflect that those years were but a fraction of a long reign of thirty-five years, and of a public life which covered at least half a century; when we call to mind, that the man who put forth the Statutes of Acton Burnel, Rhuddlan, Westminster the Second, and Winchester, was the hero of the Barons' War, the Crusader, the framer of the Hundred Rolls and the guide of the Quo Warranto enquiry, the conqueror of Wales, the arbiter of Scotland, the organiser of the coast guard, the unflinching opponent of Papal aggression, and the summoner of the Model Parliament; when we remember, that his name was as great abroad as at home, that he ranked as the equal of Philip of France, and the superior of the Kings of Aragon, Castile, and Sicily, and of the princes of the Netherlands; when, finally, we discover, that the mighty statesman was also the faithful and affectionate son and husband, the wise and patient father, the patron of merit, and the supporter of true piety; then we shall realise that few such monarchs, nay, few such men, have held up the pattern to poor humanity. It is easy to say that Edward draws the credit which of right belongs to his ministers. Doubtless, much of the wisdom of his legislation was due to the advice of his officials, who knew exactly the weak points in the ship of State. But there is also much reason to believe that, among Edward's troubles, were too often to be reckoned the follies of those who should have been his support and stay. Robert Burnel was a notorious profligate, even though he was Chancellor of England and Bishop of Bath and Wells. Antony Bek was a turbulent priest who, but for Edward's steady watchfulness, might have proved a second Becket. Ralph Hengham, Thomas of Weyland, and their fellow judges were, as we shall see, heroes of the greatest judicial scandal in English history. Adam of Stratton, one of the chief officials of the Exchequer, was a corrupt scoundrel. If, in spite of these notorious exceptions, Edward managed to attract able and upright servants, the credit is surely due to him. A King usually gets the ministers he deserves.

So we part from the brightest chapter in Edward's

career. The years between 1285 and 1289 seem to have passed with a monotony which speaks well for the peace of the country. A good deal of the time Edward spent abroad, in Gascony, where, in 1288, he had another of those narrow escapes from death which gave him his reputation for a charmed life. He was sitting with his wife, his back to a window, when the lightning passed between them, and struck dead two ladies who were standing before them. Grateful for his escape, Edward solemnly renewed his promise to start a new Crusade, and obtained from Pope Nicholas IV. a grant of the clerical tenths for a period of six years, the money to be devoted to the expenses of the expedition. But Edward's work lay nearer to hand. In the summer of the year 1289 he was disturbed by rumours of a fierce quarrel between the Earls of Gloucester and Hereford, the scene of which was laid in that very dangerous neighbourhood, the Welsh border. Bending his steps homewards, the King landed at Dover on the 21st of August, 1289, to face, if he had but known it, one of the fiercest and longest political hurricanes which have ever burst upon a ruler's devoted head.

Edward's escape from death.

CHAPTER X

SCOTLAND

1289–1292

IT was soon clear that Edward had lingered too long in pleasant Gascony. Immediately on his return, he was assailed with fierce complaints of the conduct of his officials during his absence. He promptly appointed a commission to enquire into

The judicial scandal.

the truth of the charges, ordering the sheriffs to proclaim, that all who had grievances to allege should lay them before the commissioners at Westminster at Martinmas. Whether this plan was best calculated to reveal all the secrets of official corruption may well be doubted; but at least it had a startling result. In

1290.

the following year, the English judicial bench was purged by a wholesale dismissal of its members, accompanied by a series of enormous fines. Thomas of Weyland, the Chief Justice of the Common Bench, was forced to abjure the realm, and his ill-gotten gains were confiscated.*

* Anticipating his fate, he had managed, by a clever piece of conveyancing jugglery, to save some of his land.

Lovetot, Brumpton, and Roger of Leicester, his colleagues, were mulcted in the penalties of £3000, £6000, and 1000 marks respectively. Hengham, Chief Justice of the King's Bench, an author of repute, was fined £8000; but he was ultimately received back into favour. Solomon of Rochester, and three of his colleagues, justices in eyre, paid sums varying from one to three thousand marks. Littlebury, the Master of the Rolls, a high Chancery official, paid a thousand marks. But the heaviest punishment (save that of Weyland) fell, and fell deservedly, on Adam of Stratton, Baron of the Exchequer, who was compelled to disgorge no less than 64,000 marks (upwards of £42,000).

Adam of Stratton.

Adam of Stratton was a very bad case, but only too typical, it is to be feared, of the royal official of the thirteenth century. Born in a humble sphere, on one of the manors of the Countess of Albemarle, he succeeded, with her assistance, in obtaining an university degree, and entering holy orders. His patron, who, as widow of the sixth Earl of Albemarle (William of Forz), grand-daughter of Gilbert of Gloucester, and daughter and ultimately heiress of the Earl of Devon, was related to the greatest families of the kingdom, had little difficulty in finding employment for her protégé. She seems to have had a somewhat mysterious claim to the office of Chamberlain of the Exchequer; and this was sufficient to obtain for Adam an entry to the great field of official ambition, the royal Exchequer. Before the year 1266, he had succeeded, by dint of rather sharp practice, in securing the small office of Weigher. Two years later, he was invested by Henry III. with the valuable privileges of an Exchequer official, which exempted him from the jurisdiction of all but his official superiors, and allowed him to hold any number of livings without residence. He was employed in the congenial task of superintending the workmen on the various royal works, an occupation which gave him unrivalled opportunities of plunder. He seems also to have acted as the Countess' attorney in her dealings with the Exchequer, and, in 1276, he obtained a grant of her important office of Chamberlain. Thus secure in his position, he deliberately started on a campaign of spoliation. One of his first acts was to extort, with oppressive harshness, a surrender of her lands to the Crown by no less a person than Aveline Forz, the daughter of his patron, and the betrothed of Edmund Crouchback, the King's brother. This outrageous act probably led to his first check, a great scandal and enquiry which took place in 1279, and from which, it is to be feared, he escaped by official connivance. In the new enquiry of 1289-90, he defended himself with a cool audacity and unscrupulous craft which certainly speak well for his ability, though they dispose of his last shred of pretension to even elementary morality. Forgery, violence, sorcery, even murder, were freely charged against him; and there can be little doubt that the charges were true. Ultimately, he was convicted of outrageous extortion and forgery at the expense of the Abbey of Bermondsey; and his attaint of felony was followed by the forfeiture of the whole of his vast and ill-gotten gains to the Crown. Being a cleric, he could not be hung; but he spent the rest of his life in disgrace, though, it is to be feared, Edward stooped to make use of his services in the excellent bargain which he made with the old Countess of Albemarle in the year 1293.*

Hardly less serious than the official scandal, was the quarrel in the west between the Earls of Gloucester and Hereford, previously alluded to. The Earl of Gloucester (Clare) wished, apparently, to seize by force a piece of land to which he laid claim, situated within the geographical limits of the lordship of Brecknock, or Brecon, then vested in the Earls of Hereford. The Earl of Hereford (Bohun) not unnaturally objected; and his objection was upheld by Edmund Crouchback, who had acted as Regent during his brother's absence, and who forbade Clare to carry out his plan, at least until the King's return. Edward, on his arrival, had tried to make peace by betrothing his daughter, Joan of Acre, to Gloucester; but all in vain, for, in February, 1290, the Earl's followers burst out of the Clare lordship of Morgannon, or Glamorgan, invaded Brecknock, displaying the Gloucester standard, and wrecked the church of Penrhyn, carrying off the sacred vessels, slaying the inhabitants, and driving away cattle, horses, sheep, and swine. The jury which reported on the case, at the Brecknock Lent As-

Quarrel of Gloucester and Hereford.

26th June, 1289.

The raid on Brecknock.

* The King acquired the Isle of Wight, and the manors of Lambeth and Vauxhall, for six thousand marks of silver.

sizes of 1290, expressly exonerated the Earl of Gloucester from any personal share in the sacrilege; but, as he was proved to have received one-third of the plunder (in accordance with the pleasing custom of the Marches), he can hardly be acquitted of complicity, at least after the event. It soon appeared, however, that Clare's rival, Hereford, had been by no means the patient sufferer that his pleaders represented; and the King, after a long and careful examination, at length, in the Epiphany Parliament of 1292, held in the intervals of the Scottish lawsuit, came to the conclusion, that the affair was a border quarrel of the true feudal type, in which both parties were wrong. He accordingly dealt out even-handed justice, by taking into his own custody, during the lifetime of the earls, the rival lordships of Glamorgan (Clare) and Brecknock (Bohun), and by clapping the earls and their chief followers into prison, whence they were only released on payment of heavy fines.* The haughtiness of the Clare family is well illustrated by two petty incidents of the time. In the first, Bogo Clare, a cadet of the house, had the audacity to serve a citation on Edmund of Cornwall, the King's own cousin, while he was in attendance on the Parliament of 1290. For this gross breach of privilege he was sent to the Tower, and only released on payment of a heavy fine. By way of revenge for this indignity, Clare's servants seized a messenger, John

Bogo Clare.

* It seems clear that Gloucester was chiefly to blame, for he had to pay 10,000 marks fine, and £100 damages to Hereford, while the latter only paid a fine of 1000 marks.

Wallace, who was armed with a similar document intended for Bogo, and compelled the wretched man to eat both the parchment and the seals. Bogo himself, on this occasion, escaped by professing entire ignorance of the transaction.

Other troubles.

In addition to the judicial scandal, and the trouble in South Wales, there were innumerable other quarrels going on—quarrels between the Bishop of Coventry and the Justices of the Forest, between the Bishop of Lincoln and the University of Oxford, between the King and the Bishop of Winchester concerning the patronage of the Hospital of Southampton, between the burgesses of Newcastle and the Prior of Tynemouth, between the Queen and the Earl of Pembroke, between the Cinque Ports and Yarmouth, between the Abbey of Westminster and the King's Justices respecting the franchises of the Abbey, and many others. But all were, of course, as nothing in importance compared with the great quarrel of the Scottish succession, to which we must now turn our eyes.

The Scottish Kingdom.

The early history of Scotland, like the early history of Wales, had consisted in the obscure struggles of rival chieftains for power and precedence. But, unlike Wales, Scotland had succeeded, at least as soon as England, in combining the somewhat diverse elements of her population into a more or less compact kingdom under the descendants of Malcolm Ceanmore.* For at least

* An important intermediate stage is represented by the fourfold division of the country (in the early 11th century) into (1) the Scot-

two centuries, there had been close family alliances between the Crowns of England and Scotland. Malcolm himself took to wife Margaret of England, the sister of Edgar "Atheling." Matilda, Malcolm's daughter, had married Henry Beauclerk. Her brother, David I., from whom the reigning monarch was descended, had taken to wife the daughter of the Saxon Earl Waltheof, nephew by marriage of the Conqueror. Alexander II. had espoused Joan, eldest daughter of John Lackland. As we remember, Henry III. had absurdly chosen to be offended by Alexander's second marriage with Mary of Coucy; but his son by this last marriage had been married to Margaret, Edward's own sister (see p. 235), and Henry had taken the young couple into his favour. Their daughter Margaret had been born in England, and had married Eric, King of Norway, whose house had maintained a steady friendship with both England and Scotland. But she had died in the year 1283, leaving another Margaret, the "Maid of Norway," her infant daughter, the sole heiress of the Crowns of Norway and Scotland; for the only surviving son of Alexander III. had predeceased his sister by thirty days.* Alexander III. himself, who had lost his wife, Edward's sister, in 1275, not unnaturally anxious that the Crown of Scotland should not become an appanage

Irish Dalriada in the west, (2) the Pictish Moray in the north, (3) the Teutonic Bernicia in the south-east, and (4) the British Strathclyde in the south-west.

* There had been another brother, David, who had died in 1280. The brother who died in 1283 was named, like his father, Alexander.

PEDIGREE OF THE KINGS OF SCOTLAND.

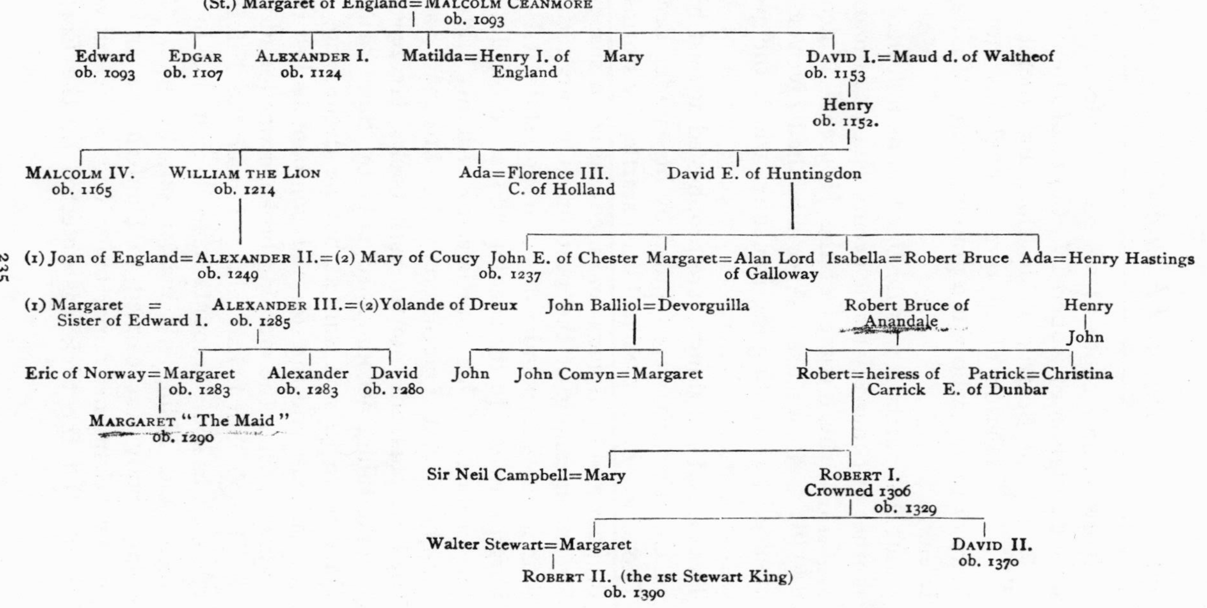

of Norway, now chose, as his second wife, Yolande, second daughter of Robert IV., Count of Dreux, and of Beatrix of Montfort, and, therefore, a relation of his own through his mother, Mary of Coucy, who was a granddaughter of Alix of Dreux.

1st Nov., 1285.

But the marriage was destined to be followed by another of the many tragic events which had marred the fortunes of the House of Malcolm Ceanmore. Alexander had given some offence by restricting the franchises which the great see of Durham claimed to exercise north of the Tweed, and evil things were prophesied against him, which, of course, were fulfilled by his sudden death. The winter of 1285–86 had been startled by storms of thunder and lightning; and men waited in suspense for the meaning of the portent. On the 18th of March, 1286, Alexander dined in high state at Edinburgh Castle. In the evening he started off, despite the protests of his courtiers, to visit his bride at Kinghorn. At Queensferry, the boatman vainly tried to persuade him to turn back. He reached Inverkeithing, accompanied only by three squires. Once more he was warned, but he dashed on. In the darkness and the storm his companions lost their way, and, when the morning broke, it was found that the King's horse had plunged over the Fifeshire cliffs, or, as some accounts have it, stumbled in the deep sand, killing his master on the spot. The King's body was carried to Dunfermline, and his widow, seizing her opportunity, feigned herself with child. But the trick was detected by the Earl of

Death of Alexander III.

Buchan, and the Queen fled to France, where she soon married Arthur of Brittany, bringing him the Montfort inheritance, and becoming the ancestress of the Montfort Dukes of Brittany.

The position at Alexander's death.

Edward's heart must have quickened when he heard the news; for the line of Malcolm Ceanmore was dwindled now to a feeble thread in the person of the little Maid of Norway, and there is small doubt that his mind was already bent on the union of the two countries. But he was too wise to force matters; and he left the Scottish nobles to arrange for the guardianship of the realm. The temptations of so rich a prize proved too much for concord, and it might have fared ill with the little Maid, had she not been safe at Bergen, under her father's care. In April, 1289, Edward reaped the fruit of his steady friendship with Eric and his dead father, Magnus; for the Norwegian King, evidently unwilling to trust his daughter in the hands of the Scottish nobles, and equally unwilling to leave his own kingdom, practically placed the conduct of the negotiations for the marriage and establishment of the little Queen in the hands of the English King. It was a great triumph for Edward, and, so far as the evidence goes, it was obtained by no unworthy means.* In the autumn of the year a meeting took place between the Bishops of St. Andrews and Glasgow with Bruce of

The marriage negotiations.

* There is some trace of a modest distribution of pensions by Antony Bek, one of Edward's representatives in Norway. But they are on too small a scale to be anything more than the usual diplomatic compliments of the day.

Anandale and John Comyn, as representatives of Scottish interests, and the Bishops of Worcester and Durham, with the Earls of Pembroke and Surrey, at Salisbury; and it was there agreed that the Maid should be sent to England (not Scotland), free from all marriage engagements, to remain under Edward's care until the state of Scotland permitted of her safe residence there. Even in this event, the Scottish commissioners undertook that she should not marry without the consent both of Edward and Eric. In truth, the Scottish nobles had themselves been reduced to beg Edward's help. In September, Duncan, Earl of Fife, the chief Regent, a cruel and avaricious tyrant, had been murdered by his own followers, and the realm was in confusion. In reply to the request for help, Edward merely bade the people obey the surviving Regents, promising to visit the country in the following year. But he had already made up his mind as to the line to be pursued, for, on the 16th November, he obtained from the Papal Chancery a dispensation for the marriage of the Maid of Norway with his eldest son, Edward of Caernarvon, afterwards Prince of Wales.

1289.

So obvious, indeed, was this solution of the problem, that the Scots themselves seem to have raised little objection, merely making conditions to secure the independence of their kingdom. On March 10, 1290, a very full meeting of the Scottish Estates, consisting of the four Regents,*

Treaty of Brigham.

* These were the Bishops of St. Andrews and Glasgow, John Comyn, and James Stewart.

ten bishops, twelve earls, thirty-four abbots and priors, and forty-eight of the lesser barons, and including both the Bruces (but not John Balliol), solemnly agreed to a marriage between the young Queen and Edward's son, upon terms to be settled between a Scottish deputation and the King, at a Parliament to be held at London the approaching Easter. The conference was duly held, and, after a solemn interchange of missions between England, Norway, and Denmark, the terms of the arrangement were recorded in an elaborate document bearing date the 18th July, 1290. The laws and customs of Scotland were to remain unaltered by the personal union of the two Crowns; if the marriage proved childless, the Crown of Scotland was to go as though the union had never taken place; during the marriage and after, there was to be no hint of subjection on the part of the northern kingdom; the King, as guardian of his infant son and daughter-in-law, was to name a deputy to reside in Scotland and hear the complaints of the widow and orphan; no Scottish official and no Scottish Parliament was to be compelled to cross the border; no castles were to be built to overawe Scotland; none of the Scottish national relics or charters were to be removed.

Death of the Maid.

Alas, for the vanity of human schemes! Hardly had Antony Bek, the great Bishop of Durham, received his appointment of deputy under the treaty of Brigham, when there arose an evil rumour (only too well founded) of the death of the little Queen, who had been put

Robert Bruce.

20th Sept., 1286.

ashore on the Orkneys to break the hardships of a long sea voyage. At once the forces of anarchy were loosed. Robert Bruce of Anandale, the most formidable claimant to the Scottish throne, aided by the Earls of Mar and Athol, was already in arms; John Comyn (who had succeeded to the earldom of Buchan) and John Balliol, rival claimants, were stirring; the perennial quarrel of the Campbells and the Macdonalds was flaring up again in the western isles. Of all these dangers, the rising of Bruce was by far the most serious. Himself an old official of Edward's father, who had suffered for his loyalty to the throne in the Barons' War, he had no love for Edward, who, it would appear, had treated him coldly after the victory of Evesham. More than fifty years before, his hopes had been stirred by Alexander II., who, then despairing of issue, had recognised him as heir to the Scottish throne; and, on the death of Alexander III., this recognition had been tacitly renewed in a secret "bond of manrent," entered into by the Bruce, the Stewart, the Dunbar, and the Macdonald families at Turnberry Castle. By his marriage with Isabella Clare, daughter of the old Earl Gilbert of Gloucester, and aunt of the Red Earl, Bruce was connected with the most powerful families in England and Ireland; and there is at least a strong presumption, that he was aided in his plans by no less a person than Richard Burgh, Earl of Ulster, whose English relations were allied by marriage with the Clares. Despite his eighty years, Bruce was too formidable a rival to be neglected.

And Edward did not neglect him. When the news arrived, the King was holding a Parliament at Clipstone in Nottinghamshire; but he at once gave orders for stores to be collected at Berwick-on-Tweed, and, as soon as the session was over, himself started northward for the scene of action. But he was almost immediately checked in his march by a terrible blow, —the Queen dying at Hardby, near Lincoln, on the evening of the 28th November, 1289. Edward at once abandoned his journey. The body was embalmed and moved to Lincoln Cathedral; whence, on the 5th December, it started on that mournful procession to London which is marked by twelve great crosses erected by the sorrowing King, at Lincoln, Grantham, Stamford, Geddington, Northampton, Stony Stratford, Woburn, Dunstable, St. Alban's, Waltham, West Cheap, and Charing, each on the spot where the body rested on its journey. The Queen was laid in her tomb in Westminster Abbey, in the newly erected chapel of Henry III., amid the profound and genuine grief of a sorrowing nation. Not until March of the following year did the King take up again his journey to Scotland. At midsummer he also lost his mother, the aged Eleanor of Provence, who had long lived in retirement at Amesbury, where she had been visited by her son in the winter of his grief.

Edward moves.

The Queen's death.

1290.

But the work of the State cannot be postponed to private sorrow, and Edward, with his wonted courage and energy, bent his mind anew to the Scottish question. Deprived, by the course of affairs, of his cherished hopes of union, he had now to act the dignified part of arbiter, which the common consent of the rivals for the Scottish throne conferred upon him. There were no less than twelve of these claimants; but only three of them need to be taken seriously. The first was, of course, Robert Bruce of Anandale, whose strong position has already been described, but whose exact claim to the throne was based on the fact that his father, also a Robert Bruce* of Anandale, had married Isabella, second daughter of David of Huntingdon, himself the younger grandson of David I. of Scotland, and youngest brother of William the Lion. The line of William was extinct, or survived only in the daughters of John Burgh, the grandson of his daughter Margaret, who were too remote to be seriously considered. The second claimant was John Balliol, the son of another John Balliol (of the French barony of Bailleul in Picardy) who had married Devorguilla, daughter and heiress of the Lord of Galloway by *his* marriage with Margaret, elder daughter of David of Huntingdon, and, therefore, elder sister of Robert Bruce's mother. The third was John Hastings of Bergavenny, whose grandfather, Henry, had married Ada, the third and youngest daughter of David of Huntingdon. Apart from legal questions, Hastings was by far the weakest candidate, for he was, in character

Renewal of the Scottish journey.

* There are, to the terror of historians, no less than four "Robert Bruces" in the story: viz. (1) the husband of Isabella, who died in 1245, (2) the claimant, (3) his son, known, from his marriage with the heiress of Carrick, as "Bruce of Carrick," (4) the latter's son, the ultimate King.

PEDIGREE OF SCOTTISH CLAIMANTS

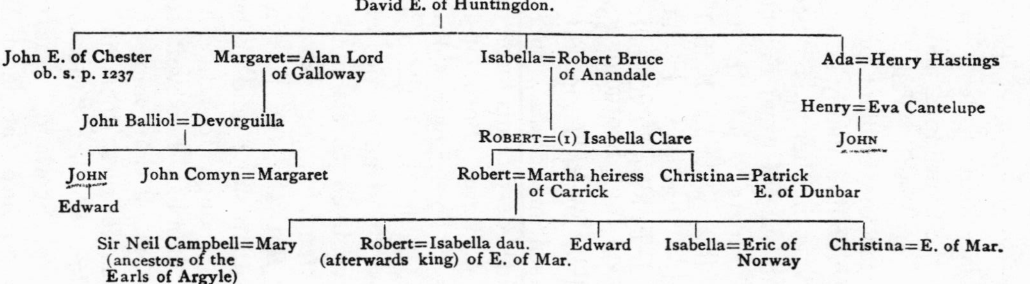

and position, an English baron pure and simple, whose father had made a great match with the heiress of the Cantilupes, and thus made him a rich landowner of South Wales. He seems never to have coveted the brilliant prize to which his legal claims were so undeniably strong. Of the two most serious rivals, neither was a Scot of long descent, both being issue of great French houses which had sent their cadets to join the forces of William the Bastard. But, whereas Balliol had only acquired the Scottish lordship of Galloway through his father's marriage with a daughter of the native earl, Bruce's forefathers had been Lords of Anandale for at least two hundred and fifty years. The rising national sentiment was, therefore, naturally on Bruce's side, despite his former connection with the Court of Edward. Both, it is not immaterial to observe, were border barons, Bruce by his lordship of Anandale, Balliol by his fief of Barnard Castle.

Attitude of the parties.

The position of all parties was delicate. Edward would have liked to claim the rôle of arbiter by feudal right, as overlord of Scotland. But the rivals trumped his hand by prompt submission; and Edward could not be ungracious enough to refuse their offer. He demanded, however, some recognition of

1291.

his position; and, on the 5th June, nine of the competitors (including the three serious rivals) admitted that "the sovereign seignory of the realm of Scotland" was vested in him. We need not go into the legal justification of this admission. No doubt the Norman barons who made good their footing in the Lowlands were, in a sense, lieges of the Crown of England, just as were the Marcher lords of Wales. No doubt there had been dealings,* even between the line of Malcolm Ceanmore and the line of William of Normandy, which might be construed into a recognition of the overlordship of the latter. But the aspirations of national feeling are not to be measured by the technicalities of feudal documents; and Edward, it is to be feared, laid too much stress on the search for precedents which he caused to be made in the charter-rooms of the great monasteries, and too little on the growth of national unity beyond the Tweed. He was gratified by the submission of the candidates, which was followed by the surrender of the kingdom into his hands. The "issues," pending Edward's decision, were to remain in the coffers of the Chamberlain of Scotland (Alexander Balliol) and of deputies appointed by him and Edward jointly. Edward and the Chamberlain agreed amicably upon the Bishop of Caithness, who was also Chancellor of Scotland, and William of Amersham; but the King strained his position somewhat by demanding from the Earl of Angus the surrender of the castles of Dundee and Forfar. He, however, gratified the Scots by agreeing that the trial should take place in Scotland, but fixed upon Norham, which, even then, could hardly be said to satisfy the

* The chief of these are: (1) the Treaty of Falaise in 1174, (2) the release by Richard of England in 1189, and (3) the renewal of allegiance by Alexander II. in 1217. But whether this last was for the kingdom or the private possessions of the Scottish King in England is much disputed.

description, as it was one of the strongholds of the see of Durham, and actually on the south bank of the Tweed. Moreover, Edward shewed a suspicious caution, by protesting that even this concession to Scottish sentiment was not to be taken as a precedent, and by directing the justices of the Common Bench to recognise writs dated from Scotland, "because the two kingdoms are now conjoined."

The preliminaries of the trial lasted from the 10th May to the 13th June, when the questions at issue were referred to a judicial commission of 104 persons, forty nominated by Balliol and Comyn* (who had thrown in his lot with his brother-in-law), forty by the Bruce, and twenty-four by the King. The hearing was fixed for August the 2nd, not at Norham, where the preliminaries had taken place, but on the neutral ground of Berwick-on-Tweed, which, until long after this date, occupied an anomalous position as regards jurisdiction. A sporting element had been introduced into the proceedings by the tardy arrival of a claim by Eric of Norway, in right of his deceased wife and daughter. But this claim was not treated seriously; and the court met on the appointed day, for the consideration of the claims of Bruce and Balliol. Meanwhile, Edward had been strengthening his position, by exacting oaths of fealty from the Regents (which, however, they declined to give, except on Scottish

The trial. 1291.

*Comyn, though a direct descendant of Donald Bane, had, of course, no legal claim to the throne, on feudal principles. But he was of the blood royal of Scotland, and, therefore, a powerful factor in the struggle.

ground*), and by proclaiming his peace. He then directed the competitors to appear at Berwick on the 2nd August with formal statements, or petitions, setting forth the details of their respective claims. The direction was duly obeyed, and, on the 3rd August, 1291, the twelve petitions were solemnly rehearsed in the great hall of the castle of Berwick. Whereupon, the King, anxious, no doubt, for a respite from the exacting claims of the suit, adjourned the proceedings to the 2nd June in the following year (1292).

The issue.

The two legal questions involved were extremely simple to state, extremely difficult to answer. The first was, whether, as between sisters, any right of primogeniture could be recognised? It will be remembered, that Balliol was descended from the eldest daughter of David of Huntingdon, Bruce from the second. The other query may be thus stated: Is the remoter descendant in the superior line to be preferred to the nearer in the inferior line? This question, it will be observed, implies an affirmative answer to the former. It was important, because Balliol was only the grandson of David's eldest daughter, Margaret, while Bruce was the son of his second daughter, Isabella.

At the present day, there would be very little difficulty in answering either of these questions. But this certainty has probably been produced as much by the memorable decision at Berwick-on-Tweed as by any other cause. Before that decision

* The place chosen was Upsetlington, just across the river, "opposite the castle of Norham."

14th October, 1292.

was given, the matter really depended largely upon the further question, what system of law was deemed to govern the disputants; and this was by no means an easy preliminary to settle. That Edward realised this truth is clear from the fact that, on the resumption of the proceedings, after a preliminary discussion of the claims of Bruce and Balliol by the commissioners, he put three legal questions to the assembled Parliament—(1) By what laws and customs is the decision to be governed? (2) Suppose there to be no provision for the case in those laws and customs, what then? (3) Does the kingdom of Scotland go as earldoms, baronies, and other tenures?

1292.

To these questions the assembly of the 14th October, which comprised, not only the chosen judges, but a large number of English magnates, replied unanimously—(1) That the King was to be guided by the laws and customs of his own "kingdoms." (2) That, if these failed, he was to take counsel with his lords and magnates, and "found" (*condere*) a new law. (3) That the Kingdom of Scotland was governed by the same rules of inheritance as earldoms, baronies, and other indivisible tenures.

Feudal principles to prevail.

These were true feudal answers, and they sealed the fate of Bruce. In their first assertion, the assembled magnates had probably only intended to repudiate any recourse to the great system of Roman, or "imperial" law, represented by Edward's favourite jurist, Accursi. By the third, however, they aimed a side thrust at the Celtic or Pictish usages to which Bruce's counsel had appealed, and which, if they did not sanction a division of the chiefship among women, at least afforded awkward precedents for the preference of the nearer representative of a younger line to the remoter member of an older. Feudal customs allowed the partition of land amongst women of an equal degree; but any "honour" attached to the inheritance was always deemed to be, as the magnates had hinted in their answer, "unpartible."

Edward's attitude.

Edward had chosen his position with masterly skill. He had probably made up his mind to decide for Balliol; but the course of events appeared to make him simply the mouthpiece of his Parliament. In order, however, to give a decent appearance of deliberation, he once more adjourned the session to November 6th. In the autumn of the previous year he had lost his faithful, though not very reputable adviser, Robert Burnel; but it is not probable that he felt any serious doubt of his course. On the day fixed, Edward solemnly pronounced the decision of the Court against Bruce; and, a few days later, gave judgement upon the somewhat lukewarm claim of Hastings by declaring that the kingdom was not divisible, as Hastings' petition had urged. On the 17th November, the kingdom was solemnly awarded to Balliol, with the significant injunction to govern it so well that there should be no need for Edward's own interference. On the 20th Balliol received seisin of the land and

1292.

The award.

its castles, doing fealty to Edward therefor. On the 30th he was crowned at Scone. At Christmas he did solemn homage to Edward at Newcastle. In both fealty and homage, the feudal superiority of Edward was unmistakably recognised.

The King returns to England.

Edward then set off for London, where his presence was urgently needed. During his absence on the affairs of Scotland, the Normans had plundered Dover, probably in the course of one of the many Channel feuds which marked the long-standing hostility between the French and English fishermen. The Cinque Ports had replied in vigorous fashion; and Edward found himself drawn into a French quarrel, which was fomented by the spite of Charles of Valois. There had been a treaty with Flanders in May, 1292; but this was counterbalanced by the alliance entered into between Bruce and the Count of Holland * during the Scottish lawsuit. The peace of the kingdom had, however, been perceptibly strengthened by the capture of Rhys ab Meredith, who was tried at York in June, and solemnly hung as a traitor. But there was a furious quarrel going on between the turbulent Bishop of Durham and his metropolitan of York, on the thorny subject of the Palatine rights of the Bishop. Eric of Norway was begging for the arrears of his wife's dower, and intimating that, as Edward was deciding the fate of Scotland, he ought not to

* The Count (Florence V.) was, nominally, a competitor for the Scottish throne. His great-great-grandfather had married Ada, daughter of David I. of Scotland. He was the son of that William of Holland whom the Pope had set up as a rival of the Emperor Frederick II.

forget such matters. The fact that Robert Bruce, son of the competitor, after sulkily absenting himself from Balliol's coronation, had resigned his earldom of Carrick in favour of his son, the future King, and retired to Norway, did not improve the prospects of peace; and, although Edward somewhat foolishly gave the earl a safe conduct to Norway, he probably repented of his rashness when he heard, as he soon did, of the marriage of the earl's daughter, Isabella, with Eric, the widowed King. For this marriage, which took place in November, 1293, was, no doubt, one of the preliminaries of that formidable alliance between Scotland, Norway, and France, which was to prove such a danger to Edward in the coming years.

14th July, 1293.

But a surer sign that the work of the tribunal of Berwick had not settled the Scottish question is to be found in the ominous fact that, in less than a year, Balliol was at feud with the King, to whom he had sworn homage. There can be little doubt that the fault lay with Edward. He could not bring himself to leave Scotland alone. The superiority recognised by Balliol implied, in strict feudal law, a right of appeal from Balliol's Court to that of Edward; and of this rule the English King took full advantage. Though the Scottish charters and the disputed lordship of the Isle of Man were ceded to Balliol, though the latter held a Parliament at Scone in February, 1293, Edward seized the opportunity of complaints by Scottish litigants to summon him to Westminster "for defect of justice." Of course there were many people only too ready to

Quarrel with Balliol.

stir up bad blood. Macduff, the new Earl of Fife, Alfrica, heiress of Man, the Abbot of Reading, and others, put in their appeals. Swallowing his resentment, Balliol journeyed to Westminster, and his submission was rewarded by the grant to him, in the English Parliament of October, 1293, of the English possessions of Alexander of Scotland. But, at the same time, he was forcibly reminded of his duty to satisfy the pecuniary claims of the King of Norway; and Edward, as King and "superior lord of the kingdom of Scotland," lost no opportunity of insisting upon his overlordship. On the outbreak of the French war, Edward, in his straits, affected to use the resources of Scotland as his own; and thereby goaded both Balliol, and, which was much more important, the Scottish nation, into an attitude of hostility, which, at the crisis of his fortunes, very nearly turned the scale against him. But, to understand the importance of this event, we must glance for a moment at the troubled sea of foreign politics.

CHAPTER XI

THE FRENCH WAR

1293–1298

IT is not easy to strike the key-note of the last years of Edward's life. Hitherto he had usually been occupied, at any given period, with one subject of overwhelming importance—the Barons' War, the Crusade, the pacification of Wales, domestic reform, or the fate of Scotland. Having dealt singly with all these great subjects, he was now to face a revival of them all at once. Happily, with all save one he dealt successfully; but the extreme difficulty of telling the tale is a fair reflection of Edward's own difficulties.

The French War.

In those easy-going times, a maritime war might often go on, in fact, for months, or even years, before its existence would be admitted in official circles. But matters in the Channel soon grew beyond the limits of freebooting. A casual brawl in a tavern of Normandy led to an outrageous vengeance by the Norman fishermen upon the crews of two English ships, whom they hung, with every species of insult, to the yard-arms of their vessels. The outrage was followed by reprisals on the port of

Sluys, and these again by a challenge to pitched battle; and, on the 14th April, 1293, in a storm of snow and wind, a great victory was won by the English and their allies at a spot marked in mid-channel by the mooring of an empty ship. The English sailors were supported by the Irish and the Hollanders; whilst the Normans had for allies their fellow subjects, the French, as well as the Flemings, and the Genoese. According to the English chronicler, Walter of Hemingburgh, the English plundered no less than 240 ships.

Philip seizes Gascony.

Be this as it may, it was clear that matters could go no further without some official recognition; and the initiative was taken by Philip of France, who, having long cast covetous eyes on Edward's hereditary duchy of Gascony, chose to allege that the Gascons had been implicated in the sea-fight of the previous April, and to summon Edward, as his vassal for Gascony, to give an account of the proceedings. This was a cunning move on the part of the French King; for, while it did not amount to a declaration of war with England, it practically enabled him to treat Edward as a rebel. Edward saw that it was necessary to proceed with extreme caution, and he at once sent his brother Edmund, in January, 1294, to offer his humble submission as Duke of Aquitaine and Gascony. Edmund, who was no match for the French lawyers, was tricked into an actual surrender of Edward's duchy, as a preliminary to the trial of the alleged misconduct of Edward. The English King, who knew something of the subtleties of feudal law, was preparing to present himself in person at the French Court, where a proposal was on foot to marry him to the French King's sister, Margaret, when he heard of a plot to seize him on the road to Amiens. Quite naturally, he changed his plans; and Philip, throwing off all disguise, declared Gascony forfeited.

Easter, 1294.

There was now nothing for it but to fight, or to yield a rich province; and Edward was not the man to hesitate between such alternatives. Throwing himself upon the friendship of his Gascon subjects, with whom he generously assumed the blame of his brother's folly, he collected all his resources in England, Wales, and Ireland, and, as has been before hinted, began to make his overlordship a very real thing in Scotland, by issuing direct summons to the Scottish barons to serve in the English army. But his activity did not stop there. He at once entered upon treaties of alliance with the Emperor (Adolf of Nassau), the King of Castile (Sancho IV.), the princes of Savoy and Burgundy, and his own powerful Gascon neighbour, the Count of Foix. The Count of Bar had been already secured, by his marriage with Edward's eldest daughter, Eleanor.

The King collects forces.

But all this preparation required money, and, in his need of money, Edward ran the serious risk of offending his own loyal subjects, the English. Summoning a great Parliament of clergy, barons, and knights, for the autumn,* he laid his

1294.

* The clergy and the laity did not sit together on this occasion. The former were summoned for 21st September, the latter for 12th November.

troubles frankly before it. From the clergy the King demanded no less a sum than one-half of their goods. As he had, earlier in the year, seized the hoarded treasures of the churches and the wool of the merchants (a good deal of which was held on account of the clergy), this demand was terrible; and the clergy, weakened though they were by the vacancy of the see of Canterbury and the absence of the bold Bishop of Durham, made a vigorous protest. But Edward, who seems to have lost his self-control in the extremity of his danger, turned so fiercely upon their messengers that the Dean of St. Paul's fell dead in his presence. As the King was inexorable, the clergy tried to get a relaxation of the Mortmain statute in return for their sacrifice; but even this concession was sternly refused. With the laity the King could not use such high-handed measures, and he had to be content with a tenth from them, except in the case of the boroughs, which, though not specially represented, were forced to pay a sixth. London gave him a handsome subsidy, for which he was duly grateful.

Thus furnished with money, or with the prospect of money, Edward had sent out a fine army of five hundred knights and twenty thousand infantry to Gascony, under the command of John St. John, John of Brittany, and that very brave soldier, William Latimer. He had intended to follow them at an early date; but, at the critical moment, an awkward renewal of the Welsh troubles, under Madoc, son of Llywelyn ab Gruffyth, sent him in hot haste to Conway.

October, 1294.

Welsh insurrection.

Edward's lieutenant, the Earl of Lincoln and Salisbury, hastily summoned from Portsmouth, had received a rather severe defeat in November; and the King himself, for some time after his arrival in Wales, was in straits. But a vigorous winter campaign reduced Madoc to sue for peace, which he purchased by the disgraceful surrender of his accomplice, Morgan; and by the spring of 1295 Edward was once more free to turn his attention to the French War.

The Gascon expedition.

1294.

Things had at first gone fairly well with the English expedition. After one false start, occasioned by bad weather, it had reached the Gironde about the end of October, and received the surrender of Castillon. Returning towards the mouth of the estuary, it quickly captured Macau, and, in spite of the presence of the French garrison, the important town of Bourg. The fall of Blaye soon followed; and then the fleet proceeded to attack the great city of Bordeaux, the key of the duchy. At first the English were baffled; but, the little town of Rions having opportunely surrendered, they were able, for the first time, to disembark their horses and get into real working order. Dividing the force into two sections, Edward's lieutenant, John St. John, marched himself to the relief of Bayonne, leaving a substantial force with John of Brittany and William Latimer to continue the conquest of the country round Bordeaux. The expedition of St. John was successful; the citizens of Bayonne welcomed their old governor with open arms, and before Christmas Gascony was once more in English hands.

But this easy progress did not last. The real struggle was to come. Apparently, the French King had been ignorant of the strength of the English army, and he now set about the conquest of Gascony in good earnest.

Arrival of the Count of Valois.

Arriving before Rions on Palm Sunday, the French army took advantage of a disgraceful scene of riot among the English and Gascons, to capture and destroy the town, making several important prisoners, amongst whom was one Thomas Turberville, afterwards notorious as a French spy. The French, under Charles of Valois, afterwards received, however, a check before St. Sever on the Adour, and both sides appear, by the arrival of Easter, to have been willing to think of a peace, or, at least, a truce.

1295.

In the general state of European confusion, in which almost all the Powers were pledged to one side or the other, the obvious mediator was the occupant of the Papal throne. Unhappily, that occupant had, until lately, been Celestine V., a man of saintly and amiable private life, but totally unfitted for his position. However, at the previous Christmas, Charles of Valois had persuaded Celestine to retire, and, by a somewhat suspicious juggling with the election machinery, Boniface VIII. (Benedict of Gaeta), a masterful spirit, who longed to continue the policy of Hildebrand and Innocent III., was seated in the Papal chair. His presence soon made itself felt; and, when Edward returned from Wales in the spring of 1295, it was to meet the two Cardinal envoys of Boniface, who came to arrange a peace.

Offers of Papal mediation.

FRENCH KNIGHT OF THE THIRTEENTH CENTURY.

(*From Viollet le Duc's " Dict. du Mobilier Français."*)

Edward was far too wise to incur the anger of the new Pope by any disrespect to his ambassadors. The Cardinals arrived on the 29th June; and, so soon as he heard of their approach, Edward summoned a Great Council of the magnates to meet at Westminster on the 1st August, and accord them a fitting reception. The Council, which comprised, in addition to the permanent officials, eighteen bishops, fifty-three abbots and priors, twelve earls, seventy-eight barons, and the heads of the three great religious orders of the Hospitallers, the Templars, and the Gilbertines, duly assembled; and in it Edmund Crouchback and the Earl of Lincoln temperately stated the English case for the benefit of the Cardinals. Edward firmly refused to grant a peace, or even a truce, without consulting his ally, the Emperor; but eventually, in spite of an ill-timed attack of the French on Dover, he seems to have consented to a suspension of hostilities until the beginning of November.

Arrival of the Cardinals.

The King had need of all his caution and all his strength. For, probably during the proceedings of the Council, he had become aware of an understanding formed between Balliol and the French Court. On the 3rd July, Balliol had definitely authorised his agents to treat for the marriage of his son with a daughter of Charles of Valois, the French King's brother, and Edward's deadly rival; and this ominous advance ripened rapidly into a treaty of alliance between Scotland, Norway, and France, which was signed on October 22nd following. Edward did not openly

Alliance between France and Scotland.

break with Balliol at once; but the state of his mind is clearly shown by the fact, that in mid-October he took into his own hands the border castles
1295. of Berwick, Roxburgh, and Jedburgh.

Before this, however, Edward had taken two memorable steps of infinite importance, which will forever make the year 1295 famous in English history. Both of them, no doubt, arose out of the presence of immediate necessity; both were, nevertheless, destined to be graven in the rock of English national life. The first of these was the organisation of the coast guard; the other, the casting of Parliament into its permanent mould.

The coast guard.

Edward had long been anxious about the defence of the coast; and the repeated attacks on Dover had not failed to teach him a lesson. The danger was complicated by the presence in the southern counties of numerous foreign ecclesiastics, who were strongly suspected of sending useful information across the Channel. As temporary measures, Edward, in September, 1295, ordered these suspicious persons to be placed under native guard, and their ships drawn up on the beach and deprived of tackle. He also, by a counter-stroke of genius, produced a cloud of useful spies upon French movements by granting permission to the sailors of Holland, Friesland, and Iceland to fish off the eastern coasts. But his systematic scheme for the defence of the coasts was the important measure. It began with a complete organisation of the counties of Norfolk, Suffolk, and Essex, under Peter of Dunwich, in the autumn and winter of 1295, and was afterwards gradually extended throughout the entire coasts. In each maritime county there was to be a warden in charge of the coast defences at a salary of two shillings a day. A list of the harbours in each Hundred was to be drawn up; and at each harbour a guard of four, six, eight, or even twelve foot-soldiers was to be stationed, each man receiving twopence a day. In each Hundred there was to be an official at threepence a day, and over every two or three Hundreds a supervisor of knightly rank at sixpence. Thus there would not only be a watch at each vulnerable point, but a machinery which could immediately concentrate at a given spot in the event of an attack. The whole of the county was to be assessed for the maintenance of the guard.

The Great Parliament.

The other momentous step of the autumn of 1295 was the assembling of the Model Parliament. The dangers which were crowding round the King threw him on his safest and soundest support—the trust of his own people. Whatever his motives, Edward shewed both his courage and his wisdom in determining to bring together a Parliament which should be thoroughly representative of all the great interests of the nation. That, in so doing, his great object was to secure money rather than advice is perhaps true. Even the principles of feudalism did not demand that a king should consult the ordinary landowners of his kingdom, still less the burgesses of the chartered boroughs, upon questions of foreign policy. But they did demand that he should consult his immediate supporters, his "tenants-in-chief"; and the vital point in the growth of the national spirit in England during the thirteenth century was that the feudal right of revolt, the last and dangerous remedy of a vassal against his lord who broke the spirit of the feudal bond, had been extending, under the favourable influences of agricultural prosperity and commercial success, far beyond the limits of the King's immediate vassals, the "tenants-in-chief."* The change in the ranks of the landowners is sharply marked by the contrast between the "all others who hold of us in chief," who, by the famous clause of the Charter of 1215, were to be summoned by the sheriffs of the counties to take part in the Common Council of the Realm, and the mere knights who, by the writs of 1261, 1264, and 1290, were to be chosen by the freeholder of the County Court, and who, since the middle of the thirteenth century, had superseded for Parliamentary, though not for military purposes, the smaller "tenants-in-chief." The introduction by Simon of Montfort into his famous Parliament of 1265 of the still newer class of burgesses, marks, of course, a yet further breakdown of the exclusiveness of feudalism, and a yet further advance towards the national ideal. In adopting both these changes in his famous Parliament of November, 1295, Edward was honestly and wisely following the trend of public opinion.

The knights.

The burgesses.

But the King had special reasons for making his Parliament yet more comprehensive. He knew that

* Edward had taken skilful advantage of the silent change in sentiment, when in 1278 he had insisted upon knighthood being assumed by all freeholders of £20 a year, "of whatsoever lord they hold."

the darling policy of the Papal see, the separation of the clergy from the laity, as a caste outside the nation, had a strong champion in the newly elected Pope, Boniface VIII.; and he determined to checkmate it by an adroit move. He knew, also, that the provinces of Canterbury and York had recently organised themselves into two formidable provincial synods or convocations, consisting of the bishops, the abbots, the priors, and the archdeacons of the province, and the "proctors," or agents of the cathedral and parochial clergy. It was the plausible argument of the clerical party, that all the affairs of the clergy should be discussed and settled only in these bodies, which so far recognised the existence of the secular arm, that they only assembled with the King's license,* but which were, of course, purely clerical bodies. Edward determined to include both the Convocations at one swoop in his National Parliament. The bishops and greater abbots had long been accustomed to receive summons to Parliaments as "magnates," *i. e.*, in their capacity of great feudal landowners. But, on this occasion, each bishop found, appended to his usual writ, a clause "warning" him that his attendance alone would not be sufficient, but that he was to take care to bring with him the prior (or dean, as the case might be) of his cathedral chapter, the archdeacons of his diocese, one proctor or agent for his cathedral chapter, and two for his diocesan clergy.†

The clerical proctors.

The *Præmunientes* clause.

* Edward himself had established this rule.

† Of course this statement is not literally correct. Some of the cathedrals had no chapters at this time.

Thus was constituted the great and famous Parliament, which assembled at Westminster on the 27th November, 1295. Two archbishops, eighteen bishops (including those of the four Welsh sees), sixty-six abbots, three heads of religious Orders, nine earls, forty-one barons, sixty-three knights of the shire,* and one hundred and seventy-two citizens and burgesses,† besides the clergy representatives, met to consider the national crisis. It is one of the vivid realities of history that we know the actual names, not merely of the prelates and great nobles, but even of the humble burgesses and clerical proctors, who came flocking to Westminster in the dark days of November, 1295. The language of the summons was worthy of the occasion. Touching briefly upon the dangers which threatened the realm, it quoted the great principle of self-government, that what concerns all should be discussed of all; and, though this may have been intended as a mere rhetorical flourish, it is to us the keynote of the drama. After a century of struggle and experiment, a great National Parliament had come into

Importance of the occasion.

Language of the summons.

* Apparently there are no returns for Durham (as a palatine), Chester (the like), Monmouth (not yet formed), Leicestershire, Norfolk, Suffolk, Warwick, Westmoreland, Wiltshire, and Worcestershire. But, with the exception of the first three cases, this is no doubt merely from accidental loss of documents. Bedford seems to have sent three knights, Hampshire four; the remaining shires two each.

† These represent eighty-six boroughs, very unevenly distributed. Yorkshire includes eleven, Hampshire nine, Devon and Sussex six each. Devonshire, apparently, held fresh elections after the prorogation, when one member was taken away from Totnes and given to Exeter.

being, to serve as a centre and focus of national life for at least six centuries. For more than five centuries of this period, the legal form of the Parliament remained theoretically unchanged. It is true that the minor clergy ceased actually to form a part of the sitting Parliament from the middle of the fourteenth century; but they long continued to assemble at the commencement of the session, and, even at this day, the *præmunientes*, or "warning," clause appears in the writs of summons to Parliament addressed to the bishops.* At any rate, Edward gained his point—that the clergy were an integral part of the nation, and bound to bear their share of the national burdens. The abbots, of course, disappeared with the Reformation; but this was a measure of ecclesiastical, not of Parliamentary reform. The county elections were slightly regulated by statute in the fifteenth century, but no substantial change was made, either in numbers or qualifications. The Welsh shires and the counties of Chester and Monmouth were added in the sixteenth century, the county of Durham in the seventeenth; but these steps involved no new principle. The storms of the Civil War passed away, leaving Parliament as it had been before

* Until the 17th century, beneficed clergymen could neither vote for nor be elected as members of the House of Commons, on the ground that they were already represented by the clerical proctors. At the Restoration, Archbishop Sheldon, on behalf of the Church, gave up the formal right to vote the clerical taxes in Convocation, and the beneficed clergy were admitted as freeholders to electoral rights for and in the House of Commons. They were again disqualified from sitting by Act of Parliament in 1801.

them.* The number of boroughs represented varied, owing to local causes, till the end of the fifteenth century; and was increased by royal charters in the sixteenth and early seventeenth. But the varied and picturesque anomalies of the old borough franchise remained untouched, till they degenerated into the mass of festering corruption which was swept away by the Reform Act of 1832.

The Model Parliament voted Edward a subsidy of one-eleventh of the goods of the nobility and the landowners, and one-seventh of the goods of the burgesses. But it by no means banished his troubles. All through the autumn he had been making strenuous efforts for the war in Gascony, raising 25,000 crossbowmen from the southern counties, and ten thousand infantry from Ireland. Though the King consented, at the request of the Pope, to send a mission to Cambrai at the New Year to treat for peace, he despatched a strong fleet of 250 ships from Plymouth a fortnight later; and this fleet, after plundering St. Mathieu in Brittany, attacked Brest, and, reaching the coast of Gascony, revived the hitherto unsuccessful siege of Bordeaux. But Edward himself dared not leave the country until he had settled with the Scots. He had ordered the Earl Marshal to muster the forces of the northern counties at Newcastle on March 1, 1296. On the 31st, John Comyn, the younger,† invaded

Renewal of the war.

1296.

The Scottish campaign.

* Of course there were endless changes between 1641 and 1660; but these were quietly ignored at the Restoration.

† *I. e.*, the son of John Comyn, Balliol's brother-in-law. At least

England at the head of a Scottish army, reaching Carlisle, where, however, he was turned back. Hurrying north, Edward captured Berwick, inflicting great loss on the Scots, and then, pushing on with vigour, came up with the main Scottish army, which was attempting to relieve Dunbar, then besieged by the English advance guard. **Battle of Dunbar.** The actual credit of the battle (of which there is not very much, for the Scots seem to have fled at the first charge) fell to the Earl of Warenne and Surrey, the English general, who, with the Bishop of Durham, had preceded Edward. But the King came up in time to receive the surrender of the castle; and the fall of Dunbar was followed by the fall of Roxburgh, Edinburgh, and Stirling. At this juncture (midsummer) Edward was 1296. joined by large reinforcements from Ireland and Wales; and the Scottish resistance completely collapsed. It had been a baronial quarrel all through, with a strong French influence. The leading Scottish nobles had set up a Court of Twelve Peers, in imitation of the French model, and had looked for support to the French King, who now abandoned them in their hour of need. Balliol made an absolute submission, and was followed by the leading nobles, including the Bruces.* Edward's action was

---

this is probably so; but the three John Comyns are almost as much a nuisance as the four Robert Bruces. Balliol's brother-in-law was nicknamed "the Black"; his son, "the Red."

* The old Bruce (the competitor) had died on March 31st, having incurred the displeasure of the other Scottish nobles by holding aloof from the rebellion. His son, the husband of the heiress of Carrick,

extreme and injudicious. He declared the kingdom forfeited, broke the Great Seal, made a triumphal procession through the southern Highlands, and traversed the ancient kingdom of Moray as far as Elgin. Then, turning south, he visited Scone, whence he carried off the ancient coronation stone, and, finally, held a great Council at Berwick, where he received the submission of the Scottish bishops and leading nobles, in August. Many of the actual combatants, *e. g.*, Alexander Comyn, the Earls of Athol and Ross, and William Lindsay, had already been sent south in custody; and the King forbade Balliol and the Comyns to appear north of the Trent. The great offices of the Scottish kingdom were placed in English hands. The Earl of Surrey, the victor of Dunbar, was made Warden of the Realm, Henry Percy, Warden of Galloway, and Walter of Huntercombe, Warden of Edinburgh; a new Seal was struck and entrusted to Walter of Amersham. Hugh Cressingham was made Treasurer. The abbey lands were restored, and an allowance was made to widows out of the forfeited estates of their husbands. Having, as he thought, thoroughly finished his work, the King turned southwards in September. He had summoned a Parliament to meet at Bury St. Edmunds in November. To all appearance, he guessed nothing of the hostile national feeling which his proceedings in Scotland had aroused.

Edward's harshness.

now became "Bruce the Elder" or "Bruce of Anandale"; the latter's son Robert, the eventual king, is called "Bruce the Younger" or "Bruce of Carrick."

In the south, things had gone by no means prosperously for Edward. All the efforts of the English expedition had failed to take Bordeaux; and in May, the King's brother Edmund, the leader of the expedition, had died, leaving the command to the Earl of Lincoln. The Earl carried on a desultory warfare for the next twelve months, doing, in all probability, as much to incense the Gascons as to protect them, and suffering a decided defeat in the attempt to relieve Bellegarde, when the troops under John St. John were routed in the wood of Peyrehorade by the Count of Artois, and St. John himself, the seneschal of Gascony, was captured.

Failure of the Gascon expedition.

Feb., 1297.

A far more serious blow, however, had been dealt to Edward's plans by the publication, in February, 1296, of the celebrated Papal Bull *Clericis Laicos*, so called from the opening words of its contents. In it, Boniface, supported by the resolution of a Council, and appealing to his apostolic authority, roundly and absolutely forbade all clerical persons, regular or secular, and all clerical foundations, including the universities, to grant, under any disguise whatever, any material, and especially any pecuniary support, to any potentate whomsoever, without the express authority of the Papal see. It was, in fact, a declaration of war between Church and State, and, while it justified, in the most striking way, Edward's policy of the previous year, it, nevertheless, appeared to close to him one of the most prolific

The Bull *Clericis Laicos*.

sources of revenue, and to put the crown on his financial difficulties. A new valuation of clerical incomes had been made, only five years previously, on the occasion of the grant of a clerical subsidy by Nicholas IV., for the purposes of the crusade; and this new valuation had, no doubt, revealed to the King the almost boundless wealth of the Church, and raised his hopes of future taxation.

The effect of the Bull *Clericis Laicos* was speedily seen in the Parliament which met at Bury St.

Quarrel with the clergy.

Edmund's on November 3rd, 1296. This Parliament followed the elaborate model of the previous year; and contained magnates, clergy, knights of the shire, and burgesses. The French King was notoriously making great preparations for the invasion of England; in fact, there had actually been attempts on Dover and Hythe in September. So urgent was the necessity, that the magnates and the lay representatives voted a grant of a twelfth (an eighth from the boroughs). But the clergy, headed by Robert Winchelsey, the new Primate, formally refused to grant a penny, alleging, as their excuse, their inability to act in defiance of the Papal bull.

Edward was determined to accept the challenge offered by the Church; but he acted with coolness

The clergy are outlawed.

and deliberation. He placed his seals on the tithe barns of the clergy, so that they could not convert their goods into cash.

1297.

But, instead of continuing the argument, he adjourned the Parliament to 13th January, in London, bidding the clergy be ready with a better answer at that time. On the appointed day, the clergy met in Convocation,* and repeated their refusal.

This time Edward struck heavily. The Pope had threatened excommunication against anyone who should obey his temporal Prince rather than his spiritual Father. By excommunication, of course, the offender was thrust forth from the membership and protection of the Church. All that elaborate network of religious ceremony which, in medieval Christendom, wrapped about the daily life of the member of the Church, was rudely rent away. He dared not set foot in a place of worship. No priest would bless his marriage or baptise his child. In his hour of sickness, the sacramental wafer was withheld, and, on his death, his body was refused a burial in consecrated ground.† The daily Mass, the Sunday festival, the frequent celebration of the Saints, which made up so much of the brightness and joy of medieval life, were not for him. He was a spiritual outcast, naked and shivering. Very good. But Edward was determined to show that there had grown up, beside the Church, another power, which also held thunders in reserve. The precise analogy of the excommunication of the Church was the outlawry of the State. As the Church withdrew her spiritual protection from the excommunicate, so

* The see of York was vacant; and it is possible that the northern clergy gave way sooner than their brethren of the Canterbury province.

† It is true that the Bull, *Clericis Laicos*, allowed death-bed absolution; but it was a grudging concession.

the State withdrew its secular protection from the outlaw. To all appeals for help against oppression and wrong, the State would then reply coldly, that it recognised no duty to the applicant. Its courts were not for him, its officials did not admit his existence, he had no civil rights, whether he lived or died the State did not care; he was a mere animal, a *caput lupinum*, outside the King's peace.

This terrible weapon the King turned at once against the whole of the clergy. His own officers seized their goods, for they no longer had property which the State would recognise. Anyone who liked might plunder their houses, and attack their persons; for the King's courts would not listen to their complaints, and no other tribunal could protect them. This was the point which Edward wished to bring home to the Church. If the clergy despised the royal courts, and clung to their own clerical tribunals, let them see what the latter were worth—whether they could restore the Primate's horses, or punish the open violence which the clergy suffered on the highways.

It was a bitter lesson; but it was speedily learned. Under cover of a polite fiction, the archbishop-elect of York (Henry of Newark), and the bishops of Durham, Ely, and Salisbury, paid a fifth part of their goods. The Primate stubbornly held out, and lived for a while, attended by a single priest and a single clerk, under the sheltering roof of a humble parson. He even went so far as to beg his bread on the highway. But it was of no use. Such melodrama might have moved the weak

The clergy give way.

heart of Henry III.; Edward viewed it with a scornful curl of the lip. Before long, the Sheriff of Lincoln, acting in friendly collusion with the bishop, seized a fifth of the episcopal goods; the monasteries had to pay a fourth to get their lands out of the custody of the King's officials. On the 1st March, 1297, the King issued commissions to the sheriffs of the counties, to receive the submission of the clergy, on the hard terms of paying double the amount of taxation demanded in the Parliament of the previous autumn. By the end of the month, even the stubborn Primate had given in, saying: "Let each man save his own soul."

Significance of the struggle.

Whatever may be thought of the wisdom or the morality of Edward in this matter, the importance of the question and the courage of the act are beyond doubt. The King's victory virtually anticipated, by two centuries, the struggle of the Reformation. He could now feel that the Crown, the State, was the strongest power in the land. In his desperate courage, the King determined to go still further, and prove that the Crown was stronger than all the other powers in the land combined. But here he was mistaken, as the sequel will show.

Quarrel with the earls.

For, whilst he had been seizing the goods of the clergy, the King had also made a daring attack on the wool of the merchants. Bidding the latter bring down their whole stores to certain ports, he seized every fifth sack, and demanded from its owner a "maletolte,"* or tax of

*This was, of course, an addition to the "ancient custom" of half a mark granted by the Parliament of 1275 (see p. 174).

18

forty shillings, as the price of its release. In the face of the storm excited by these proceedings, the King had the courage to come before a Parliament of magnates at Salisbury on February 24th, and coolly detail his plans for the campaign.

1297.

Following the example of the clergy, the earls and barons defied the King. For the last five years they had cherished a grudge against him, ever since, at the first Parliament of 1290, he had taken an effective revenge for the Statute *De Donis* (see p. 208). It had long been a vexed question of the law, whether a feudal tenant had the right, without his lord's consent, to sub-grant the whole, or part, of the land granted to himself by that lord. The King's judges, as we gather clearly from the language of Bracton, had leaned in favour of liberty of action by the tenant. But the great feudal landowners complained, that this liberty rendered it almost impossible for them to collect their feudal dues, by raising all kinds of complicated questions as to who was really liable to pay them. To a lawyer, it is clear that the magnates had a real grievance; but it would hardly be possible to explain it in detail without going into technicalities. On the other hand, the feudal tie was becoming less and less real; and feudalism, from being a principle of social and political organisation, was dwindling into a special, and rather cumbrous, form of landownership. In the interests of commerce, it was especially necessary that all landholders, and especially the

The Statute *Quia Emptores*.

smaller landholders, should be able to alienate their lands.

The great landowners, however, thought otherwise; and, just as they had largely succeeded in spoiling the Statute of Merchants by the counterstroke of the Statute *De Donis* (see p. 208), so they had proposed, in the Parliament of 1290, to neutralise the tendency of the King's courts, by obtaining a formal declaration against the alienation of land. They, accordingly, presented a petition, in which the evils of the practice of *subinfeudation* were detailed. The petition was accepted by the King, who ordered his officials to turn it into a statute. But, when the roll came to be examined, it was found that the officials, whilst gravely recording the proposal of the Statute by the "magnates and other lords," and solemnly forbidding the process of *subinfeudation*,* had expressly authorised the far more sweeping practice of complete alienation to a purchaser who stepped completely into the shoes of the seller, and became immediate tenant of the lord in his place. In other words, whilst forbidding *subinfeudation*, the Statute expressly authorised *substitution*. Thus the Statute *Quia Emptores*, instead of being, as its promoters had fondly hoped, the bulwark of feudal exclusiveness, virtually made land an article of commerce, by allowing it to be freely bought and sold.†

* The prohibition of subinfeudation only applied to the creation of sub-tenures "in fee simple." Subinfeudation for life, or "in tail" was not forbidden.

† The truth of this account of the Statute, though resting mainly on internal evidence, is proved by the fact that the Statute was never

It may readily be imagined, that the baronage became more and more incensed against the King, as the results of the Statute *Quia Emptores* became plain. And now, whilst Edward was unpopular with the clergy and the merchants, and his hands were tied by a foreign war, they saw their chance of revenge. And there was a certain poetic justice in the fact, that they used as their weapon a plea more technical even than Edward's own manœuvre of 1290. The King requested certain of the earls to cross with their forces into Gascony, where, as we have seen, the English army was in sore straits. The earls refused; and, when pressed for reasons, Norfolk (the Marshal) and Hereford (the Constable) alleged that the Court offices they held, being originally of a domestic character, entitled them to remain in personal attendance on the King. With the King they would go; without him they would not stir. This did not suit the views of Edward, who proposed himself to open the campaign in the Low Countries, where he had just succeeded in making a great alliance against the French King. Turning fiercely upon the Earl Marshal, Edward gave way to a wrath which fixed itself deeply on the minds of his contemporaries. "By God, Sir Earl, thou shalt go or hang." "By the same oath," replied the Earl calmly, "I will neither go nor hang." And, without obtaining leave, the earls withdrew from the Parliament, threatening to raise an army against the King.

The earls refuse to go to Gascony.

---

held to bind the Crown. The King's immediate vassals could not alienate without license till 1660.

Things now looked as black for Edward as they well could do. But he seized the opportunity of the submission of the clergy to reconcile himself with the Church, and, boldly disregarding the threats of the earls, he appeared in London, where, on the 14th July, he held an informal gathering of the magnates, clergy, and citizens before the great hall of Westminster. Many of the magnates did fealty to the young Prince Edward, whom his father, with striking confidence, committed to the special care of his late foe, Archbishop Winchelsey. Then, turning to the assembled multitude, Edward threw himself in passionate self-abandonment on their sense of justice, freely admitting the irregularity of his acts, but pleading that his conduct had been induced, not by luxury or extravagance, but by the real and public needs of his position. Deeply moved, the assembly swore to stand by Edward in life and in death; and then, in lofty contempt of the worst that the earls could do, the King set out for the coast, where he had ordered every available soldier to meet him on August 1st. Such acts of splendid courage and insight reveal Edward's personal genius for rule, and explain much of his apparently mysterious power.

Edward appeals to the people.

But, before he left England, Edward received two announcements of a formidable character. One was, that the discontented earls were embodying their grievances in a formal document, which could not fail to remind Edward of the ominous "Articles" of his grandfather's and father's reigns. The Remonstrance reached him at Winchel-

The articles of the earls.

sea, and contained far too much unpleasant truth to be lightly set aside. The King sent, for immediate answer, that part of his Council was in London and part abroad; and that he could not be expected to attend to a matter of such magnitude in the absence of his advisers. The other item of news was that of the national rising of Scotland, the importance of which it is probable that Edward underrated. Still, it seemed sheer madness to leave the country in the face of these problems; but Edward trusted Winchelsey to deal with the barons, whilst he, no doubt, firmly believed, that the best way to stop Scottish trouble was by striking a blow at Philip of France, whom he rightly suspected to have been the instigator of the revolt of Balliol in the previous year.

The rising in Scotland.

In the matter of the English grievances, Edward's action, rash as it seemed, was fully justified. No sooner had the King sailed, than the earls came to London and forbade the collection of the taxes granted by the Parliament of Salisbury. Edward had already anticipated this source of revenue, by ordering the seizure, on July 30th, of eight thousand sacks of wool, to be paid for out of the proceeds of the grant; and he had left orders that the collection of the taxes should go on. But the earls assumed a really national position, by taking the citizens into their confidence; and Winchelsey took the wisest possible step, by summoning a Great Council,* or Parliament

Revolt of the earls.

* There seem to have been much hesitation and fluctuation in collecting the Council; but the result is that stated in the text.

of magnates and elected knights, to Rochester for Michaelmas. Here the quarrel between the King and the barons was thoroughly discussed, and the Prince, on behalf of his father, undertook to renew, in solemn form, a Confirmation of the Charters which had been issued by Edward at the Salisbury Parliament in the previous February, with the important addition of clauses designed to affirm beyond dispute the illegality of the recent seizures of Church treasure, and the "maletolte" on wool. Thereupon the Prince and the Archbishop undertook to mediate between the King and the earls; and the assembly granted a subsidy of a ninth, which was afterwards confirmed by the citizens of London (somewhat irregularly) on behalf of the boroughs. On the 5th November these arrangements were formally approved by the King, who was then at Ghent; and the Confirmation of the Charters, with its appendant articles, took its place on the Roll in due course, as a great landmark of constitutional progress. A somewhat imperfect paraphrase of the articles, known as the Statute of Tallage, seems to have been circulated soon after; and this document was declared by the Court of Exchequer Chamber, in the famous Ship Money case, decided in 1638, to have the force of an Act of Parliament.*

Confirmation of the Charters.

Meanwhile, the futile and costly French war was

* The six judges who took this view based their conclusion mainly upon the fact that the document had been explicitly recognised as a statute in the famous Petition of Right, accepted by Charles I. in 1628.

coming to an end. Philip knew that he had committed a gross outrage in seizing Gascony; he had now realised that Edward was not the man to submit to injustice. The English King had raised up a formidable league, against which Philip's Norwegian and Scottish alliance could do little. On the other hand, Edward wished to be back to deal with the growing trouble in Scotland. In these circumstances both parties agreed to accept the mediation of Benedict of Gaeta, who in public life was, it will be remembered, no less a person than Pope Boniface VIII. This harmless fiction enabled Edward to avail himself of the good offices of the man who had issued the *Clericis Laicos*, without acknowledging the claims of the Holy See. The Pope's award was not published until midsummer, 1298; but every one knew that it must compel Philip to disgorge his plunder. The way was smoothed by the plan of a double marriage, between Edward himself and the French King's sister, Margaret, and the Prince and the same King's little daughter, Isabella.* The Scots were left to their fate. Edward had returned to England in the middle of March, and at once prepared to march northward.

End of the French War.

* The definitive treaty was actually not signed till 1303 (20th May) at Paris. But Edward married Margaret in 1299; and peace was assumed to exist from the spring of 1298.

CHAPTER XII

CLOSING YEARS

1297—1307

THE last ten years of Edward's life proved to be a terrible punishment for the one great mistake in his career. Had he not attempted the fatal and impossible task of destroying Scottish independence, he might, to all appearance, have reaped the fruits of a noble life in a peaceful and glorious old age. His second marriage proved far happier than might have been expected. Though Margaret of France could never replace the wife of his youth, the brave and gentle Eleanor of Castile, she seems to have loved her husband. She bore him children; and, as far as can be judged, escaped the odium which a French marriage had brought upon the King's unhappy father, and which another French marriage was destined to bring on his yet more unhappy son. But the doom which drove Edward to pursue to the bitter end his hopeless struggle with Scotland, poisoned all the peace of his latter years, and all but lost him the well-earned love of his English subjects. Whilst we cannot fail to admire the indomitable courage and endurance which sustained the old King during his Scottish campaign, we cannot but mourn the waste of so much splendid energy. The only bright features of the period are the steady growth of national unity in Scotland, and the steady growth of popular freedom in England. For both of these results Edward is in a way responsible; but they were due to his failures, not to his success.

The national rising in Scotland.

So confident had Edward been, that his work in Scotland was done, that, in July, 1297, he had released many of his Scottish prisoners, on condition that they should accompany him abroad. But at Michaelmas of that year came news from the North, which showed that the struggle had only passed into a new and far more serious stage. The disappearance of the Scottish baronage from the scene had left the leadership of the Scots open to any one strong enough to assume it, and, at the critical moment, there had appeared, as the national champion, Sir William Wallace, a simple knight, but descended of a good family which, probably Welsh in its origin, had settled in Ayr and Renfrew some hundred and fifty years before. Whilst Balliol had been amusing himself by carving out new sheriffdoms for his noble supporters, and trusting to the broken reed of a French alliance, Wallace had been slowly collecting a mass of sturdy yeomen, who, in the autumn of 1297, drew together in the Ochil Hills, and threatened the English forces in Stirling. The Earl of Warenne, Edward's viceroy, disdainful of

Wallace.

the new Scottish champion, whom the aristocratic officials of both countries persisted in regarding as a mere freebooter, determined, in spite of the earnest warnings of his generals, to charge the Scottish forces across the narrow bridge of Cambuskenneth, which spanned the river Forth below Stirling. Wallace, whose forces were concealed in the woods of the opposite bank, quietly allowed him to send across the bridge so many of the English troops as he felt well able to master. Then, swooping down, he easily blocked the passage of the main army, whilst he surrounded and cut off the five thousand helpless English who were forming up on the northern bank. The rout was complete. The Earl of Warenne fled, panic-stricken, to Berwick; while Wallace overran the Lowlands, and, dashing across the border, carried fire and sword into the counties of Northumberland, Cumberland, and Westmoreland. A counter raid by Robert Clifford upon Anandale brought the year to a close, without any very decisive action; but it was clear that Wallace and Moray, who styled themselves "leaders of the Army of the Scottish Kingdom in the name of Lord John," could not be allowed to remain at large, if the English supremacy was to be maintained.

Cambuskenneth.
Sept. 11, 1297.

The Prince and his guardians did the best they could in Edward's absence. Although the King was demanding more men for service in Flanders, they directed the assembling of a great army of knights and infantry at Newcastle on December 6th. The reconciliation with the earls

The Prince's measures.

having, fortunately, just taken place, there was a prospect of united action; and the appointment to the
1297. supreme command of the Earl of Warenne,
despite his defeat at Cambuskenneth, shows the respect which was paid to Edward's arrangements, even in his absence. The Scottish nobles were summoned to the Parliament fixed for York on
1298. February 14th. Not unnaturally, they
failed to appear; but the English nobles, cheered by the sight of the vast number of English soldiers who had assembled in obedience to the royal writs,* and by the news that Edward himself was coming to take command of his troops, determined to begin the attack. Moving forward with deliberation, the English army reoccupied Berwick, and then sat down to await the King's arrival.

Having summoned a Parliament of knights and burgesses† to assemble at York on May 25th, the
Arrival of Edward. King journeyed northward, and reached
the border about Midsummer Day. He had moved the Exchequer and the Bench to York,
1298. and, as usual, meant business. Pressing
forward in good order, the English army crossed the Tweed, and marched through the Lothians, capturing a few castles on the way. So deliberate were its movements, that Wallace conceived the scheme of starving it into retreat; but his plans were

---

*These are placed as high as 3,200 cavalry and 100,000 infantry.

†The magnates were already in the north; but the King took the precaution of sending special summons to the lately reconciled Earls of Norfolk and Hereford.

betrayed, and he found himself compelled to give battle near Falkirk on July 22nd, 1298. Wallace's position was admirably chosen. His rear was protected by a hill, and his front by a "moss," or morass. His numerous pikemen were drawn up in four dense "schiltrons." Behind them lay his small body of one thousand horse; a few archers were on the flanks of the schiltrons. The King attacked in the customary three "battles," himself leading the centre, with the Earls of Norfolk and Hereford on the right, and the warlike Bishop of Durham (Antony Bek) on the left. The English right was very nearly lost in the morass; but managed to save itself by a long circuit, which brought it on the left flank of the Scottish army. Bek, on the left, did not fall into the trap, but led his troops to the left, clear of the morass, where he wisely resolved to halt them till the arrival of the centre, which was following him. But his insubordinate feudal followers insisted on hurling themselves at once on the Scottish right wing, just when the Earl of Norfolk was making a similar attack on the Scottish left.

Falkirk.

The double onslaught produced little effect on the solid masses of the Scots, though it drove away their horsemen in disgraceful rout; and the issue of the battle hung in suspense when Edward arrived on the scene. In a flash he formed his plans. Halting his cavalry, he brought his sturdy archers to the front, and these took deliberate and deadly aim at the huge masses of the schiltrons. The Scottish pikemen dared not break their ranks, for they knew it was hopeless to charge the main body of the English horse; and the English archers would have vanished long before they came within reach of the Scottish spears. In a few moments awful gaps began to show in the schiltrons, and into these the English knights charged home. The pikemen broke and fled, the battle became a rout, the rout a massacre. Many thousands of the Scotch were slain or drowned; the English suffered little.

For the moment the Scottish resistance was at an end, and the King proceeded leisurely eastwards to

Edward's policy.

St. Andrews, laying waste the country. Lack of provisions, however, soon drove him south, where he had summoned a Council of magnates for Pentecost at Carlisle. At

1299. this Council he assumed openly the character of conqueror, distributing the Scottish lands amongst his English followers, but reserving a few estates, as a bait to attract the return of the wavering Scottish nobles. The curious position occupied by the latter is well shown by the fact, that the younger Bruce, who had served under Antony Bek at Falkirk, had deserted Edward soon after the battle, and shut himself up in the castle of Annan.

From Carlisle, Edward made his way south to London, where he held a Parliament of magnates,

Second Confirmation of the Charters.

knights, and burgesses, at the beginning of Lent. The earls were again mutinous, and demanded another Confirmation of the Charters, which Edward at length granted, though with a saving of the rights of the Crown, which aroused discontent. The King, in his want of money, had given much offence by levying heavy fines for alleged trespasses within the bounds of the royal forests; and he had to consent to the appointment of a commission of nine, for the purpose of ascertaining the forest boundaries. A useful but severe reform of the coinage added to the popular ill-will. A diversion was, however, created by the arrival, at the beginning of July, of the Papal legates, bearing the award of the Pope in the dispute between England and France. With the contents of this award we are already acquainted (see p. 280); but the legates had another message to deliver, to the effect that Boniface, having looked into the pages of history, had decided to end the Scottish question by claiming Scotland as a fief of the Papal See.

The Papal claim on Scotland.

Edward appears at first to have treated the claim as a jest; for he not only carried out the terms of the award, by celebrating his marriage with Margaret of France, but he even consented to hand over to the Papal envoys the ex-King of Scotland, John Balliol, who had long languished in the Tower, and now disappears from the scene.* It is just possible that Wallace, who had escaped from the slaughter of Falkirk, had employed his time in stirring up continental diplomacy against Edward, by visits to Paris and Rome. At any rate, he maintained a hitherto unexplained retirement during the five years which followed the battle. But Boniface was in no position to make good his preposterous claim. In the same year, he was defeated in a naval

The Pope's difficulties.

* He lived many years abroad in obscurity.

battle by Frederick of Sicily, a descendant of the ancient enemy of Papal pretentions, the Emperor Frederick II. He was known to be so hard pressed, that the Franciscans offered him a sum of 40,000 florins to be relieved from the rule of their Order which forbade them to acquire land. Boniface asked them where the money was. They replied incautiously, "In the hands of the merchants." Whereupon the Pope, reminding them of their vow of poverty, which forbade them to acquire money, no less than land, absolved the merchants from their trust, and compelled them, under pain of anathema, to hand over to him the funds entrusted to them by the Order. Such a foe was unscrupulous; but he was not likely to prove very dangerous to Edward, who seems to have treated the Papal claim to Scotland more as a means of arousing support in England than as a serious danger.

The rest of the year 1299 was employed in strenuous preparation for another attack on Scotland, and, at Christmas, Edward summoned a great Parliament, on the complete model of 1295, to meet at London on the 6th March following. The Parliament duly assembled, and Edward found himself attacked on all sides by complaints of irregularities. The Forest Commission had been dilatory and unsatisfactory. It was now replaced by a systematic visitation of fifteen counties, with a view of receiving complaints of violation of the Forest Charter. Somewhat later, special commissions were issued to three justices for each county, to hold a summary enquiry

The Parliament of London.

1300.

concerning breaches of either Charter, and of the Statute of Winchester. To crown all, the King not only republished the Charters, and directed them to be proclaimed four times every year in each county, but added to them a list of nineteen Articles dealing with new grievances, which, in reality, amount to a second Charter of Liberties. So strong was the critical spirit in this Parliament, that Edward does not seem even to have asked for a grant, which may be one reason why, after a somewhat inglorious summer campaign, he consented, at the request of the French King, to a truce with the Scots until Whitsuntide, 1301. Unhappily, the documents do not show by whom the Scots were represented in the proceedings.*

The Articles upon the Charters.

It had been arranged, in the Parliament of 1300, that a very full assembly of the estates of the realm should meet at Lincoln on January 20th, 1301, to discuss the returns of grievances which were expected from the enquiries of the previous summer and autumn, and to compose a formal answer to the Pope's claim on Scotland. In a sense, the Parliament of Lincoln may be looked upon as an adjournment; for the King directed that the same knights and burgesses should serve as in the previous year. But it has an interest of its own, for it contained not only a very full list of magnates,

Parliament of Lincoln.

* It would appear, from other sources, that the negotiations with Philip of France were conducted by John Comyn, John Soulis (who called himself "Warden of the kingdom") and the Bishop of St. Andrews. Many of the Scottish nobles were in Paris, whence, in 1303, they addressed an encouraging memorial to their compatriots.

councillors, officials, knights, and burgesses, but representatives of the two universities of Oxford and Cambridge, "wise persons and very skilful in the written law." The previous winter had been spent in a thorough search of the archives of the monasteries, with a view to the preparation of a crushing answer to the Pope's claim; and medieval views of history may be studied in the elaborate document produced by Edward to the Parliament, and perhaps forwarded to the Pope. Herein, after sketching the history of the island of Britain, from its conquest by Brutus of Troy in the days of Eli and Samuel, and its division by that potentate into three parts, England, Scotland, and Wales, the King touches lightly on an invasion of the Huns, which gave its name to the district of Humbria, and passes to the admitted supremacy of Arthur as overlord of all Britain. After this, the exploits of Alfred and Athelstan appear tame; and the King descends gradually to the forged charter attributed to Malcolm Ceanmore, and the sordid details of comparatively recent history.* The letter of the magnates, far shorter and more dignified, calmly rebuts, in terms which inevitably suggest the struggles of the Reformation, all claim to disposing authority over the realm of Scotland by the "mother church of Rome," and distinctly repudiates any liability of an English king to answer in respect of any secular rights to any tribunal, ecclesiastical or civil. In conclusion, the barons,

The answer to the Papal claim.

* There are various versions of this extraordinary document, and some doubts as to whether it really was sent to Rome.

speaking as representatives of the nation, go so far as to say that they could not "permit" the King, even if he should wish it, to recognise the Papal claims.

In fact, cordiality reigned between the King and his Parliament on all points. The King invited free discussion, and as, one by one, the grievances of the realm were stated, and suggestions made for their reform, the King graciously assented. So pleased were the members, that they changed the grant of a twentieth, originally made, into a grant of a fifteenth, but prescribed the method of its collection. The prelates, supported by the rest of the magnates, made a feeble attempt to shelter themselves again behind *Clericis Laicos;* but the King unequivocally refused his consent.

Reconciliation of King and people.

Abroad, the King's affairs were prospering greatly. The Pope, who had already a Sicilian war on his hands, drifted into war with France in the year of the Lincoln Parliament; and Philip, rashly invading Flanders, which had been rather shabbily treated by its English allies, suffered, in the summer of 1302, the terrible and crushing defeat of Courtrai, which completely incapacitated him from giving further trouble to Edward. The Pope, his hands full, gave up the Scots, and denounced his agent, the Bishop of Glasgow, as a fomenter of discord. A generous charter granted by Edward to the Gascon merchants put them in the best of humours, and, no doubt, paved the way for the grant of the "new" custom, payable by the foreign merchants, in 1303.

Foreign affairs.

But at home things went by no means so smoothly for Edward. Although the interesting Constable's

Trouble at home.

Roll which has come down to us shews that feudal service was, even at the date of the muster of Carlisle, still a genuine thing, desertions from the English army were frequent,

1300.

and special measures to punish them had to be taken. A long-standing quarrel between the Bishop and the Prior of Durham burst out again in the summer of 1301, and revealed a dangerous weakness on the Scottish border. Wallace was back again in Scotland, and the submission of that country seemed as far off as ever. Even England was in a disturbed condition, owing, probably, to the number of discharged soldiers; and "Commis-

1300.

sions of Trailbaston"* were issued for the apprehension and summary punishment of felons and disturbers of the peace. That this latter measure made a great impression, and was rigorously carried out, is shown by the popular poetry of the period, in which the outlaw bewails the absurd severity of the authorities.†

Meanwhile, the Scottish war had dragged on.

The Scottish war.

Edward had made an unprofitable campaign in the summer of 1302, and had returned to England, when, in the following January,

---

* There has been much dispute as to the meaning of the word "Trailbaston" in this connection. It is probably used to describe the kind of ruffian the Commissions were intended to catch—the man who lurked near highways and smote his victim with the staff, or *bâton*, which he trailed behind him.

† *The Political Songs of England*, ed. Wright (Camden Society), 1839. See p. 231 (*The Outlaw's Song of Trailbaston*).

he was startled by the news of fresh outbreaks, with which his lieutenant, John Segrave, seemed unable to cope. Shortly afterwards, Segrave was defeated at Rosslyn; and this defeat was followed by the fall of Stirling, which was captured by the Scots under John of Soulis, after a desperate siege. Thoroughly awake now to the difficulties of his task, Edward completed the pending negotiations with the foreign merchants, whereby, in exchange for a charter which gave them numerous privileges, he received a promise of a "new" Custom, consisting of forty pence on each sack of wool and each three hundred woolfells exported, twice that sum on every last of hides, sums varying from one to two shillings on each piece of cloth and quintal of wax, and a general poundage of threepence on each silver pound's worth of goods exported or imported in their names. All this was to be in addition to the "old" or "great" Custom; and Edward, elated by his success, endeavoured to procure the acceptance of the change by the native merchants, at a general gathering of them held at York at Midsummer. Though he was unsuccessful in this hope, he had secured a substantial permanent addition to his revenue, and, with a good heart, he set out on the Scottish campaign, capturing Brechin Castle in August, ravaging the country as far as Caithness, and going into winter quarters at Dunfermline "amongst the bears and tigers."

Rosslyn.

Fall of Stirling.

The Carta Mercatoria.

So manifest was his determination, and so hopeless the chance of succours from abroad, that the

Scottish nobles, represented by John Comyn,* made submission before the spring. But Stirling Castle, under William Olifard, held out stubbornly until July 20th. Edward, now (it must be remembered) sixty-five years old, performed prodigies of valour, riding round the walls within easy bowshot, and daily encouraging his men by his example. He had more than one marvellous escape. Once a bolt from a springald passed between his legs, actually pierced his doublet, and lodged in his saddle, without wounding man or beast. On another occasion, a mass of stone hurled at him, fell between his horse's feet. Every engine of medieval siegecraft was employed. The English constructed a "ram" and a "wolf" to batter down the gates; both sides used catapults of various kinds for hurling stones and bolts. As a last resource, Edward ordered up a supply of materials for Greek fire; and this seems to have frightened the besieged into submission. At any rate, they surrendered on July 20th, and were leniently treated by the King. A far more important event for Edward, even than the fall of Stirling, was the capture of Wallace, who, in the following year, led a foray into Northumberland. He was captured † (or betrayed) by the Earl of Menteith, in the house of a man named Ray, at Hexham, and taken to Lon-

The Scottish nobles surrender. 9th Feb., 1304.

Capture and death of Wallace.

* This seems to have been John Comyn the younger, the son of Balliol's brother-in-law, who had died in 1299.

† It seems to be beyond question that Edward paid money rewards for the capture of Wallace. But, of course, these may have been given only to his own subjects for their exertions.

SIEGE WEAPONS OF THE THIRTEENTH CENTURY.

(*From Hewitt's "Ancient Armour."*)

in life, he had directed that his body should accompany his troops until the final conquest of Scotland. But his wishes were disregarded; and he was taken, first to Waltham Abbey, then to Westminster, where, on October 28th, he was worthily buried. One of his last official acts had been to forbid the citizens of London to annoy his wife by burning fires near the Tower. At the time of his death, he had lived sixty-eight years, two weeks, and five days. The last offices were rendered by his turbulent, but attached subject, Antony Bek, Bishop of Durham and Patriarch of Jerusalem. On his simple tomb in the Abbey, are inscribed the words:

EDWARDUS PRIMUS SCOTORUM MALLEUS HIC EST
1308. PACTUM SERVA.

(Here lies Edward the First, the Hammer of the Scots, 1308. Keep troth.)

MARRIAGES OF EDWARD'S CHILDREN.

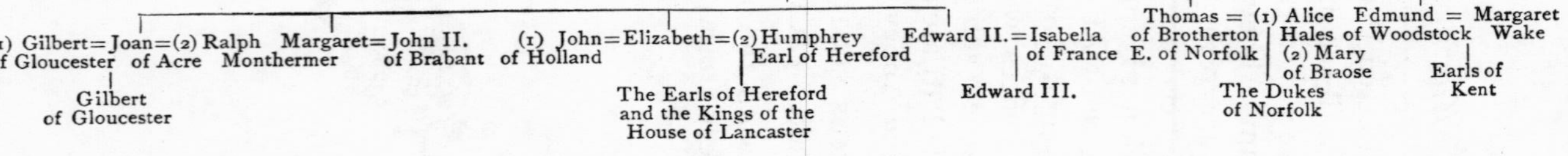

GREAT SEAL OF EDWARD I.

(*From Hewitt's "Ancient Armour."*)

CHAPTER XIII

THE KING AND HIS WORK

EDWARD of England is not, of course, one of the colossal figures of the world's history. Alexander, Julius Cæsar, Mahomet, Charles the Great, Akbar, Napoleon, were founders of empires which, short-lived as some of them were, made their masters for the time the most conspicuous actors in the human drama. Edward belongs to the less brilliant, but more profoundly important class of rulers who, out of scattered and disjointed materials, have called into existence compact and united nations. He ranks with Alfonso Henriques and Sancho I., of Portugal, with Philip Augustus, with Ferdinand the Catholic, with William the Silent, with Peter of Russia, and with Victor Emmanuel of Italy.

A great ruler is not necessarily in private life an attractive man; but Edward's personal character was as noble as his public career. That he was physically brave is shown by his conduct at the time of his attempted assassination, no less than by his fearless bearing in war and the chase. His affectionate nature shines through the wonderful patience and respect

Personal character.

Brave.

Affectionate.

with which he treated his worthless father, his absolutely unbroken relations with his mother and both his wives, and the care which he bestowed upon the education of his fickle son, Edward of Caernarvon. If he looked to advance his political interests by the marriages of his children, we can hardly blame him for yielding to the pressure of forces which have proved too strong even for the most saintly rulers; and the pardon which he granted to his daughter, Joan, for her secret marriage with Ralph Monthermer, shows that he was ever ready to let the father in him triumph over the king. It is also one of

Just.

Edward's greatest glories, that his affectionate nature never betrayed him into favouritism, one of the most besetting dangers of kindly kings. Though his ministers were very far from blameless in their conduct, there is no proof that Edward chose them for anything but their abilities; and the foresight with which, in the last year of his life, he banished Piers Gaveston from the land, deserved a better reward than it met with

Chaste.

at the hands of his worthless son. In his relations with women, Edward's conduct was, so far as evidence goes, absolutely stainless; and the absence of scandal, in such a case, is almost proof conclusive.

In an age in which scepticism of a very subtle kind was making great headway, Edward remained free

Devout.

alike from superstition and irreligion. Whilst always respectful toward genuine piety, and even punctilious in the performance of his religious duties, he kept a firm hand on all attempts at clerical aggression, whether they took the form of Papal interference in national concerns, or of episcopal arrogance. Even Antony Bek, the Bishop of Durham, one of the ablest of his ministers, he twice chastised for insubordination in secular matters. He was also entirely free from that childish vanity which led Henry of Winchester to waste on relics and ecclesiastical adornments the revenues which were needed for the government of the realm. In spite of the evil example set by his father, to which he did, perhaps, in the days of his youth, give way, Edward's personal expenditure, after he reached man's estate, was regulated with wisdom and frugality. Even in the midst of his direst financial straits, in the summer of 1297, he could boldly challenge his people to say that his troubles were caused by his own luxury or domestic extravagance. And yet no foreign ambassador or gilded visitor ever found Edward's Court lacking in dignity or splendour; and Edward knew full well, that a monarch who wishes to impress his subjects must treat them to occasional displays of magnificence.

Frugal.

It was, indeed, more than anything else, Edward's noble dignity which, in his mature years, kept in check that fiery temper which, on rare occasions, betrayed him as the true son of Eleanor of Provence. The unfortunate Dean of St. Paul's and the haughty Earl Marshal succeeded in breaking down his guard; but such outbursts were rare, and were, obviously, due to the awful strain of public anxiety then pressing upon the King. Their

Dignified.

occurrence only brings out into clearer relief the habitual self-control of Edward Plantagenet.

Closely allied with this strong sense of personal dignity, must be reckoned that feature of Edward's character which is expressed in his death-motto: *Pactum serva* ("keep troth"). It reminds us pleasantly of that other great English King, Alfred of Wessex, with whom *wed-bryce* was one of the deadliest sins. And if Edward saw that, in the social revolution which was enacting before his eyes, adherence to the plighted word was as essential to the salvation of society as respect for the armed hand and the sacred relic had been in the days before, then indeed he showed himself, not merely an upright man, but a political genius of the very first order. That Edward's motto should have served him rather as an ideal than as an unfailing rule of practice, may be freely admitted. But that, in the thirteenth century, he avowed such an ideal, and kept so closely to it, is not the least of his virtues.

Faithful.

We approach the border line, often so difficult to draw, which separates virtue from vice, strength from weakness, when we speak of Edward's perseverance. The indomitable energy which has left behind it such a record of work as few rulers have to show, which thought no exertion too great, no self-denial too severe, was apt to degenerate into a blind pertinacity which, at best, became almost mathematical in its action. Whether it was ambition, or vanity, or greed (to take the most unfavourable view), or whether (to adopt the other attitude) it was a strong sense of public duty which led the

Persevering.

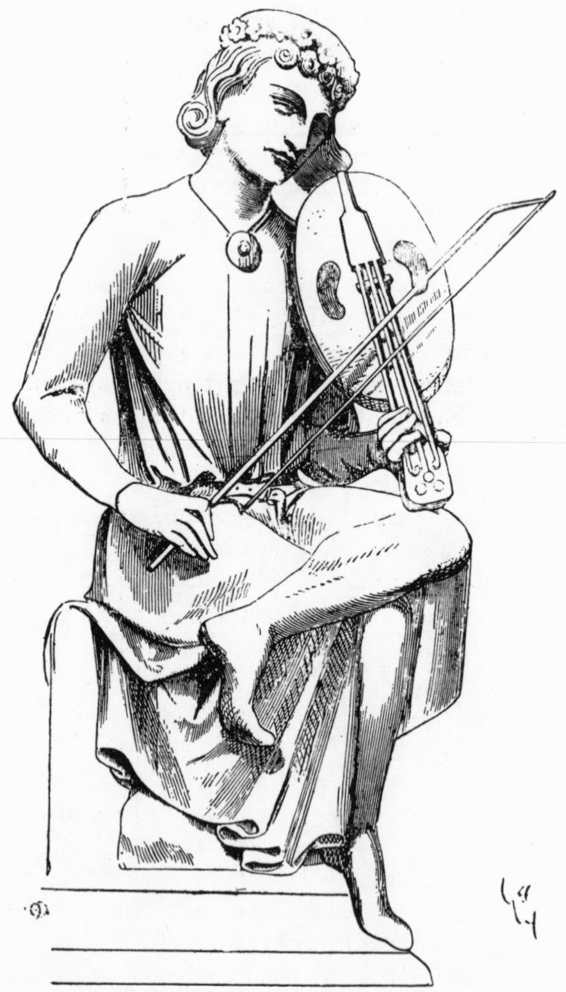

VIOL OF THE THIRTEENTH CENTURY.

(From Viollet le Duc's "Dict. du Mobilier Français.")

King to undertake the Scottish crusade, it is quite clear that he pursued his plans till success was hopeless, and till he positively endangered for ever the fulfilment of his dream of an united kingdom. And yet, as will be suggested later, there was nothing, in Edward's relations with Scotland, of the morbid obstinacy of Philip II. of Spain, or the flatulent vanity of Louis XIV. of France. That the struggle with Scotland brought out the worst features in Edward's character, his rare lapses into cruelty and bad faith, may be freely admitted. But it was the one great blot on a noble career.

Sympathetic.

To crown all, Providence had gifted Edward with that magnetic charm of sympathy, without which all other virtues in a ruler are so sadly wasted. He was no demagogue; and he had not the smallest intention of playing the part of a puppet. But he had just that human feeling for his people, which commanded their steady affection, and enabled him to appeal, in moments of supreme crisis, to their instinct of trust. There are few grander scenes in English history, few which reveal more clearly the secret of national greatness, than the meeting between Edward and his subjects before the great hall of Westminster on the 14th July, 1297 (see p. 277). Everything seemed to be against the King—the Church hostile, the barons mutinous, the people discontented, danger in the north, and the most powerful prince of Europe in arms against him. Yet, in a moment, the King found his way to the hearts of the multitude; and those who had come to curse remained to bless. It was the most triumphant vindication of Edward's character; and the most supreme testimony to his national position.

Brave, affectionate, just, pure, devout, frugal, dignified, faithful, persevering, and sympathetic—it is a great and humane character. With little of the saintly self-abnegation of Louis IX. of France, Edward's contemporary, it was a character far more suited to a king in the world of his day. The age of the crusade and the cloister was passing away; the age of national life and commercial greatness was setting in. St. Louis was the man of the past, Edward was the man of the future. His greatness assumes an almost miraculous air, when we reflect, that he was the son of Henry of Winchester and Eleanor of Provence, the grandson of John Lackland and Isabella of Angoulême, the father of Edward of Caernarvon. It seems almost as though the stem of Plantagenet, like the American aloe, had blossomed but once in a hundred years.

No saint, but a great man.

We turn from the King to his work, and, beginning with the circumference, proceed inwards to the centre.

With Gascony we are not seriously concerned; for the Gascons formed no part of the English nation. Moreover, it so happens that the splendid materials for the study of the English administration of Gascony, which undoubtedly exist, are, for the most part, yet unpublished.* But we know enough to feel fairly confident that Edward's

Gascony.

* The Gascon (or Vascon) Rolls for the years 1242–54 have been edited by M. Francisque Michel; those for 1273–1290 by M. Bémont (*Documents Inédits sur l'Histoire de France*). An interesting fragment

government of Gascony was, at least by comparison, a success. The condition of the country was peculiar, and full of bewildering contrasts. Alongside of the most intensely feudal barons—the Counts of Bigorre and Périgord, the Viscounts of Béarn, Limoges, Ventadour, and Turenne, the Lords of Albret and Buch—stood the free communes of the ancient cities of the Roman province—Bordeaux, Tarbes, Bazas, Bourges, Rions—with those of the more modern growths of La Réole, Bayonne, and Orthez. These cities, believing themselves to inherit the tradition of Roman municipal self-government, were strong to oppose, both the pretensions of feudal arrogance, and the more regular discipline of royal control. Rapidly becoming rich and popular with the tide of increasing commerce, they were developing a new system of maritime and commercial law, which bade fair to set an example to Western Europe. The code of the little island of Oléron, which, in spite of Henry III.'s defeat at Taillebourg, still clung to the English, is the basis of the modern maritime law of Europe. Outside the cities there were yet many sturdy yeomen who disdained all feudal protection, and claimed to hold their lands by the old independent Roman title of allodialism. Such materials as these required the most careful handling; and Earl Simon's administration, vigorous and just as it was, very nearly lost Gascony to the English Crown. The unanimity with which the Gascons sought Edward as their lord, may have been only an expression of the same feel-

from the Roll of 1305 will be found in Appendix II. to Professor Maitland's edition of the Parliament Roll of that year (Rolls Series).

ing which, no doubt, had much to do with their preference for English over French rule. They saw that, under a distant ruler, their chances of being allowed to govern themselves in their own way were greatly increased. But the facts remain that, under Edward's rule, we hear of few complaints from Gascony, that the duchy was, on more than one occasion, a source of wealth to the King, that it steadily resisted the determined attempt of Philip to incorporate it in the French kingdom, and that, in spite of its manifest destiny, it continued, for a century and a half after Edward's death, to belong to the English Crown. Edward would have been a poltroon, if he had surrendered Gascony to Philip, just as Bruce would have been a poltroon had he renounced his claims on Scotland to Edward.

Ireland.

In estimating the King's work in Ireland, we are at once struck by the fact, that the sister island comes rarely into prominence during his career. We should, in fact, have had to interrupt the thread of the story to bring her in. Therefore it is necessary to review briefly the evidence which exists for our conclusions.

Early history of English settlement.

When Edward took up the reins of government, less than a century had elapsed since the Norman knights of Henry Fitz Empress had first set foot in Ireland. Henry's self-imposed penance for the murder of Becket led to a royal visit, and a rapid conquest and organisation of the eastern districts. A central administration on the Norman model was set up, consisting of justitiar, constable, seneschal or steward, butler, chancellor, and chamberlain, with their subordinate officials. A municipality was founded at Dublin, recently won both from the Danes under Haskulf Thorgilson, whose Ostmen (Eastmen) have left their traces on the neighbouring township of Oxmanstown, and from the native Irish at Castleknock. But Henry was tempted to repeat the policy of his predecessors in Scotland and Wales, by allowing Hugh Lacy to carve out for himself the lordship of Meath, and Richard Fitz Gilbert ("Strongbow") the lordship of Leinster; whilst John Courcey soon effected what he was pleased to consider a conquest of Connaught. In 1186, Lacy came to an untimely end through his unseasonable anxiety to instruct an Irishman in the use of the pickaxe; but his family flourished, and his son, another Hugh, having treacherously slain John Courcey in the year 1200, acquired the lordship of Connaught, whilst that of Ulster was granted to him by King John in the year 1205. The enormous inheritance of the Lacys broke up on his death in 1242, when the earldom of Ulster passed to the Burghs, in whose hands it was destined to prove such a powerful factor in the politics of the neighbouring kingdom of Scotland. The marriage of Isabella Fitz-Gilbert with the "old Marshal" in 1189, raised up another powerful feudatory in Leinster; and already, in the year 1246, we find King Henry's advisers fixing the Exchequer permanently at Dublin, and ordering the administration of justice to be carried on "as it was

Palatine lordships.

Hugh Lacy.

The Burghs in Ulster.

The Marshals in Leinster.

before the Earls Marshal began to usurp the royal franchises."

In the same reign, an attempt was made to assimilate the legal procedure of the two countries, by framing the forms of the Chancery writs at

1246.

Dublin on the English model, and by setting up a "Bench," and holding periodical "eyres" and "circuits" in such of the country as had been broken up into shires.

Dublin.

Dublin was treated with great liberality. At first handed over to the control of the citizens of Bristol, it had received, in 1185, a charter which conferred upon it the most cherished municipal privileges of the period, whilst, during the troubles of 1215, the boon of self-government was virtually conferred upon the citizens by the grant of the "ferm," or issues of the city, at an annual rent of two hundred marks. In the year 1229, the seal was put upon the municipal independence of the city, by the grant of the right to elect an annual mayor. Already there were legally authorised fairs, not only at Dublin, but at Donnybrook, the Droghedas, Waterford, and Limerick. The mixed national character of the adventurers who flocked over in the reign of John and his successors is well illustrated by the case of the illustrious family of the Geraldines, who were, originally, the Gherardini, of Florence, in which city their ancient tower still stands (or till recently stood) in the Via Santa Porta Maria.

The Friars.

Yet other foreign elements were introduced by the arrival of the new Orders of Monks and of the Friars; by the end of the thirteenth century, there were no less than thirty-four Cistercian abbeys in Ireland. Yet the mixed blood of the settlers did not prevent their combining to obtain from the young Henry's ministers, in 1216, a grant of a Magna Carta similar in terms to that of Runnymead.

Magna Carta.

Edward's first direct connection with Ireland was in the year 1249, when, as nominal governor of Gascony, he received a grant of two years' issues of the Exchequer of Dublin towards the expenses of Earl Simon's administration. In 1252 a standing Order, addressed to the Irish treasury, directed that the sum of a thousand marks should always be kept ready for the service of Gascony. Four years later, Edward, as we have seen, received a formal grant of the Lordship of Ireland, in view of his approaching marriage; and at once directed the Irish revenues to be paid into his treasury at Bristol. This, it must be confessed, is the keynote of Edward's Irish policy. His rule appears to have been, after the first few years, successful and humane; but there was no thought of spending the surplus of Irish revenue in or for the benefit of the country. Men and money were freely drawn from Ireland for service in Wales, Scotland, Gascony, and Flanders. English money never found its way to Ireland, except in the form of wages of Irish foot-soldiers, or in payment for Irish goods.*

Edward and Ireland.

Within this modest ambition, however, there is no reason to doubt that Edward governed Ireland

* Welsh bowmen were often employed to garrison the Irish castles; but their wages were paid out of Irish revenues.

well. Almost immediately after the grant of the lordship, disturbances broke out in Ulster, where Walter Burgh was oppressing the native Irish, and extending his attacks into the neighbouring province of Connaught. Edward acted with promptness and decision; but he was hampered by the interference and opposition of his father's officials. In 1256 the actual administration was made over to him; and he at once superseded the existing staff by a body of fifteen chosen advisers whom he sent over. At this time it was confidently expected that Edward himself would visit the country; and, indeed, he was ordered by his father to do so. But the troubles of the approaching Barons' War probably prevented him; and there is no evidence that he actually went. There are references in the documents of 1262 to an Ordinance made by Edward for the administration of Ireland, but the details have not survived; and, shortly afterward, the Prince was practically deposed by the successful barons. Resuming the administration after the battle of Evesham, Edward again deserted it on his departure for the Holy Land; and there was a good deal of trouble during his absence, especially with the Archbishop of Dublin, who claimed extraordinary "franchises" in the city.

Success of Edward's administration.

On his return, however, Edward seems to have had little difficulty in restoring order. The turbulent archbishop was dead, and though the Mandevilles, in league with Irish septs, were making it unpleasant for Edward's lieutenant, William Fitzwarren, in Ulster, the Justi-

Resumption of control by Edward.

tiar, with the help of the bishops of Meath and Waterford, soon patched up a peace. By the year 1277 the reports from Ireland were distinctly encouraging, and Edward was consulting with Robert Ufford, the Justitiar, on his project for introducing English law into Ireland, a privilege for which, so it appears, the "community of Ireland" (probably a Council of Anglo-Norman barons) had offered to pay no less a sum than 8000 marks. In the year 1284 Edward had trouble with a defaulting official, Stephen Fulbourn, who appears to have been an Anglo-Irish Adam of Stratton; and a more serious complication in the hostility aroused among the Anglo-Irish by the adoption, on the part of the Irish Church, of a steady policy of hostility to foreigners. Notwithstanding this tendency, Edward's Council appointed the Archbishop of Dublin "keeper" of the kingdom, on the death of the Archbishop of Tuam in 1288; and his administration, though somewhat stormy, seems to have restored order. (See Appendix A.)

Results of Edward's rule.

From these accounts it will be abundantly clear that Edward's task in Ireland was no easy one. Yet there is reason to believe that the King treated the country generously, according to the standard of the times, and that the results were, on the whole, satisfactory. In 1285 he confirmed the municipal privileges of Dublin; and, in the same year, an interesting parallel to the Convention of Royal Burghs in Scotland was started by the agreement of the burgesses of Dublin, Waterford, Cork, and the two Droghedas, to meet triennially at Kilkenny. Dublin was speedily included in the list of boroughs privileged to record "statutes merchant" under the terms of the Ordinance of Acton Burnel. But the great proof of the prosperity of Ireland under Edward's rule is the steady rise, not merely in the revenue, but in the surplus of revenue over expenditure. At the beginning of his reign the annual income was less than £5000; and this barely covered the outgoings. In six years the revenue had increased to upwards of £6000, while the outgoings were considerably less; and though Irish finance suffered by the failure of the Ricardi and the Betti firms in 1294, the improvement was maintained. On the other hand, there seems to be no trace of increased taxation until the introduction of the "alien" custom in 1303. But, it must be again admitted, the praise which is undoubtedly due to Edward's Irish administration, is largely counterbalanced by the fact that, especially in his later years, the handsome balances in the Irish treasury were steadily drafted over to England, to pay for the expenses of the Scottish and Gascon wars.

Scotland.

In speaking of Scotland, we touch, of course, upon the capital failure in Edward's career. By whatever standard he may be judged, the verdict of history must go against him. It may be reasonably urged that a statesman, especially a statesman who is also a ruler, cannot be expected to strive after the abstract ideals of justice which guide the conduct of a philosopher. Nor is it unreasonable to urge also in Edward's defence, that an ethical standard which is suitable even to the average man, in his private affairs, is too high for the conduct of the business of the State. It is a lamentable, but perfectly undeniable fact, that the morality of the State is, and always has been, below the morality of the individual. But a statesman fails, beyond dispute and beyond appeal, if he misjudges hopelessly the possibilities of the situation, and if his policy, instead of achieving his own object, merely renders that object more unattainable than ever. Yet this is precisely Edward's position with regard to Scotland. He wished, obviously, to unite the two countries. At first, circumstances seemed to favour his plans. The marriage of Edward of Caernarvon with the Maid of Norway might have produced an heir to both kingdoms, who would have anticipated James VI. by three centuries. Even when it was ordered otherwise, Edward at first behaved wisely. There is nothing in the conduct of the Scottish trial which convicts him of bad faith, though his excessive precautions to establish his title show the longing inclination of his soul. Up to the Christmas of 1292, Edward had done nothing to alienate our sympathy—rather everything to win it. Luck had done a good deal for him in placing his favourite candidate on the Scottish throne ; yet, by the strictest of strict legal arguments, the title of John Balliol was superior to that of Robert Bruce.

Edward's lapse.

But, at the critical moment, Edward failed to maintain his wise attitude. He could not honestly bring himself to leave Balliol a free hand, or trust Scotland to work out her own destiny. Doubtless he was technically justified in summoning Balliol to his bar; but he acted unwisely, if he hoped to maintain his impartial position. Inevitably the Scottish barons, and, so far as they understood the question, the Scottish people, believed that Scotland was being degraded to the rank of an English province. Doubtless, Balliol was a weak man, and might not have kept his country in peace. But there had been weak kings in England; and Englishmen had overcome the difficulty in their own way. Just as the English barons in 1216 had resented, whilst they made use of, the help of Philip Augustus, so the Scottish barons who disliked Balliol resented, whilst they made use of, the help of Edward. And when Edward began to enforce his help by the aid of fire and sword, of Welsh archers and Irish footmen, he kindled in Scotland a dull flame of resentment, which soon spread beyond the narrow circle of the Lowland baronage, and which, though often apparently quenched, flamed out into fiery and terrible revenge on the day of Bannockburn. Edward was, in truth, calling into existence, in both countries, that new national spirit which was destined to replace the dying principles of feudalism. But whereas, in England, he was arousing it by a generous trust in his people, and a steady resistance to feudal aggression, in Scotland he was awakening it by the hard methods of persecution. Therefore, in England, the national spirit was his friend; in Scotland, it was his foe. And his condemnation in Scotland is, that, in his last ten years, he drove further and further away that very union which he was striving, with might and main, to bring about.

With Wales, the case was different. The great outburst of Welsh literary activity in the twelfth century had enkindled a people, but it had not created a nation. The one inflexible condition of national existence in the thirteenth century—unwavering obedience to a central authority—was not attained by the Welsh. Though they acknowledged a vague claim of leadership in the house of Llywelyn ab Jorwerth, the scattered clans which still maintained their independence were unwilling to submit to anything like settled government. The rule of the Marchers on the east and south had effectually broken up any tendency to cohesion which had previously existed. Consequently, it was really a choice between falling into the hands of the Marchers and falling into the hands of Edward. Again and again the family and tribal quarrels of the Welsh gave them, an easy prey, to the English armies. And when the conquest was effected, the English rule, stern as it was, was better, even for the Welsh, than the anarchy of the old days. Edward's Statute of Rhuddlan is no fierce code of terror for a conquered land, but a wise and statesmanlike measure. The pity of it was, that the King did not feel himself strong enough to suppress the Marcher lordships, and bring all Wales under the rule of Justice and Sheriff. The real blot on the English connection with Wales is the brutal legislation with which Henry IV. strove to stamp out the rising under Owen Glendower; but for this Edward cannot be held responsible. And the final incorporation of

Wales.

1284.

Wales with England, by a king in whose veins ran Welsh blood, was only the natural and fortunate result of a Welsh policy which had striven to gain its ends by supporting, first one party and then the other, in the Wars of the Roses.

England.

So we come at last to England, Edward's true sphere of action. And here it is impossible to dispose, in a single paragraph, of the results of his work. We must glance at the four conspicuous sides of Edward's national position, as a soldier, an administrator, a ruler, and a legislator.

Edward's military greatness.

As a soldier, his success is clear, and his achievements great. It is not merely that Edward was a great general, so that, after the disastrous lesson of Lewes, he never knew defeat. His masterly strategy in the campaign of Evesham, when he pinned his old instructor ruthlessly behind the barrier of the Severn, till he could make a brilliant dash at the careless garrison of Kenilworth; his orderly and crushing attack in the battle which followed; his masterly conduct of the great Welsh campaign; his flash of genius at Falkirk; his unconquerable activity at the siege of Stirling; all these show him the great general in the field. But his adoption of the Welsh longbow, his careful combination of horsemen and archers, his organisation of the coast guard, his commissions of array which collected the sturdy English infantry and carefully provided for their wants—all these things mark a departure from the old freebooting ways of feudal armies, with their ineffectiveness, their extravagance, their uncertainty. They are important steps in the process which led to the English victories at Creçy, Poitiers, and Agincourt, and which made England, for a time, the leading military power in Europe.

Administration. As an administrator, Edward's position is far more open to criticism. But his reign is, none the less, epoch-making. True it is that, in more than one respect, the old feudal ideas of administration had been replaced by more modern methods, wellnigh a century before Edward mounted the throne. Roughly speaking, the feudal view was, that every administrative post ought to be given to a warrior, who would undertake to return for it to the King a "ferm," or fixed sum, year by year, the King asking no questions as to the way in which the work was done, or the profit made out of it by the official. The acute Angevin clerks who surrounded Henry II. convinced the King of the folly of this plan; and the elaborate organisation of the Exchequer, and the financial "eyres", were the results.* There grew up a new class of officials, men sprung from the ranks, who held their posts entirely at the pleasure of the King, and who were at least supposed to render a rigorous account of every penny they received. Even the older classes of officials, for example, the sheriffs, though they continued to render a "ferm," or lump sum, for the ancient sources of revenue,

New officials.

* These "eyres" (*itinera*) were, at first, merely visitations of the King's local officials by his confidential messengers. The latter used their privilege of summoning juries of the inhabitants, to keep a check on peculation by sheriffs and escheators. Out of this practice grew up the "assizes" of modern times.

were held strictly to account for the newer items of taxation which were coming into vogue. After the great quarrel with the sheriffs, the taxes were usually
1170. collected by special officials of the Exchequer, who journeyed round the shires, and assessed the payments according to the verdicts of local juries.

Before Edward's accession, too, it had become clear, that the ancient revenue, from the Crown lands
New sources of revenue. and the "ferm" of the shires, was becoming hopelessly inadequate; and new devices were being introduced. Those ancient items, originally payable in kind, had, unfortunately for the Crown, been commuted for fixed sums; and, as the purchasing power of money was steadily falling,
New royal functions. their real value was becoming less and less. On the other hand, the business of government was rapidly increasing; and, though some of this new activity, such as the administration of justice, paid its own cost and something over, other parts of it, such as the Coast Guard and the new infantry, were sources of great expense.

Quite naturally, the kings and their subjects took different views of the situation. The kings said that
Fiscal questions. they must have more money; and the simple political economy of the day failed to explain why even a careful and frugal king like Edward, no less than a careless and extravagant king, like his father, was continually in need of supplies. The people—barons, clergy, merchants, peasants—all grumbled that the King ought to "live of his own," *i. e.*, on his ancient revenue. Upon

this apparently simple issue, the great constitutional question of the thirteenth century was fought. Leaving, for the moment, the constitutional machinery produced by the struggle, we may notice briefly the desperate efforts made by the Crown to evade the unwelcome conclusion, that taxation could not be imposed without the deliberate and express consent of the nation, given in formal assembly.

Irregular taxation.

The latter principle seemed to have been expressed in terms as clear as daylight by the Great Charter of 1215. "No scutage * or aid (beyond the three customary aids) may be placed upon our kingdom except by the common counsel of our kingdom"; and the nature of this "common counsel" is explained in clear terms, to which we shall hereafter have to refer. But the Crown was not easily beaten. There were, for example, the Jews, hated and despised by the people amongst whom they lived, and practising that trade of usury which, according to medieval theology, was a deadly sin. Gathered together in their "Jewries," they trembled at the sound of the cries which told them that some ruffian debtor had egged the citizens on to plunder and slay amongst the yellow gaberdines. Gladly would they pay large sums to a powerful king to be protected from the wrath of his subjects. Fat with the spoils of rich manors, pledged by reckless Crusaders, the Jews

The Jews.

* Scutage, or shield money, was a composition for military service due from feudal tenants of land. But the documents show pretty clearly that scutage, even when exacted, did not really free the man who paid it from personal service.

were a tempting object to a needy ruler. Edward was not above the temptation. In 1271 his uncle Richard lent him 2000 marks; and the money was secured by a pledge of the Jewries for a year. In 1278, under allegation of coinage offences, the King hung nearly 300 Jews, and seized their goods. In 1287 he extorted from them a sum of £12,000. It was probably a good thing for both parties when, in 1290, the King yielded to popular clamour, and expelled the Jews from his dominions.* Then Edward turned to the Italian and Cahorsin bankers, to whom he mortgaged forthcoming revenues for large sums.

The Italian and Provençal bankers.

Another means of supply was the revenues of the churches. Not only could the King, by prolonging the vacancies of bishoprics and abbacies, draw large sums from their custodians, but he did not hesitate to press the extreme view, which had considerable vogue in medieval Europe, that, in the dire need of the State, the Church was bound to restore part at least of the wealth which royal benefactors had so liberally showered upon it. The growing merchant class also offered a rich source of revenue, which might be drawn either by way of payments for the grant of municipal privileges, or by the more brutal method of the *maletolte*. Especially with the alien merchants, almost as much in fear of national jealousy as the Jews, good bargains could be made, as we have seen;

Ecclesiastical revenues.

The merchants.

* It is strange that the Jews were expelled from England by one of the greatest of her rulers, and restored by another, almost, if not equally, as great.

for, in those days, men would hardly realise that the alien custom would eventually fall, in part at least, upon the native producer.

The solution of the problem.

But nearer and nearer grew the day on which it would be recognised that there was but one source of legitimate taxation; and Edward, even if he did not desire this result, did much to bring it about. He set a good example with his first Parliament, in 1275; but that inexperienced body made the mistake of granting the Customs in perpetuity, instead of for a single year. When he tried to repeat the experiment with the native merchants at York in 1303, they flatly refused. Every one of the "tenths," "fifteenths," and "twentieths," which the King demanded so often in his later years, strengthened the growing principle, that each demand for money was to be considered on its merits by a national assembly, and granted for one occasion only. The King profited by the vast increase in the movable wealth of the country; the nation profited by the increased unity and co-operative power which it obtained by the practice of parliamentary action. The keenness with which Edward watched fiscal developments is shown by his repeated Ordinances for the management of the Exchequer, and by the thoroughly scientific way in which his taxes were collected.

Parliament.

Through the fiscal question we naturally approach that great development of parliamentary machinery, which is one of the most striking features of Edward's life and reign. Hitherto all the organs of the central government had grown out of one simple germ — the feudal council which surrounded the first Norman King. It was a fundamental principle of feudalism that, on the one hand, the feudal lord could take no step of importance without consulting his immediate vassals; and, on the other, that he was entitled to their presence and advice when he asked for them. His immediate vassals were his *curia*, or "court"; and the word included in germ all that we now mean by the ceremonial court of His Majesty, his judicial courts, and his Council.

The Feudal Council.

Gradually, however, this *Curia Regis* assumed three more or less distinct forms. As an almost permanent body, it comprised only the few household officials who habitually attended the person of the king, and who, by virtue of their nearness to his person, probably knew more of his affairs than anyone else. Very gradually and tentatively this body began to speak of itself as the "king's council," or his "ordinary" council, or, finally, as his "private" or "privy" council. But it was long before the king dared to take any great step without consulting his immediate vassals as a whole; and the next development was really caused by the unwillingness of the poorer and less important of these vassals to travel long distances to the royal presence. Gradually the attendance becomes confined to the "great men of the realm," the "greater barons," as they are called, or the "magnates." What first drew the line between a "greater" and a "lesser" baron, we do not know; but in the thirteenth century

Three forms.

The Privy Council.

The Magnates.

the legal distinction was, that the former paid his feudal dues direct to the Exchequer, while the latter paid his to the sheriff of his county. Thus appears, by the middle of the twelfth century, a Council of Magnates, or "Great Council," which, we observe, does not call itself the "Council of the King," but the "Council of the kingdom." This body met pretty regularly once a year, and would not in the least have hesitated to assemble of its own accord, if the King had refused to summon it. It was by far the most independent body in the land, consisting, as it did, not only of the bishops and greater abbots, but also of the chief feudal potentates of the kingdom, each of whom claimed a right of individual access to the King. But it could fall back, if need were, on the humbler ranks of the baronage; and then it became, as the Great Charter expresses it, the "Common Council of the kingdom."

The Common Council.

Somewhere in the early years of the twelfth century, there branched off from the first of these three bodies a permanent committee or office, known as the Exchequer of the King. We cannot go into the disputes as to whether this famous institution took its rise in England, Normandy, or Sicily *; anyway, it was a Norman device. It was, of course, supposed to be concerned with revenue matters only; and it marks the date at which the personal expenditure of the King was beginning to be distinguished from the expenditure

The Exchequer.

* There were Norman rulers in Sicily from the middle of the eleventh century till the middle of the thirteenth.

of the State. We know a great deal about it from a description drawn up by one of its officials in the later twelfth century.* From it there branched off yet other bodies, notably the Court of Common Bench, or Common Pleas, which at first consisted merely of those officials of the Exchequer who, in their financial circuits through the country, or, in their sessions at Westminster, began to hear private causes, between subject and subject. It was put on a permanent footing in 1178; and the Great Charter provided that it should always sit "in some certain place," instead of following the king about all over the country. Soon after, other Exchequer officials, jealous of the fees received by their former colleagues, got themselves recognised as a judicial court, the Court of Exchequer; but they were never called "justices," only "barons." Finally, the King's Council, to which an appeal originally lay from the Court of Common Bench, threw off yet another body, the King's or "Upper" Bench, and thus the "three Courts of Common Law at Westminster"† came into existence. This last development was closely connected with the appearance of Parliament.

The (Common) Bench.

The Court of Exchequer.

The Upper Bench.

* The *Dialogus de Scaccario* may be seen in Stubbs' *Select Charters*. An English translation is to be found in Henderson's *Select Historical Documents of the Middle Ages*, p. 20.

† It was some time, however, before they were really fixed at Westminster. The articles upon the Charters (see p. 279) expressly provide that the King's Bench shall follow the king wherever he goes. The technical name for the King's Bench was *Coram rege* court.

don. There, after a brief trial before a special commission of justices, he was executed with the savage rigour of the law of treason, an offence which it was the merest quibble to attribute to him. Accusations of personal cruelty were, no doubt, freely brought against him by his enemies; and it is possible that, in the course of a war which often threatened to degenerate into a series of border raids, he had not been altogether free from blame. But it was, beyond question, the terror inspired by his name which caused Edward to mete out such different fates to him, and to the baronial leader of the Scottish armies, John Comyn.

August, 1305.

Two remarkable Councils were held in the year 1305. The first was a full Parliament of magnates, clergy, knights, and burgesses, which met at Westminster in February. Very full accounts of its proceedings survive; and one striking feature is the appointment of a Committee to receive and distribute the vast mass of petitions, which prove to us, beyond all doubt, that Parliament was now rapidly assuming one of the most important of its modern functions, the discussion of grievances. The Committee was directed to arrange the petitions received by it into four bundles, one representing England, a second Scotland, a third Ireland and Guernsey, and a fourth Gascony. The last three were distributed again among three corresponding committees. All the members of these Committees, be it observed, were royal officials, not, as we should call them, "private members." On the 21st March, all members except those who were "of the Council

Great Parliament.

of the King," and those who had special business, were allowed to depart, with a warning, however, to hold themselves in readiness for a second summons. Then the Council proceeded to general business. Officials were appointed for Gascony: John Havering as Seneschal or Governor, Richard Havering as Constable of Bordeaux, Peter Arnold as Provost of Bayonne, William Dene as Seneschal of the Agenais. On April 5th, the question of clerical taxation was discussed on the united petition of the laity, and a statute, afterwards attributed to the Parliament of 1307, was made, which prohibited the remittance abroad of money or goods, under any pretext, by any member of a religious foundation. This was, of course, another reply to *Clericis Laicos*. The affairs of Scotland were debated; and it was decided that the Scots should choose a body of ten representatives, to meet a similar number of English at a conference to be held in London at midsummer. In due course less important petitions received their answers. Not less than 480 were dealt with.

Conference on Scottish affairs.

The Council for the affairs of Scotland did not meet until 15th September, after the capture and execution of Wallace. It was attended by the Bishops of St. Andrews and Dunkeld, the Abbots of Cupar and Melrose, the Earl of Buchan (Alexander Comyn), John Mowbray, Robert Keith, Adam Gordon, and John Inchmartin, on behalf of the Scots. The Earl of Dunbar was also to have come, but he failed, and his place was taken by John Menteith. There were twenty English representatives, mostly prelates, earls, and offic-

Settlement of Scotland.

ials. The Assembly, after a discussion lasting twenty days, produced an elaborate scheme for the permanent settlement of Scotland. John of Brittany was to be Warden and Lieutenant, Sir William Bevercote Chancellor, Sir John Sandale Chamberlain, and Sir Robert Heron Controller. For judicial purposes, the country was to be divided into four circuits—the Lothians, Galway, the "Scottish Sea" (between Forth and the mountains), and "Beyond the Mountains"; and, to each of these, two justices were to be assigned. The justices actually named were mostly Scots, but they were to be removable by the joint resolutions of the Warden, the Chancellor, and the Chamberlain. The sheriffdoms were to be increased to twenty-four, and the sheriffs might be either Scottish or English; they were to be appointed, according to ancient custom, by the Chamberlain. The custody of the great castles was fairly divided between English and Scottish hands, perhaps with a leaning in favour of the former. The office of coroner was to be reformed, and disturbers of the peace banished. Finally, a most important clause provided, that the Warden should at once hold a general assembly for the ascertainment and record of the "laws which King David made, and also of the amendments and additions since made by the kings." These, after being considered by a Council containing both English and Scots, were to be sent to Edward for final confirmation at the next year's Parliament. The Scottish delegates swore to observe the terms of the Ordinance, at Sheen, in Surrey.

It was not an unfair scheme, save for its authorship. Edward determined to keep the highest offices in his own hands, at any rate for a time. But the daily administration of justice, in great and small affairs, was left largely to native officials: and national sentiment was given free play by the adoption of the national law. Edward might well hope that, at last, the Scottish question was in a fair way of being settled. Abroad, things were still going all in his favour. Boniface, his enemy, had died in the autumn of 1303. His successor, Benedict XI., had been poisoned at Perugia in the following July. Benedict had been succeeded by Clement V., who, as Archbishop of Bordeaux, had been Edward's own subject, and who manifested a willingness to accede to Edward's requests, which was more complaisant than dignified.* At home, the King had drawn the teeth of two of his most dangerous subjects, by marrying the Earl of Hereford to his daughter Elizabeth, and by obtaining a resettlement of the Norfolk estates, which left the immediate reversion in the Crown. He had taken a somewhat spiteful, but not excessive revenge upon Archbishop Winchelsey, by entrapping him into a confession of treasonable correspondence during the French campaign. It is to be hoped that this little success at last removed from Edward's mind the grudge which he had so long borne the Primate for his conduct over the *Clericis Laicos*. In spite of a drought and

Criticism of the scheme.

* He began by releasing Edward from his oath to observe the Charters. Happily, Edward did not make use of the absolution ; but he should never have sought it.

murrain of sheep, followed by a severe winter, the King might dream, at the Christmas of 1305, that his troubles were ended.

But, from that dream, there came a rude awakening. In the previous summer, Robert Bruce, grandson of the Competitor, had met the Bishop of St. Andrews on the historic ground of Cambuskenneth, and agreed with him to strike a bold stroke for Scottish freedom. The Bishop of Glasgow (Wishart) and the Bishop of Moray, with the Abbot of Scone and others, had joined the league, and, in the spring of 1306, the news came to Edward that the leaguers had murdered John Comyn the Red, Edward's supporter, in the Franciscan church at Dumfries, and that the Bruce had been crowned at Scone on Lady Day. The great Scottish nobles for the most part held aloof from the rising; but the Bruce seems to have stepped into the place left vacant by Wallace, and to have developed into something like a national hero.

Coronation of Bruce.

Feb. 10th.

Edward saw now the gravity of the crisis, and set about raising men and money. He determined to seize the opportunity of his eldest son's majority to confer on him the rank of knighthood, an occasion which gave him an orthodox reason for demanding an "aid" of his subjects. He summoned a Parliament of magnates, knights, and burgesses for Trinity Sunday (May 29th), with this object, but, in the meantime, the ceremony was hurried forward in view of the Scottish campaign. At a splendid gathering held at Westminster on Whit-Sunday (May 22nd) the young Prince, with

Preparations.

three hundred companions, arrayed in gorgeous robes, received the Order of Knighthood, the Prince being also created Duke of Aquitaine.* Two swans, trapped in golden nets, were then brought into the Palace, and the King swore upon them to avenge the death of Comyn, and the injury to Holy Church. Receiving from the Parliament, on the following Sunday, a grant of a thirtieth for the "aid," † he marched northward, preceded by his lieutenant, Aymer of Valence, who, on June 25th, inflicted on the Bruce a sudden defeat at Methven, compelling him to fly to Cantyre. Hither he was pursued by the English, who captured his brother Nigel, and his wife Mary, daughter of Burgh, the Red Earl of Ulster. Nigel was sent to Berwick, where he was hanged; but the lady, who had from the first thrown cold water on Bruce's pretensions, greeting him as a "summer's king," was suffered to depart in peace. The main English army easily overran Scotland. The Earl of Athol,‡ and Christopher Seaton, with his two brothers, were captured and executed, and their lands distributed among Edward's followers. In the autumn, the Bruce reappeared, and collected his Michaelmas mails in Carrick, while Henry Percy, who strove to

Bruce defeated at Methven.

* Tents were pitched for the candidates in the Temple Gardens; and most of them kept their previous watch in the well-known church of the Templars.

† This was less than the orthodox amount of an "aid." The merchants, however, voted the usual twentieth.

‡ He pleaded his royal blood as a reason for forgiveness. Edward's answer was to direct that he should be hung on a gallows higher than those of his friends.

capture him, was roughly handled. Bruce's two brothers, Thomas and Alexander, however, attempting a raid on England in the spring of 1307, were captured, and executed at Carlisle.

Nothing daunted, Edward procured Bruce's excommunication by the obliging Pope, obtained, from the same source, liberal grants of clerical revenues in England, Ireland, Scotland, and Wales, gave directions for the assembling of a great fleet at Perth, began a vigorous prosecution of the Bishop of St. Andrews before the Papal Court, and summoned a full Parliament to meet at Carlisle on the 20th January, 1307. The King made Lanercost his headquarters during the autumn; which he spent in busy preparations for the approaching campaign.

Edward's activity.

A good deal of private business was done at the Parliament of Carlisle; but the main concern of the assembly was to enter a vigorous protest against the rapid resurrection of the Papal exactions, which the understanding between Edward and Clement V. had produced. The Pope's agent in England was one William Testa; and against this unfortunate man and his subordinates, the lay members of the Parliament drew up a terrible indictment. The King could not openly face the storm. He had to consent to the holding of a systematic enquiry on the subject throughout the kingdom, and to the republication of the Statute of 1305, which forbade the exportation of clerical property. But, as soon as Parliament was dissolved, he virtually annulled these steps by granting letters of protection

Parliament of Carlisle.

to Testa, upon which the latter had the audacity, in the following May, to petition the Council, then sitting in London, to assist him in the discharge of his duties. Thus the King's duplicity could not fail to appear; and it is probable that death alone saved him from a very awkward situation.

For Edward's days were drawing to a close. The winter was barely over, when the Bruce issued once more from the western Highlands. There speedily gathered round him a crowd of men whom the English chroniclers describe as outcasts of society, but who were, very probably, nothing worse than humble peasants. In other words, Bruce was gaining a stronger hold upon the affections of the Scottish people. Edward's forces were divided into three sections, commanded by Henry Percy, Aymer of Valence, and the young Earl of Gloucester, respectively. Valence was defeated by Bruce at Loudon Hill, and Bruce then attacked Gloucester, shutting him up in Ayr Castle. The news roused Edward to a final effort. Hastily summoning fresh forces to Carlisle, he determined to march once more at the head of his troops. Though he was suffering from dysentery, the indomitable old man quitted Carlisle on the 3rd July. On the following day he actually insisted on riding two miles; but the effort was too great, and on the Wednesday he was unable to move. On the Thursday he was carried to Burgh on Sands; on the Friday, July 7th, he died as he was being raised by his attendants to take his place at table. Dauntless in death as

Edward's last campaign.

For a long time the word "Parliament," which means, of course, merely a "talking," was used to describe any important or public discussion—notably that held by a Council of Magnates in the presence of the King. For a long while the magnates were content to rely on the unwillingness of the "lesser barons" to attend meetings; and it is doubtful whether the clause of the Great Charter of 1215, which directed the summoning of a "Common Council," was ever really acted upon, except when it was desired to collect a feudal army. But still, the Great Charter had started the idea of connecting a grant of special taxation with a specially full gathering of the King's lieges, and had provided that the humbler part of this gathering should be summoned through the sheriffs of the counties, to whom they paid their taxes. The idea was seized by the Reformers of the middle of the thirteenth century; but, instead of confining their summons to the King's "tenants-in-chief," they merely directed the sheriffs to cause two knights to be chosen in the county court, perhaps meaning that only tenants-in-chief should be chosen, and willing to excuse the irksome attendance of the great majority. This was done in 1254, 1261, 1264, 1265, 1275, and 1290; and, when the practice became established, no mention was made of tenants-in-chief. By this omission, intentional or accidental, the shire representation ceased to be feudal, and became national. Then, in 1265, Earl Simon, as we have seen, added the famous clause requiring the sheriffs to send

Developments of Parliament.

Knights of the shire.

Burgesses.

burgesses as well as knights of the shire; and, finally, Edward himself, in 1295, put the coping stone on the growing fabric, by summoning the deans, archdeacons, and proctors of the humbler clergy. It was some years before the name "Parliament" was confined to this elaborately collected body. But more and more the model of 1295 was followed. And when people spoke of a "Parliament" in the middle of the fourteenth century, they probably meant a body of the kind rendered famous by Edward's assembly in November, 1295.

Clerical proctors.

But it would be a great mistake to suppose that Edward created, or intended to create, a Parliament in the sense in which we now understand the term. At the present day Parliament performs four great functions. It legislates, it ventilates grievances, it criticises the details of administration, it provides money. The last of these functions alone was assigned to it by Edward, at least so far as the elected members were concerned. The orthodox form of the summons to the shire and borough members, as settled by Edward's ministers, and consecrated by six hundred years of practice, invites them "to do" what shall be ordained in the premises. There can be no doubt, in the circumstances of the case, that the phrase "to do" (*ad faciendum*) was merely a polite form of the cruder expression "to grant money," and equally little doubt that, however long the phrase has been a mere fiction, it originally expressed a genuine truth. The clearest proof of this

Functions of the Parliament.

Supply.

lies in the fact, that when the King really did desire the counsel of humble persons, he knew how to ask for it, as when he summoned an assembly of citizens in 1296 to advise him on the settlement of the borough of Berwick-on-Tweed. Not for nearly four hundred years did the elected members of Parliament make good their claim, except in times of revolution, to criticise the royal administration, or to cause the removal of the King's ministers.

Ventilation of grievances.

As a matter of fact, the elected members were far more anxious to establish another right, and their anxiety was wise. In all probability they had not the knowledge necessary to make them useful critics of the royal administration. But they were an admirable machinery for the collection of popular grievances. The right of presenting petitions to a monarch is so useful to the ruler himself, that it is very rarely denied, even by Oriental despots. Nothing is so dangerous to the security of a throne as the existence of secret discontent, which the sufferers despair of being able to bring to the royal ear. Long before Parliament came into existence, the English kings received petitions from their subjects. But the fate of the petitions was precarious. First the king had to be found; and only students of history can realise the activity and elusiveness of a medieval king. When found, the king had to be approached, often through a crowd of courtiers and officials, who were none too anxious to help the suppliant. Then there was the weary waiting for a reply. All these difficulties disappeared, as by magic, with the institution of Parliament. The Parliament was summoned to meet the king. Its presence could not be ignored. The distant petitioner could entrust his plaint to the hands of his elected knight or burgess. The wages of the knight or burgess could be stopped if he did not do his duty; for they were paid by his constituency, not by the royal treasury. Above all, the knights and burgesses soon found that they had a powerful weapon in their hands. They could refuse to grant taxes until the petitions which they had presented had been carefully considered and properly answered by the Crown. Thus the great constitutional principle, that redress of grievances precedes supply, came slowly to light in Edward's reign. Thus, also, we see the meaning of the careful apportionment in the Michaelmas Parliament of 1280, and so often afterwards, of the numerous petitions presented at the assembling of Parliament, among special officials or specially appointed committees, and the appearance of the Receiver of Petitions as a regular Parliamentary official. In fact, the merest glance through the records of Edward's Parliaments is sufficient to convince the student, that the main business of the session was the discussion and remedy of individual grievances, while specially difficult or specially "prerogative" lawsuits form the other great item of work. These latter, after a few years, constituted the sole contents of the *coram rege* Rolls of the King's Bench; while the private petitions which play so large a part in the records of Edward's Parliament disappeared from the rolls, and became the "private bills" of a later day. Thus the "public bills," which are so

Petitions.

scanty on the rolls of Edward's time,—the bills or petitions promoted by the King's ministers, or by the magnates, or by the "community" or "communities" of the realm,—at last became the staple material of the Parliament Rolls, being engrossed in their final shape on the Statute Roll of the Kingdom. For that was the final work accomplished by Parliament. It fused the thousand diverse interests of shires and boroughs, clergy and laity, magnates and humble folk, into one national whole; and made possible the existence of national legislation.

Legislation.

And so we come, finally, to Edward's position as a legislator, and to the title which he has acquired, of "the English Justinian." Like most other popular titles, it covers a certain amount of truth. Justinian, reigning over an empire whose civilisation had been growing for a thousand years, summed up the legal history of that civilisation in a series of works, which has become one of the priceless possessions of Western life. In the Digest, or Pandects, he summarised, by a ruthless process of excision and compression, the works of that famous body of Roman jurists which was the boast of the earlier Roman Empire. To this he added a Code, or collection of imperial statutes, the second edition of which has been accepted as an integral part of the *Corpus Juris Civilis*. These again he supplemented by an admirable little Primer of Law, or Institutes, founded on the similar treatise of a great Roman jurist, who had been dead three hundred years when

The Corpus Juris.

The Digest.

The Code.

The Institutes.

Justinian ascended the throne. Finally, he himself contributed upwards of a hundred "Novels," or new statutes, to the legislative activity of the Byzantine Empire. With the authority of one who still believed himself to be the world's master, he forbade all criticism of his completed work, and all reference to other sources of authority. Within the covers of the *Corpus Juris* would be found, he insisted, an answer to every legal difficulty which could possibly arise to vex the minds of his subjects.

The Novels.

The work of Justinian was, in itself, a great work, and would, at all times, have commanded the respect of the world. But, owing to the special circumstances of its fate, it achieved a success such as has not been secured by more than a dozen other books in the world's history. It became, in fact, the secular Bible of Christendom, second only in authority and influence to the Sacred Scriptures. The age which produced it was a literary age, the ages which followed it were rude and ignorant. Even in its decay, the mighty Roman Empire contrasted forcibly with the crowd of petty princedoms into which it broke up. The rude barbarian princes of Europe listened with awe to the pages which spoke to them of a civilisation so far above their own. At first the *Corpus Juris* was known to them only through hasty and crude adaptations, made by the orders of the conquering chieftains of the Teutonic invasions; but, gradually, as Europe settled down after the storms of the Dark Ages, the pure text was received into

Justinian's work.

the homes of the new learning, and ardent students of the precious volumes carried the fame of their wisdom from the schools of Bologna, Pisa, and Padua, to the Courts of Europe. At first the Church had no word of blame for the new movement; for the Byzantine Empire, though schismatic according to later Western ideas, was a Christian Empire, and Justinian's Code accorded due honour to Bishop and Church. And, even after the Church, pursuing her new policy of isolation, had forbidden her priests to study the "secular" or "imperial" laws, and had set up a formidable rival in the Canon Law, the enthusiasm of the students of the Roman Law abated not a whit. In fact, the sincere flattery of imitation was accorded to Justinian's work by the Papal legislators, who compiled their *Corpus Juris Canonici* on that very model which the *Corpus Juris Civilis* had seemed to render inevitable. And, in drawing a sharp line between the professors of the Civil and the Canon Laws, the Papacy made one of its most fatal mistakes, by alienating from its service a body of men who, for the first time in the history of Western Christendom, made a serious inroad upon the intellectual monopoly of the Church.

Influence of the "Corpus Juris."

As a very natural result, the nations of Western Europe, or rather their rulers, began, at the end of the Middle Ages, to look upon the *Corpus Juris* of Justinian, not merely as a monument of Roman greatness, but as a complete code of conduct for the guidance of secular affairs. Realising fully, that the barbarous local customs of their own peoples, and even the general maxims of feudalism, offered no satisfactory guides for the new world of commerce which was growing up around them, they turned more and more for the solution of new and complicated problems to the ever ready pages of the Digest and the Code.

Spain.

In some cases, as in Spain, the Roman Law spoke of a past which men were proud to contrast with the present. There, the compilation of the *Siete Partidas*, modelled on the seven years of the legal curriculum in the Roman Law schools, was the Christian's badge of defiance to the hated but impressive Saracen. In others, as in Southern France, the continuity between the city life of the

France.

Roman provinces, and the city life of Gascony and Aquitaine, was at least a cherished tradition; and it was natural that Southern France should be a *pays du droit écrit*. But, that Germany

Germany.

and Scotland* should accept the *Corpus Juris* of Justinian is, apparently, so wild a freak of history as to deserve at least a passing

Scotland.

wonder. And this wonder is increased by the discovery that England, so closely allied with Scotland and Germany in the course of history, so like them in civilisation, so near them in geographical position, at the critical moment, re-

Its rejection by England.

jected the Roman Law, and went off on an entirely different course. And this critical moment is the reign, or at least the lifetime, of Edward Plantagenet.

* It was, of course, long after the thirteenth century that Germany and Scotland received the Roman Law. But the fact is none the less striking on that account.

The explanation is twofold. It lies partly in the notion which men then held of Law, partly in the circumstances of English history. It would be very easy to wander gradually into speculations as to the nature of Law, which would land us in a hopeless quagmire of confusion.

Explanation of the difference.

"Law" is one of those familiar words which everybody thinks he understands, until he tries to explain them. But, briefly speaking, the notion of Law, in the thirteenth century, vibrated between three different conceptions. One was, that Law was a divine or, at least, a philosophical ideal, which could only be discovered by great wisdom and patient study. Men ought to conform their lives to a high ideal. And, as the Scriptures dealt mainly with principles and generalities, a system of Law was necessary to define details. The supporters of this view urged the adoption of the *Corpus Juris* as the required ideal. Nowhere else, they urged, was it possible to find such profound wisdom applied to the details of secular affairs. The revival of learning tended to give immense weight to the writings of the ancients; and Europe in the thirteenth century was far too uncritical to distinguish between the dates of Aristotle, Virgil, and the Roman jurist, Gaius. They were all "ancients," and that was enough.

Conception of law.

The philosopher's view.

But it is doubtful whether the *Corpus Juris* would ever have obtained its immense success, had it not itself ostensibly maintained a second conception of Law, which had always found favour with a certain very important, if limited, class

The military view.

of persons. "The pleasure of the Prince has the force of Law," is one of the best-known maxims of the *Institutes;* and we can well imagine that the sentence would not be unacceptable from the lips of a courtier. As a fact, of course, the *Corpus Juris* of Justinian had been compiled in the days of a despotism the completest, though, it must be admitted, also the wisest, which the world has ever seen. In the system of the later Roman Empire, everything centred in the person of the Prince, and his will was final and absolute.

Narrowness of the escape.

How near, how very near, England was to the adoption of a system based on the principles of the *Corpus Juris*, few but professed historians know. Two facts, small in themselves, but very significant, reveal the possibilities of the situation more clearly than pages of vague description. One is, that Edward for years maintained in his pay, as his trusted adviser, Francesco Accursi, himself a learned student and professor of the Roman Law, and the son of the still more famous Accursi, the author of the *Great Gloss*, and the contemporary and fellow townsman of that Azo to whom Bracton was indebted for so much of his language. The other is, that an anonymous, but highly popular law book, compiled in the late thirteenth century, figures the Law as issuing from the mouth of the king. Evidently, there were symptoms, in the thirteenth century, of a very powerful alliance between the philosophical and the military conceptions of Law.

The humble alternative of these two lofty notions is the view, that Law is nothing but the formal expression of the common sense of the average man, as evidenced by his daily practice. In other words, Law is the formal shape into which the customs of average men are translated by the processes of legislation and judicial decision. It may be said that the conduct of the average man is influenced unconsciously by the teachings of religion and philosophy, and, consciously, by the commands of authority. That may be so; and yet, just as it is true that the average man's conduct never precisely conforms either to the ideals of the philosopher or to the wishes of authority, so it is true, that custom always differs substantially both from religious and philosophical teaching, and from the injunctions of the most minute arbitrary directions. But it is not true, as has been superficially argued, that a system of Law which, like the English, is based on custom, is merely licensed anarchy. On the contrary, it acts somewhat severely on all abnormal persons, whether they be, like thieves and murderers, mere laggards in the march of civilisation, or, on the other hand, men with advanced ideas, who make their fellow-men uncomfortable by too rapid progress. To use a very simple simile, drawn from the practice of the examiner, Law, on this principle, aims at reproducing the best works of the second class, leaving out of account the geniuses in the first rank, and the dullards in the third.

The popular view.

This conception of Law, it must be admitted,

offers to the ruler of a country which adopts it a somewhat humble position. He cannot pose as the Heaven-sent deviser of an ideal system, which he imposes at the sword's point upon a stupid and ignorant people. But his task is, for all that, an important one, none the less important that it makes no superhuman demands upon the intellect. To put it briefly, he has to collect, to harmonise, and to formulate. It is only in quite recent years that we have known how these humble processes went on in England during the lifetime of Edward. For the first two he can hardly claim the credit; the last has won him the title of the English Justinian.

The function of the legislator.

One of the essential conditions of Law is uniformity. But this condition did not exist in the England of the early twelfth century, when the royal justices first began those circuits of the shires which have been one of the most important features in the domestic history of the country for the last seven hundred years. These justices found that each county, almost each district, had its own local customs, differing, ever so slightly perhaps, but still differing, from the customs of its neighbours. As more and more cases came before the royal courts, as more and more juries delivered their verdicts in answer to royal enquiries, more and more clear did this truth become. But, on the other hand, more and more did the royal officials come to know of the customs of the land. The clerkly skill of the Norman and the Angevin official made ever more and more plain

Collection of the materials of English law.

the habits and practices of the people. Greater and greater grew the collection of Plea Rolls which accumulated in the King's Exchequer. Thus the materials for a Common Law were collected.

Bracton.

Then came a man with a great love of order and symmetry, a man capable of casting the work of the previous century into a compact and harmonious form. This man was Henry of Bratton, or, as we call him, "Bracton." No man could have been better fitted for the task. In spite of his borrowings from Azo, and his references to Digest and Institutes, he did not, perhaps, know very much of Roman Law. But he knew something of it, and, as a cathedral chancellor, he must also have known something of the Canon Law. But, above all, as an experienced royal justice, deeply learned in the practice of the royal courts, he had unique qualifications for his task. The vital point in his work is that, whilst occasionally borrowing the language and arrangement of the Roman Law, whilst courtly in his references to the King, and civil to his brother ecclesiastics, he draws the body and bones of his work from the records of the Bench and circuit courts. This fact, long suspected from internal evidence by intelligent students, has been finally established, within the last twenty years, by the discovery of the very materials used by Bracton in writing his great book. Having access, by virtue of his official position, to the Plea Rolls, he made from them a collection of some two thousand cases,* and from this

* The MS. containing these cases was discovered by Professor Vinogradoff in the British Museum in 1884, and has been lucidly

collection he drew the rules which compose his book. For a century the work of assimilation had been going on throughout England, no doubt largely through the efforts of the justices themselves. A nation had been slowly born, with a consciousness of unity, and a willingness to give up minor differences for the sake of that unity. How much of the process was due to Bracton, how much to his predecessors, it is not possible to say, though, in many cases, we know the very names of the men to whom he attributes those decisions which have become part of English Law. But to him, at least, is due the credit of having cast into harmonious and enduring shape a huge mass of material which had been slowly accumulating. Still the different local customs lingered on, in the local courts of the manor, the borough, and the shire. But these were every day dwindling beside the vigorous growth of the royal courts; and for the royal courts there was now a Common Law, a law common to all the realm.

Edward's task.

Bracton's book was given to the world only a few years before Edward ascended the throne. Edward's task was to give it free play. For the first time, English Law could be thought of as a whole, as a body which could grow and develop. Bracton's treatise had stated, not only the rules of conduct themselves, but the legal procedure by which they could be enforced. In so doing, it had revealed some anomalies and many imperfections. These it was the peculiar province of the

edited by Professor Maitland, under the title of *Bracton's Notebook* (Cambridge Press, 1887.)

King to remedy; for the courts which they affected were his courts. It is astonishing how much of Edward's celebrated legislation is concerned with matters of procedure. In the substance of the Law there were still moot points. These the King could settle, as he did in the case of *De Donis* (see p. 208), where he had to take the reactionary side, and in the case of *Quia Emptores* (see p. 274), where progress won a decided victory. But, perhaps unconsciously, he did the greatest thing for the future of English Law when he called into existence the National Parliament. For, better even than the judges on circuit, the elected members of Parliament knew the customs of the people, and, with the aid of their counsel and advice, future kings could formulate from time to time the rules of English Law. And thus provision was made for the perpetual continuance of that process of collection which had been begun by the King's justices, and which had to be done over and over again if Law was to keep abreast of national progress. Not until Edward is dead do we find in the statute book the honoured formula which describes the King as enacting "with the advice and consent of the lords spiritual and temporal and the commons in Parliament assembled"; * but this consummation became clearly inevitable, from the day on which the Model Parliament assembled at Westminster in November, 1295. To explain all that it means it would be necessary to write the comparative history of the States of Western Europe, and to show how the history of

* The first equivalent seems to be the preamble of the Statute of York in 1318. But the Statute of Carlisle came very near it.

England has been so different from the history of France, of Italy, of Germany, and of Spain. Briefly put, to close an already overlong chapter, it meant the creation of that national and political unity which, until quite modern days, was the highest achievement of European statesmanship; it meant the appearance on the world's horizon of that new star, which was to light the nations on their march to freedom. For the ideals and principles adopted by the English people under the rule of Edward, were not merely the ideals and principles which nerved the arm of the Puritan soldier, and raised the banner of defiance against Napoleon. They were the ideals and principles which, despite the excesses of the French Revolution, struck the fetters of tyranny from the limbs of Western Europe, and breathed the spirit of justice and freedom into the mighty Commonwealths of America and Australia.

APPENDIX A

PERHAPS a brief account of the Archbishop's two years of office will reveal the character of English rule in Ireland in the thirteenth century, as well as any other description.

Leaving Dublin on July 20th, 1288, the new Justitiar started for Connaught, where the royal officials had of late been insubordinate. But, before he started, he ordered a muster of the King's forces at Kildare for September 9th, with a view to proceedings against the Irish of Offaly and Leix. Presumably the Archbishop succeeded in his mission in Connaught. At any rate, he reached Kildare on the appointed day, reviewed the "service of Leinster," and made arrangements for guarding the borders of Kildare county. On the 16th he heard that the Roches were up in Desmond, and immediately hurried to Carlow, where he arrived on the 18th, and, after a vigorous tour in the province, changing his quarters frequently,* he succeeded in pacifying the district by mid-October. The rest of the year he spent in thoroughly organising the defences of Leinster; and on January 14th, 1289, proclaimed the Tipperary "eyre," which was carried out under his personal supervision. But none the less he returned to Desmond to complete

* He slept four nights at Cork, three at Limerick, two at Clonmel.

his task of restoring order, a duty which occupied him till the end of January.

After this there seems to have been a lull. But before Easter the Justitiar found himself compelled to visit Meath, to fortify it against the attacks of an Irish chieftain with an unpronounceable name.* He fortified Athlone, Randown, and Roscommon; and then visited Dromore and Tuam, cutting a pass through the hills at Delvin. Then, after another hasty glance at the progress of the Tipperary "eyre," the Justitiar determined to take seriously in hand the war in Offaly; and, for that purpose, he collected a considerable army at Baltinglass in September, 1289. Apparently, the exhibition was successful; at any rate we find the records saying that, after the campaign, the Irish of Offaly and Leix gave no more trouble. From the conclusion of the campaign until Christmas, the Justitiar was at headquarters, holding the pleas of the Crown at Dublin. At the beginning of the new year† he held a Parliament of the magnates at Dublin, and another at Kilkenny in Easter week, whence he was called away by the news of a rising at Athlone. The Athlone business employed his energies until May 14th, 1290; and, a month later, the indefatigable Justitiar set off on a prolonged "eyre," lasting sixty-five days, through Meath, Connaught, Tipperary, Cork, Limerick, and Waterford. It is not surprising to learn, that these exertions resulted in the loss of nineteen of the King's horses, valued at £78. But the officials claimed that "Ireland was ever afterwards at peace."

---

* "Omalethel" or "Omalachelyn." (? "O'Malley").

† Of course, this expression is strictly out of place in this connection. In the thirteenth century, and for centuries afterwards, the "new year" began on March 25th.

LIST OF AUTHORITIES

(A) OFFICIAL.

The Statutes of the Realm. Vol. I. 1810. (Record Commission.)

Acts of the Parliament of Scotland. Vol. I. 1844. (Record Commission.)

Fœdera . . . ab ingressu Willelmi I. . . . ad nostra usque tempora. Vol. I. Pts. I. and II. Rymer. ed. Clarke. 1816.

Rotuli Parliamentorum. Vol. I. (1278–1327.) n. d.

Records of the (Lenten) *Parliament of 1305.* ed. Maitland. 1893. (Rolls Series.)

The Parliamentary Writs, etc. Vol. I. ed. Palgrave. 1827. (Record Commission.)

Pleadings in Parliament. ed. Ryley. 1661.

Rotuli Hundredorum. Vols. I. and II. ed. Illingworth. 1812. (Record Commission.)

Placita de Quo Warranto. ed. Illingworth. 1818. (Record Commission.)

Taxatio Ecclesiastica . . . Papæ Nicholai IV. 1802. (Record Commission.)

Documents Illustrative of English History. ed. Cole. 1844.

The Red Book of the Exchequer. Vols. I., II., and III. ed. Hall. 1896. (Rolls Series.)

Calendar of Documents Relating to Scotland. Vols. I. and II. ed. Bain. 1881.

—— Vol. IV. (Addenda). 1888. (Register Series.)

Documents and Records Illustrating the History of Scotland. (1278–1307.) ed. Palgrave. 1837. (Record Commission.)

Documents Illustrative of the History of Scotland. (1286–1306.) Vols. I. and II. ed. Stevenson. 1870. (Register Series.)

Calendar of Documents Relating to Ireland. Vols. I.–V. ed. Sweetman. 1871–1886. (Record Office Series.)

Rôles Gascons. Vol. I. ed. Francisque-Michel. 1885. Supplement. ed. Bémont. 1896. Vol. II. ed. Bémont. 1900. (*Documents Inédits sur l'Histoire de France.*)

Rotulus Walliæ. ed. Philipps. 1865. (Privately printed.)

(B) CHRONICLES.

Matthæi Parisiensis . . . Chronica Majora. Vols. IV.–VII. ed. Luard. 1877–1883. (Rolls Series.)

Flores Historiarum. Vols. II. and III. ed. Luard. 1890. (Rolls Series.)

Chronicon de Lanercost. ed. Stevenson. 1839. (Maitland Club.)

Chronicon . . . Walteri de Hemingburgh. ed. Hamilton. 1848. (English Historical Society.)

Chronica Monasterii S. Albani. (Chronica Willelmi Rishanger.) ed. Riley. 1865. (Rolls Series.)

Chronica de Mailros. ed. Stevenson. 1835. (Bannatyne Club.)

Annales Monastici. ed. Luard. Vol. II. (*Waverley.*) 1865. (Rolls Series.)

Liber de Antiquis Legibus. ed. Stapleton. 1846. (Camden Society.)

Croniques de London. ed. Aungier. 1844. (Camden Society.)

Brut y Tywysogion. ed. Williams ab Ithel. 1860. (Rolls Series.)

Journey of William of Rubruck. ed. Rockhill. 1900. (Hakluyt Society.)

(C) MISCELLANEOUS.

Roberti Grosseteste Epistolæ. ed. Luard. 1861. (Rolls Series.)

Liber de Adventu Fratrum Minorum. (Monumenta Franciscana.) Vol. I. ed. Brewer. 1858. Vol. II. ed. Howlett. 1882. (Rolls Series.)

Documents Illustrative of . . . Sir William Wallace. ed. Stevenson. 1841. (Maitland Club.)

Illustrations of Scottish History. ed. Stevenson. 1834. (Maitland Club.)

The Political Songs of England. ed. Wright. 1839. (Camden Society.)

Historic and Municipal Documents of Ireland. ed. Gilbert. 1870. (Rolls Series.)

Chartularies of St. Mary's Abbey, Dublin. ed. Gilbert. Vols. I. and II. 1845. (Rolls Series.)

Letters Illustrative of the Reign of Henry III. ed. Shirley. Vol. II. 1866. (Rolls Series.)

Munimenta Academica. ed. Anstey. Vols. I. and II. 1868. (Rolls Series.)

De Legibus et Consuetudinibus Angliæ. Bracton. Vols. I.–V. 1878. (Rolls Series.)

(N.B.—It must be understood that the above is only a selection from the contemporary authorities. It does not profess to be exhaustive.)

INDEX

C

G

H

I

J

K